Catholics in America

CATHOLICS IN AMERICA
A Social Portrait

Lisa A. Keister

OXFORD
UNIVERSITY PRESS

OXFORD
UNIVERSITY PRESS

Oxford University Press is a department of the University of Oxford. It furthers the University's objective of excellence in research, scholarship, and education by publishing worldwide. Oxford is a registered trade mark of Oxford University Press in the UK and certain other countries.

Published in the United States of America by Oxford University Press
198 Madison Avenue, New York, NY 10016, United States of America.

© Oxford University Press 2024

All rights reserved. No part of this publication may be reproduced, stored in a retrieval system, or transmitted, in any form or by any means, without the prior permission in writing of Oxford University Press, or as expressly permitted by law, by license, or under terms agreed with the appropriate reproduction rights organization. Inquiries concerning reproduction outside the scope of the above should be sent to the Rights Department, Oxford University Press, at the address above.

You must not circulate this work in any other form
and you must impose this same condition on any acquirer.

Library of Congress Cataloging-in-Publication Data
Names: Keister, Lisa A., 1968– author.
Title: Catholics in America : a social portrait / Lisa A. Keister.
Description: New York, NY : Oxford University Press, [2024] |
Includes bibliographical references and index.
Identifiers: LCCN 2024022925 | ISBN 9780197753675 (hb) |
ISBN 9780197753682 (pb) | ISBN 9780197753705 (epub) |
ISBN 9780197753699 | ISBN 9780197753712
Subjects: LCSH: Catholics—United States—History. | Catholics—United States—Social conditions. | United States—Ethnic relations. | Catholic Church—United States—History. | Catholics—Religious life—United States. | Catholic families—United States.
Classification: LCC E184.C3 K27 2024 | DDC 282.73—dc23/eng/20240613
LC record available at https://lccn.loc.gov/2024022925

DOI: 10.1093/oso/9780197753675.001.0001

Paperback printed by Integrated Books International, United States of America
Hardback printed by Bridgeport National Bindery, Inc., United States of America

To JWM

CONTENTS

List of Figures and Tables   ix
Acknowledgements   xiii

1. Catholics in America   1

PART I Origins, Turning Points, and Achievements
2. Social Origins   15
3. Family: Marriage, Divorce, and Fertility   41
4. Achievements: Education, Work, Income, and Wealth   68
5. Catholicism Evolving: Leaving, Joining, and Staying with the Church   97

PART II Beliefs and Attitudes
6. Religious Beliefs and Practices   127
7. Politics   152
8. Social Issues   173
9. Conclusion   195

Appendix   205
References   215
Index   245

FIGURES AND TABLES

FIGURES

1.1 Religious affiliation: Catholic stability amid change   2
1.2 Catholic ancestry, increasing diversity   6
1.3 Catholic families since the 1970s: Declining marriage, rising divorce   7
2.1 Birth cohort and religious tradition   20
2.2 (A) Women and religious tradition. (B) Men and religious tradition   22
2.3 Ancestry and religious tradition   24
2.4 Race-ethnicity and religious tradition   26
2.5 Immigrants and religion   31
2.6 Father's education   33
2.7 Growing up urban versus rural   36
3.1 Marriage   47
3.2 Cohabitation   49
3.3 Rising divorce rates   52
3.4 Divorce   53
3.5 In-group preference: Religious homogamy   56
3.6 In-group preference: Educational homogamy   56
3.7 Declining and converging fertility rates   60
3.8 Ideal number of children is more than two   61
3.9 Actual number of children   62
3.10 Age at birth of first child   63
3.11 Remaining childless   65
4.1 College completion   73

4.2 Working full time   75
4.3 Self-employment   77
4.4 Division of household labor   80
4.5 High poverty rates for Latino Catholics   82
4.6 High income   83
4.7 Investment income   85
4.8 Net worth poverty   88
4.9 High wealth   89
4.10 Homeownership   91
4.11 Inheriting   92
4.12 Self-reported class   93
4.13 Making ends meet   94
5.1 Movement among religious groups   100
5.2 Retrospective editing   106
6.1 Strength of religious belief   130
6.2 Religious practices   132
6.3 Religious experiences and evangelization   134
6.4 God, the afterlife, and the Pope   136
6.5 The Bible   138
6.6 Religion, politics, and science   140
6.7 Sex, divorce, and pornography   143
6.8 Abortion   145
6.9 Abortion complexity   147
7.1 Political party identification   154
7.2 Government spending   160
7.3 National problems   163
7.4 Charitable giving to any cause   167
7.5 Charitable giving: Amount given   168
7.6 Charitable giving to religious, health, and educational causes   169
8.1 Gender roles   176
8.2 Economic inequality and poverty   181
8.3 Suicide and assisted suicide   185
8.4 Capital punishment   186
8.5 Generalized trust and confidence in institutions   188
8.6 Volunteering   191

TABLES

5.1 Changing affiliation: Movement between childhood and adulthood   *102*
5.2 The magnitude of religious change   *103*
5.3 Multiple religious changes   *104*
5.4 Social origins and religious change   *109*
5.5 Family and religious change   *111*
5.6 Socioeconomic status and religious change   *113*
5.7 Wealth and religious change   *114*

ACKNOWLEDGEMENTS

Many thanks to Jim Moody for his support in this and all things. I am also grateful to Brent Curdy for analysis of GSS data and to Shuyi Qiu and Noah Gibson for assistance with PSID analyses. I thank Laura Tesch and Audra Dugandzic for editing and other excellent feedback. I am grateful for excellent comments and suggestions from James Cavendish, Mark Chaves, Maureen Day, Michele Dillon, Doug Downey, David Eagle, Michael Hout, Cyrus Schleifer, Christian Smith, Landon Schnabel, and Paul von Hippel. Finally, many thanks to David Grusky, Katherine Edin, and the PIs of the American Voices Project for allowing me to use their data.

CHAPTER 1

Catholics in America

More than 20% of Americans—approximately 70 million people—are members of the Catholic Church. And with more than 16,000 parishes and 34,000 priests, the Catholic Church is the single largest religious organization in the country (Center for Applied Research in the Apostolate [CARA] 2023; Smith 2021). This book provides a contemporary social portrait of Catholics that addresses questions about who Catholics are by documenting critical demographic traits, trends in these traits over time, religious practices and beliefs, and political and social attitudes. Changes in the U.S. religious landscape, the rising prominence of Catholics in important leadership positions, significant demographic changes to the U.S. population, and misperceptions about Catholic beliefs make a social portrait of them timely and relevant to understanding current affairs. Understanding Catholics also provides a window into the U.S. religious landscape more broadly.

There are at least five reasons for a serious examination of Catholics. First, Catholic Church membership is large and holding relatively steady (Figure 1.1). There has been a modest decline in Catholic Church membership since the 1970s, when approximately 25% of the population was Catholic, but Catholic Church membership has been remarkably stable in an era when membership in Protestant denominations has declined and disaffiliation has reached record levels. Overall, there are still more Protestants than Catholics in the United States, but Protestants are spread across a large number of denominations that have wildly varying approaches to both religion and secular issues. Moreover, since the 1970s, there has been a rapid decline in membership in mainline Protestant churches, and, since the 1980s, there has been a corresponding decline in membership in conservative Protestant denominations. By 2021, approximately equal percentages (about 20%) of Americans are affiliated with Catholic, mainline Protestant, and conservative

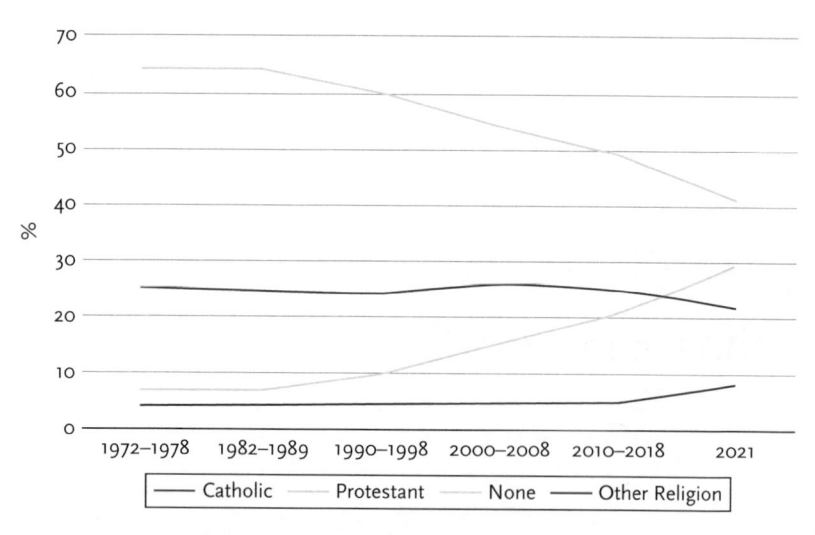

Figure 1.1 Religious affiliation: Catholic stability amid change

Protestant churches. At the same time, there has been a pronounced and well-documented rise in disaffiliation from all faiths—that is, an increase in those who claim no religious affiliation (hereafter, the *religious nones*) (Burge 2021).

Second, some particularly prominent and influential Catholics have drawn attention to the Church and its teachings. President Joe Biden is Catholic, as are nearly 30% of members of Congress (Sandstrom 2021). Before the 1980s, it was rare for more than one of the nine justices to be Catholic, but the Supreme Court is now majority Catholic: six of nine justices are members of the Church (Newport 2022a). Catholic doctrine became an important part of public conversations when internal Church debates—for example, regarding whether priests should give communion to politicians who disagree with the Church—spilled over into broader discussions about the role of religious belief in public life (Kaplan 2022; McCammon 2021; National Catholic Reporter 2021). Similarly, the 2022 overturning of *Roe v. Wade* was extraordinarily and notoriously controversial. Because this decision was in line with Catholic doctrine—and possibly in line with the religious beliefs of the Supreme Court justices who voted to overturn the law—the religion of public figures was the subject of heated debates about what Catholics believe and how those beliefs might affect public policy, legal precedent, and other aspects of social, economic, and political life.

Third, dramatic demographic changes in the United States that are mirrored in the Church may have significant social, economic, and political implications for the country. Central among these changes is the well-documented growth in the U.S. Latino population, including many first- and second-generation immigrants, increasing the proportion of Catholics who are Latino (Gaunt

2022; Gray, Gautier, and Gaunt 2014; Ramos, Woodberry, and Ellison 2017; Zech et al. 2017). Some projections suggest that, by 2043, Latino Catholics may be the dominant U.S. ethnic-religious group and may account for up to 18% of the U.S. population (Skirbekk, Kaufmann, and Goujon 2010). The correlation between religious beliefs and voting behaviors of this segment of the population may have significant political ramifications, particularly in swing states such as Texas and Florida.

At the same time, the social and economic position of non-Latino white Catholics (hereafter, white Catholics) has improved. In the nineteenth and first half of the twentieth centuries, Catholics—who were predominantly European immigrants with relatively low incomes and education levels—were widely considered by the Protestant majority to be racially and religiously inferior and to have questionable political loyalties (Wilde 2020; Zeitz 2015). As historian Josh Zeitz describes, "It wasn't unusual for respectable politicians to wonder aloud whether Catholics could be loyal to their adoptive country *and* to the Pope" (Zeitz 2015). However, increases in the education levels, incomes, and wealth of white Catholics—which were accompanied by declines in the importance of religious identification—have landed them in more influential positions in business, economics, and politics, potentially increasing their sway on important issues (Bruce 2017; D'Antonio et al. 2007; Keister 2007; Wuthnow 1990). Yet not all recent demographic changes promise more influence for Catholics. Many white Catholics have left the Church (Sherkat 2014; Smith et al. 2014), and an unprecedented number of people, particularly young people, now claim no religious affiliation (Newport 2022b; Smith et al. 2014; Smith 2021). The Catholic Church has been hard hit by the decline in religious affiliation among younger Americans (Gaunt 2022; Pew Research Center 2015; Smith et al. 2014), a pattern that raises questions about Church membership in coming decades.

Fourth, misperceptions and confusion about Catholic religious beliefs, practices, and social and political attitudes are pervasive. Accompanying these misperceptions, many people imagine that Catholics are widely allowing Church teaching to guide their beliefs, attitudes, and related behaviors. It is understandably difficult to make sense of a tradition that counts such a varied group of people among its members: the U.S. president, many well-known politicians and celebrities such as Steve Bannon and Stephen Colbert, some of the nation's poorest citizens, and new immigrants are all affiliated with this single religion. It is also difficult to classify Catholic beliefs and attitudes because they do not fit neatly into the well-defined and highly polarized political, social, and other categories that characterize most Americans. Differences between President Biden—whose politics lean left—and those of the Supreme Court justices and other politicians—who are more right-leaning—highlight this reality. Differences between high-income, highly educated Catholics and the increasingly large segment of Catholics who are working-class Latinos are likely even starker. The challenge of classifying Catholic political and social attitudes has been well documented over the decades (D'Antonio et al. 2007; Greeley 1977b; Stark 2008), and journalistic accounts suggest that it remains true today (Orcés 2022; Smith 2020). There appears to have been some change in the modal Catholic from Democrat to Republican in recent years (Smith 2020), but, even with this change, Catholics do not fit neatly into liberal or conservative boxes.

Because Catholics are hard to pin down on key political and social issues, conservatives often assume that Catholics are liberal and cite Church doctrine regarding poverty, inequality, and immigration as evidence that ordinary Catholics must be progressives. On the other hand, progressives point to the Church's official opposition to abortion, same-sex marriage, birth control, premarital sex, and divorce and assume that ordinary Catholics are comparable to conservative Protestants in having more uniformly traditional attitudes, beliefs, and practices. Progressives point to alliances between some Catholics and conservatives—both religious and nonreligious conservatives—on issues such as abortion as evidence of traditionalism (Douthat March 17, 2023; McConahay March 13, 2023; Picciotti-Bayer September 22, 2022; Smith 2020). Even Church members are unlikely to grasp fully the complexity of Catholics today, given the increasing demographic diversity of the Church's membership (Horowitz March 13, 2023).

Fifth, Catholics can provide a window into the changing American religious landscape more broadly. The evolution of religious affiliation that has characterized the U.S. in recent decades (shown in Figure 1.1) demonstrates that this is an era of considerable religious transformation. The rise of the religious nones hints at a new level of secularism that would render religion irrelevant if it were to continue. Yet the attention that religious ideology has received in many areas of public life, including politics (e.g., in the Supreme Court decision regarding *Roe v. Wade*), suggests that religion and religious ideology are still critical for understanding Americans and what they believe. By understanding how Catholics compare to other Americans, including both those with affiliations to other faiths and those who claim no affiliation, I will be able to say something about the nature of faith and social trends and how Catholics are situated within those trends.

THE NEED FOR A SOCIAL PORTRAIT

Despite these important issues, no recent work has addressed who Catholics are and what they believe about religious and secular issues, including how Catholics compare to other Americans. In the past, academics devoted considerable attention to Catholics, writing notable social profiles that highlighted issues that were once relevant to understanding the Church and its members.

These past profiles documented important differences in Catholics' socioeconomic status (SES), attitudes, and beliefs (D'Antonio et al. 2001; D'Antonio, Dillon, and Gautier 2013; Greeley 1977a). Past scholarship described Catholics as largely white, with almost exclusively European ethnic ties, an accurate portrayal at the time. Subsequent scholarship focused on understanding rising SES trends among the descendants of those immigrants, documenting significant changes in their education levels, the role of Catholic schools in facilitating upward social and economic mobility, and changes in other measures of social and economic status such as income and wealth ownership (Bryk, Lee, and Hollan 1993; Keister 2007; Sander 1995; Westoff and Jones 1979).

However, attention to Catholics has waned, with a few notable exceptions, and even these are quickly becoming dated (D'Antonio et al. 2013; Day 2018; Gaunt 2022; Smith et al. 2014). Moreover, although some of these works provide useful information about Catholics, they rely on data that include *only* Catholics and are unable to speak to how Catholics compare to other Americans. By contrast, there have been some excellent *general* treatments of American religion that include Catholics as well as members of other religious groups (Chaves 2017; Greeley and Hout 2006; Sherkat 2014; Stark 2008). These general treatments have the advantage of situating Catholics in the broader American religious landscape; however, they say little about what is unique about Catholics. The changing U.S. religious landscape, the rise of Catholics into important leadership positions, the Church's recent dramatic and significant demographic changes, and misunderstandings about who Catholics are suggest a need for an up-to-date portrait of today's Catholics.

CATHOLICS IN AMERICA TODAY

Who are Catholics in America today? No simple answer to this question can do justice to the varied demographic traits of members of the Church, their complex religious beliefs and practices, and their attitudes toward political and social issues. Indeed, the relatively stable overall percentage of Americans who are Catholic (shown in Figure 1.1) likely masks significant underlying demographic changes associated with equally significant changes in their beliefs, practices, and attitudes. The Catholic Church's well-documented doctrine fuels the idea that ordinary Catholics can be understood simply by understanding official Church policies and teaching. However, dramatic variation in major demographic traits and corresponding beliefs and attitudes suggests that this notion is not just overly simple but also that it risks mischaracterizing 20% of the American population.

Three broad demographic patterns suggest that understanding Catholics today requires exploration of differences both *among Catholics* and differences *between Catholics and other Americans*. First, changes in the ethnic composition of the Church are fundamental to understanding Catholics. White Catholics have left the Church in large numbers, and converts—albeit in smaller numbers—have joined and changed the face of the Church. Consistent with changes in the U.S. population (Sherkat 2014; Smith et al. 2014), Latino membership in the Catholic Church has grown significantly: the percentage of Catholics identifying as Latino increased from 23% in 2000 to 34% by 2021 (author's estimates from the General Social Survey [GSS]). Consistent with this change, Figure 1.2 shows the ancestry of GSS respondents over time, with a five-year moving average used to smooth over-time fluctuations. In the 1970s and early 1980s, nearly 80% of Catholics reported European ancestry, but that percentage began to decline in the 1980s, reaching only 55% by 2021. At the same time, the percentage of Catholics reporting Latin American ancestry rose from less than 10% in 1972 to more than 30% in 2021. The percentage of Latinos who are affiliated with Protestant—particularly conservative Protestant—churches or who have disaffiliated with religion entirely has grown (Mulder, Ramos, and Marti 2017).

These ethnic changes have affected a good deal about the Catholic Church, and they have the potential to affect issues beyond the Church. For example, there are now more Latinos in seminary programs and, in bishop and priest roles, their presence has increased in all geographic regions of the United States. Beyond the Church, Latinos also comprise large shares of the U.S. voting population, including in states considered political battlegrounds, such as

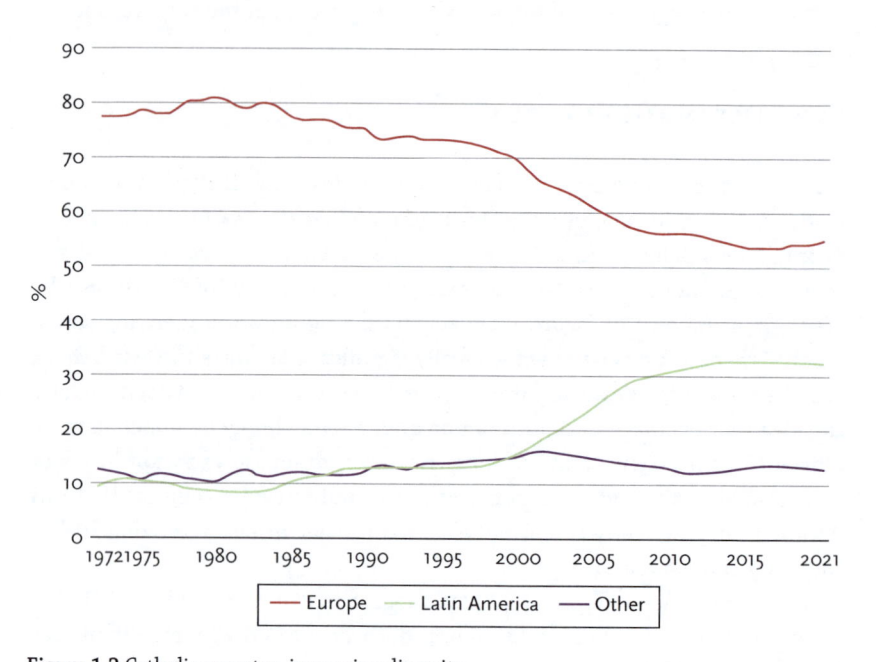

Figure 1.2 Catholic ancestry, increasing diversity

Florida, Texas, and Arizona (Igielnik and Budiman 2020). Although Latinos are politically engaged and religiously committed, their religious practices, religious commitment, and attitudes about secular issues may differ from those of white Catholics (Day 2020; Lopez, Gonzalez-Barrera, and Krogstad 2018; Taylor et al. 2012).

Second, there have been significant changes to Catholic families in recent decades, including patterns of marriage, cohabitation, divorce, and fertility. However, family patterns likely vary among Catholics—particularly by ethnicity—and between Catholics and members of other faith groups, and these are essential to understanding contemporary Catholics. Family patterns are particularly telling because they tend to be correlated with religious practices, political attitudes, and approaches to social issues such as gender roles in and out of the family (Ellison, Wolfinger, and Ramos-Wada 2013; Konieczny 2013; Perry and Schleifer 2019; Stone and Wilcox 2021). Figure 1.3 highlights marital status differences between the 1970s and 2021. In the 1970s, 70% of Catholics were married and had never been divorced. By 2021, fewer than 50% of Catholics were married and never divorced. The figure also documents the rise in the percentage of Catholics who have been divorced and either remarried or remained single. Marriage and divorce rates are associated with how men and women divide their labor in

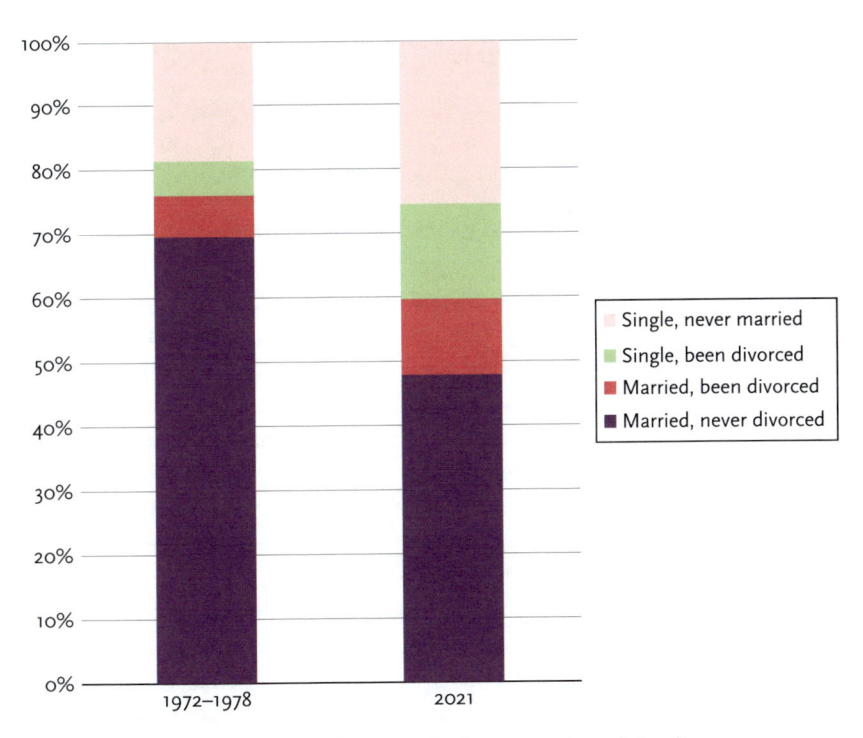

Figure 1.3 Catholic families since the 1970s: Declining marriage, rising divorce

and out of the home and with educational pursuits, careers, wealth accumulation, and other attitudes and behaviors, particularly for women (Hamilton and Armstrong 2021; Keister, Thebaud, and Yavorsky 2022). The Catholic Church has made efforts to become more inclusive in terms of marriage, divorce, and other family issues (Dillon 2018), but we know little about how the changing family is filtering into these other behaviors and outcomes for Catholics.

Third, SES—education, work, income, and wealth—differences among Catholics and between Catholics and other Americans are complex but vital to understanding Church members. SES convergence between white Catholics and mainline Protestants is well-documented, but research on this issue has slowed somewhat in recent decades suggesting that an updated SES portrait is in order. More importantly, however, prior research evidence regarding SES differences between white and Latino Catholics is limited, and these differences may be among the most dramatic demographic differences among contemporary Catholics. Evidence that Latino Americans lag behind white Americans is abundant; however, Latino Catholics—particularly those who have spent significant time in the United States—may have been upwardly mobile on measures such as income and wealth (Agius Vallejo 2012; Keister and Borelli 2013; Keister, Agius Vallejo, and Borelli 2014). Given that many of these patterns have changed among non-Catholics as well, part of my task in the remaining chapters of this book is to explore whether Catholics are unique or simply following broader U.S. trends.

A DATA-DRIVEN APPROACH

In this book, I offer a contemporary social portrait of American Catholics that acknowledges their social and demographic complexity while attempting to understand their beliefs, practices, and attitudes from their own perspectives. I situate Catholics within the academic literature, largely from sociology. I then use detailed empirical evidence to document variations among Catholics and explore how today's Catholics compare to other Americans on a large number of demographic traits, religious beliefs and practices, and attitudes about secular issues. When possible given my data, I also explore how the behaviors, beliefs, and attitudes of Catholics compare to Church doctrine to uncover whether and how Church members follow—or diverge from—the Church's official positions on critical issues.

I use three datasets, each of which is nationally representative and allows me to study Catholics closely and offer up-to-date comparisons between Catholics and other Americans. Each of the datasets was collected at approximately the same time, allowing me to compare patterns for respondents to different surveys that occurred roughly simultaneously.

First, I use the 1972–2021 GSS to provide quantitative evidence about important demographic and other trends that are relevant to understanding Catholics. The GSS is a series of nationally representative cross-sectional interviews with the adult U.S. population conducted since 1972, offering 50 years of detailed information on the U.S. population. I use the over-time GSS data to show trends, but I focus on the details available in the 2021 GSS to provide a contemporary portrait of Catholics. The GSS is widely regarded as an authoritative source of information on the U.S. population, including on religious affiliation, practices, and beliefs. The GSS is also a dependable and reliable source of information about attitudes and beliefs regarding other, more secular issues that I address. Given this combined strength, the GSS is ideal for exploring the topics I raise in this book. An added advantage is that the GSS has been the information source for past books on religion and Catholics, allowing me to document changes in important issues and highlight those areas where changes have been most pronounced. Importantly, the GSS was collected during the COVID-19 pandemic and required changes to the survey's normal data collection procedures. I conducted robustness checks to uncover data inconsistencies that might have resulted and did not discover any significant issues. However, I acknowledge that the time during which the surveys were collected might have influenced respondent answers.

Second, I use the 1997–2021 waves of the Panel Study of Income Dynamics (PSID) to provide longitudinal, quantitative information focused on income, saving, wealth ownership, and giving. The PSID is the longest-running longitudinal survey of U.S. individuals and families. Its sample includes individuals and families who were originally selected for a probability sample in 1968, with an oversample of low-income families. It also includes individuals who were born to or adopted by these original sample members, members of the families that split off from the original families (e.g., following a divorce, when a child leaves home), and those included in immigrant refreshers conducted in 1997 and 2017. This survey allows me to study topics not included in the GSS (e.g., detailed wealth ownership) and changes in the same families over time (as opposed to cross-sections of different families as in the GSS). The PSID is also useful for understanding movement into and out of religious groups over time and at key life turning points. It is well-known for providing excellent information on family structure (including marriage, fertility, and women's roles in the family) and financial behaviors and processes (such as work, income, and wealth).

Finally, I use the American Voices Project (AVP)—a unique, current, mixed-methods (quantitative and qualitative) data source—to provide fresh insights into the mechanisms underlying the empirical patterns emerging from the GSS and PSID. The AVP was collected in 2019 and 2020 and includes quantitative information about respondents as well as qualitative, survey, and experimental data. The interviews cover detailed life histories, including information about religious affiliation, beliefs, and practices. It also provides respondent descriptions of other important life events, relationships with family members and others, economic hardships and ways of handling those hardships, income and expenses, work and job experiences, and use of safety net programs. I use the AVP to create case studies of issues that illustrate patterns I find in the GSS and PSID data.

ROADMAP

My social portrait of Catholics unfolds in two parts. In Part I, I explore who Catholics are demographically. I start by providing details about their social origins (Chapter 2), including personal characteristics (e.g., birth cohort, gender, ancestry, and ethnicity/race) and class background (e.g., parents' social and economic standing, place of birth). I show in Chapter 2 that differences between white and Latino Catholics are fundamental to understanding Catholics, and I explain that studying these two groups in greater depth is empirically viable because current survey data—including the GSS, PSID, and AVP—include sufficiently large numbers of each group to make valid empirical observations. I also describe how black and Asian Catholics are unique, but I conclude that there are too few Catholics from these groups to study in additional detail. Therefore, in subsequent chapters, I focus on differences between white and Latino Catholics, and I compare how these two large Catholic ethnic groups compare to members of other American faith groups.

In Chapter 3, I examine Catholics' adult families with special attention to marriage, cohabitation, divorce, and fertility. I also look at patterns of homogamy, or marrying someone like yourself. Next, I study Catholics' SES achievements, including education, income, wealth, and related topics, such as charitable giving (Chapter 4). In Chapter 4, I also document how women and men divide work in and out of the home, given that this division of labor shapes many other behaviors, outcomes, and attitudes. To fully grasp the continued high Church membership despite underlying demographic changes requires an exploration of who has remained, left, and joined the Church. Thus, I conclude Part I with an exploration of religious mobility, or movement into and out of Catholicism and other faith groups (Chapter 5). In each of these chapters, I compare differences between white and Latino Catholics, and I compare Catholics to other American faith groups. I also explore—where possible—how Catholics' behaviors align with Church doctrine.

In Part II, I provide a unique, contemporary study of Catholics' religious beliefs and practices (Chapter 6), including the degree to which Church membership is an important part of Catholic identity, Church members' Mass and prayer participation patterns, and attitudes toward issues on which the Church has taken a stance, such as abortion. Part II then provides an in-depth study of Catholic attitudes regarding critical political (Chapter 7) and social (Chapter 8) issues. As I did in Part I, I focus on differences both among Catholics and between Catholics and other Americans in each of these chapters, and I address how Catholics' beliefs and attitudes align with official Church doctrine where possible. The final chapter (Chapter 9) distills findings, notes potential extensions of these questions, and speculates about how the current makeup of the Church may continue to change over time.

My hope is that this strategy will reveal the degree to which Catholics are, indeed, the complex individuals and families that anecdotal evidence suggests they are. By studying their social backgrounds, other demographic traits, and SES alongside their religious beliefs and attitudes about political and social issues, I hope to offer a comprehensive portrait of the contemporary American Catholic that documents some of the unique characteristics of America's largest religious group.

PART I
Origins, Turning Points, and Achievements

CHAPTER 2

Social Origins

Social origins matter for much of what people do, accomplish, and believe over their lives, and this chapter shows that Catholics are diverse on the four primary types of social origins: birth cohort, gender, ancestry and race/ethnicity, and class background. This chapter shows that differences between white and Latino Catholics are critical to understanding Catholics in the United States. I build on this conclusion in subsequent chapters by focusing on differences between white and Latino Catholics and comparing these two large Catholic ethnic groups to other American faith groups.

I use the broad term "social origins" to include both ascribed personal traits (such as birth cohort, gender, and ancestry) and other elements of background (such as parents' social and economic status) to describe the early influences on a person's life. The various components of social origins interact with each other in complex ways over time to create the trajectories on which people travel during their lives. For example, social origins can influence who people marry, when they have kids, how many kids they have, how much education they complete, what they accomplish in their careers, their other socioeconomic achievements, and their religious and secular practices and beliefs. Importantly, these processes are interdependent, with causation operating in tandem in many cases (i.e., religious beliefs affect family size and education, but family size and education can also affect religious beliefs). I do not directly address causation in this book. However, I do allow the notion of a life course—in which social origins affect later-life outcomes in a logical temporal sequence—as a guide for the topics that are important for understanding contemporary Catholics.

Given that personal characteristics and background traits are foundational for much of what happens in a person's life, I start my social portrait of Catholics by describing their social origins. I first document birth cohort

Catholics in America. Lisa A. Keister, Oxford University Press. © Oxford University Press 2024.
DOI: 10.1093/oso/9780197753675.003.0002

and gender patterns; I then provide a detailed portrayal of ancestry, ethnicity and race, and country of birth. I conclude the chapter with a description of family background, including parents' socioeconomic status (SES) (education and income) and region (urban vs. rural) of birth. Each of these components of social origin is critical for understanding who Catholics are today, and each affects the family and SES outcomes that are the subject of subsequent chapters of this book. In each section of this chapter, I document differences in social origins among Catholics and compare Catholics to members of other faith groups.

BIRTH COHORT: DIVERSITY IN GENERATIONS IN THE CHURCH

It is useful to think first about birth cohorts. I study Catholics across generational—or birth—cohorts throughout this book, and, as we will see, there are important differences among Catholics resulting from when they were born. A large literature in the social sciences studies the implications of how people born in the same birth cohort experience important social, demographic, economic, and political events at the same time (Elder 1974; Riley 1973; Ryder 1965). These shared experiences affect opportunities, trajectories, ideologies, and norms that lead to cohort differences in behaviors and outcomes that are related to but distinct from the effects of age. There is clear evidence, for example, that marriage and divorce, fertility, family size, and other outcomes vary across birth cohorts (Forest, Moen, and Dempster-McClain 1995; Stockard et al. 2009; Waite 1995; Yang and Lee 2009). There is also evidence that cohort size and norms, such as those about gender and work, affect things like whether people attend college and the types of training they pursue (Berger 1989; Brooks and Bolzendahl 2004; Connelly 1986; Smith, Crosnoe, and Chao 2016). Together, these family, demographic, and educational differences affect job prospects, career advancement, spending, and saving patterns that contribute to sizable differences across cohorts in income and wealth ownership and related behaviors and attitudes.

Six birth cohorts are relevant to understanding today's Catholics and many of the issues I explore in the remainder of this book. Although the enormous variations that characterize members of a single birth cohort are impossible to capture in a few sentences, there are shared experiences that shaped the lives of each of these cohorts and that are relevant to understanding the behaviors of many of their members. The *Silent (or Prewar) Generation*, born 1925–1945, is the oldest cohort I study, and, in many ways, this has been one of the most fortunate birth cohorts in recent U.S. history. Although many members of this generation survived the Great Depression and were forever marked by this experience (Elder 1974), this cohort is largely considered one of the more prosperous in U.S. history (Golden and Katz 2008). This was a relatively small cohort that benefitted from limited competition for education and jobs which, as we will see in Chapter 4, helped them progress through job and career milestones early and fairly quickly, earn wages and salaries that exceeded those of their parents and other older generations, and accumulate assets relatively quickly (Easterlin, Schaeffer, and Macunovich 1993; Sabelhaus and Manchester 1995). As a result, people born in this cohort had among the highest levels of income and wealth in U.S. history. The relative ease with which this cohort passed through education and career stages meant that they also married, had children, and bought homes at younger ages than previous generations.

Subsequent cohorts have encountered more roadblocks and challenges that affected their family, educational, and work outcomes and that likely shaped their religious and secular behaviors and attitudes as well. For example, it is well-documented that the *Baby Boomers* faced a unique set of challenges given the size of their cohort and the economic and social conditions in which they were born and moved through life. The Baby Boom generation is usually divided into two groups: those born 1946–1954 (older Baby Boomers) and those born 1955–1964 (younger Baby Boomers). Although there were differences between these two groups that I will explore throughout this book, both groups grew up and entered the labor market during a period of declines in labor's share of national income (Lin and Tomaskovic-Devey 2013), leading to significant shifts in job and career openings from manual to white-collar work. Of course, there were upsides to this change, including more opportunities in safe work environments, but white-collar jobs required additional education and the salaries in these jobs did not keep pace with rising prices. The size of the Baby Boom cohort also meant much greater competition for spots in universities and for jobs in all sectors.

Gender norms were changing rapidly as well as Baby Boomers entered adulthood, creating conflicting opportunities and outcomes. On the one hand, norms about women attending college and working out of the home were changing, leading Baby Boom women to apply to universities and enter the labor force in record numbers. The unprecedented number of women in both higher education and the labor market created a phenomenon known as *cohort crowding*, which reduced employment opportunities and suppressed salaries for the entire cohort. On the other hand, changing norms about gender and family also contributed to delays in marriage and childbearing, which allowed both women and men more time to finish college, find jobs, and establish careers (Easterlin, MacDonald, and Macunovich 1990). There has been considerable debate throughout the lives of the Baby Boomers about whether—and if so, how—their milestones and successes compare to those of their parents and others in older cohorts. Now that Baby Boomers are largely at the end of their careers and well into retirement, the consensus is that they did not do as well as older cohorts (Macunovich et al. 1995; Yamokoski and Keister 2006; Zagorsky 1999).

Generation X, many of whom were the children of the Baby Boomers, were born 1965–1980 and faced different challenges that have created a unique set of outcomes for this cohort. Unlike the Baby Boomers, Generation X was a fairly small cohort, but they entered the labor market in the 1980s and 1990s, when worker bargaining power was reduced even further than it had been when the Baby Boomers entered the work force. This contributed to wage and salary stagnation for many members of Generation X, particularly those in hourly jobs and other blue-collar occupations (Western and Rosenfeld 2011). During Generation X's prime working years, income and wealth inequality grew to record levels, a trend which benefitted a small number of households but meant stagnant real wages for most workers (Keister 2000; Kennickell 2000; Wolff 2002).

Both the *Millennial Generation* (born 1981–1996) and *Generation Z* (born 1997–2012) are still relatively young, and researchers are only now beginning to clarify basic facts, such as who is included in this generation and what events will influence the paths they take through life (Dimock 2019).[1] It is also relatively soon to say definitely how the lives of these younger Americans will evolve. Yet it is becoming clear that these cohorts are unique from each other and have already experienced significant social, economic, and political events. For Millennials, the September 11 attacks, the U.S. war in Iraq, and the 2007–2009 financial crisis and recession were formative events. Millennials are a relatively large cohort and—compared to prior generations—have higher levels of education, women's labor force participation, and (at least so far) incomes (Bialik and Fry 2019). However, Millennials also have more debt than their parents, particularly student debt. Many Millennials entered the labor force during the 2007–2009 financial crisis and have continued to encounter housing shortages through 2023, making it difficult for them to purchase homes and decreasing their net worth (Rodriguez 2023). Millennials are a relatively diverse cohort ethnically, they lean left politically, are delaying marriage and childbearing even more than previous generations, and appear to have high rates of disaffiliation from religion compared to other cohorts (Bialik and Fry 2019; Kaplan 2020; Smith et al. 2014; Smith 2020). Notably, this pattern does not represent a qualitative break in religiosity with this cohort. Rather, this cohort is slightly less religious than the one before, continuing a long-term trend in declining religiosity (Voas and Chaves 2016).

For Generation Z, the 1999–2021 U.S. war in Afghanistan and the ongoing global COVID-19 pandemic are likely to have lasting effects. Early indicators suggest that Generation Z is even more ethnically and racially diverse, more highly educated, and on-target to earn higher incomes and marry later in life even than Millennials. Changing patterns of immigration have been central to creating these changes. That is, there are more Latinos in Generation Z than in previous generations, and, most notably, Generation Z Latinos are less likely than Latinos in previous generations to be first-generation immigrants (Fry and Parker 2018).

Birth cohort captures an enormous amount of information about the context in which people move through their lives. For Catholics, the Second Vatican Council (Vatican II) was a critical contextual event that each of these cohorts experienced differently and that is likely to contribute to differences in how members of each cohort experience Catholicism. Vatican II, during which more than 2,000 Catholic bishops from every corner of the world met from 1962 to 1965, was a moment of epochal change in the Catholic Church and was an important juncture with ramifications for the experiences of Catholics from these six birth cohorts. Members of the Silent Generation were ages 20 through 40 in 1965. Older Catholics in this cohort would have known the pre-Vatican church well and would likely have experienced the changes as a significant transformation of their religious lives (Greeley 2004; Wilde 2007). The oldest Catholic Baby Boomers were only 19 at the end of Vatican II; although they would have some memory of the pre-Vatican Church, this cohort would largely have been raised during the years when the Council's mandates were being implemented. Catholic members of Generation X were all born after Vatican II, making them the first cohort to have no personal memory of the pre-Vatican church. For both Millennials and Generation Z Catholics, the Church has always been a post-Vatican II organization. Members of these cohorts may have knowledge of Vatican II, but for them, the Council is likely to be part of history rather than a tangible part of their religious experience and understanding of what it means to be Catholic.

Because birth cohort clearly matters—including for many of the family traits, SES, beliefs, and attitudes—it is useful to know that today's Catholic Church has large numbers of members from each of the birth cohorts I have described. Although there is not an even split of birth cohorts in the Church, as Figure 2.1 shows, each of the cohorts I mentioned above is clearly well-represented. The bars in Figure 2.1 indicate the percentage of members of each religious tradition who are members of the six birth cohorts. Within each religious tradition, the percentage of cohort members sums to 100%.

Importantly, however, the cohort distribution in the Catholic Church is relatively young, reflecting fertility differences between white and Latino Catholics (Hout 2016) and the aging of the U.S. religious population, including Catholics (Chaves 2017). That is, Catholics are slightly most likely to be Baby Boomers, who account for 31% of the total (17% young Boomers, 14% older Boomers). Millennials (25%) and Generation X (26%) are the next largest cohorts. Approximately 10% of Catholics are from Generation Z, and 8% are Silent Generation.

Catholics differ from other religious groups in many ways, as I document throughout this book, and the representation of birth cohorts within their ranks is an important initial point of difference. Catholics are more likely

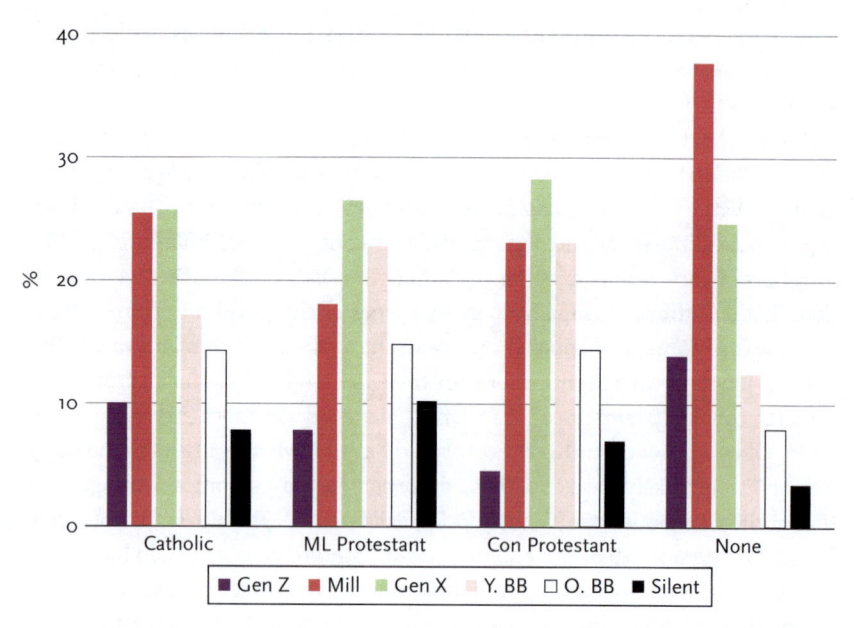

Figure 2.1 Birth cohort and religious tradition

than mainline Protestants to be young: that is, Catholics are more likely to be Millennials (25% vs. 18%) and less likely to be young Baby Boomers (17% vs. 22%). Catholics and conservative Protestants are more similar in their distribution of birth cohorts: 35% of Catholics and about 30% of conservative protestants are Generation Z or Millennials. As we will see in Chapter 3, the somewhat young age distribution for Catholics may reflect historic—and to a lesser degree—current fertility patterns. Historically, Catholics have had high fertility rates, and their families are still somewhat larger than those of other Americans. Latino Catholics have slightly higher fertility rates than white Catholics and other Americans (see Chapter 3), and this may account for the differences evidenced in Figure 2.1.

To put patterns by birth cohort and religious tradition in perspective, however, it is important to consider the "religious nones," who are clearly the youngest of the religious groups shown in Figure 2.1. Differences between Catholics and the religious nones are stark. The patterns shown in Figure 2.1 are consistent with the higher likelihood of younger Americans to disaffiliate from religion entirely. Most religious nones are Generation Z (14%), Millennials (38%), and Generation X (25%). These patterns have been well-documented in previous research and are clearly still significant. Importantly, however, some of these cohort differences reflect the age distribution of the population: more members of older cohorts have died in higher numbers leaving a smaller percentage of older Baby Boomers and, especially, the Silent Generation in each religious group.

WOMEN AND MEN: GENDER BALANCE AND CONVERGENCE

Gender is another trait that is, of course, a well-documented axis on which many social, economic, and political behaviors and attitudes vary (England, Levine, and Mishel 2020; National Women's Business Council 2012; Thébaud and Halcomb 2019). Gender affects a host of family processes including how couples divide labor in and out of the household and related issues such as how much power each person has to influence important decisions in the family regarding childcare, housework, and how to spend money (Lachance-Grzela and Bouchard 2010; Reskin and Maroto 2011). There are gendered patterns in educational expectations and the completion of schooling and in work, including the choice of jobs or careers, business start-ups, and access to leadership positions (Bergmann 2011; Jennings and Brush 2013; Saurav, Goltz, and Buche 2013; Warner, Ellmann, and Boesch 2018). Family and education, in turn, affect how much income women and men earn, leading to well-documented income deficits for women who leave the labor force to have children, barriers for women to high-income occupations, and gender differences in approaches to saving and wealth (Blau and Kahn 2017; England et al. 2016; Yavorsky et al. 2019; Yavorsky, Keister, and Qian 2020).

There is also evidence that women and men approach and live out their religious beliefs in different ways, and these differences vary across birth cohorts; as a result, religion is associated with outcomes such as education, work behavior, occupational and career mobility, income, and charitable giving in different ways for women and men (Amin and Sherkat 2013; Eagle, Keister, and Read 2017; Ellison and Bartkowski 2002; Horwitz 2022). For women, for example, conservative theological attitudes are associated with earlier marriage and childbearing, lower educational attainment, a reduced likelihood of labor force entry, lower earnings, and more time spent on housework and childcare (Glass and Jacobs 2005). By contrast, there is little association between conservative theology and men's behaviors and attitudes (Civettini and Glass 2008). Past scholarship also showed important gender differences between Catholic women and men in their religious and secular practices and attitudes (D'Antonio et al. 2001). Importantly, however, these differences are likely to have declined over time given that gender equity is more evident in younger birth cohorts. I revisit gender and birth cohort differences in financial and work outcomes in Chapter 4 and in related attitudes in Chapters 6 and 7. My goal here is to provide an initial accounting of gender and birth cohort differences between Catholics and Americans from other faith traditions.

Given the importance of gender in creating and maintaining a host of economic and social outcomes, it is noteworthy that the cohort distribution for Catholics is comparable for women and men (Figures 2.2A,B).[2] That is, of Catholics, a comparable percentage of women and men are Generation Z (9% of women, 11% of men), Generation X (26%, 25%), young Baby Boomers

(a)

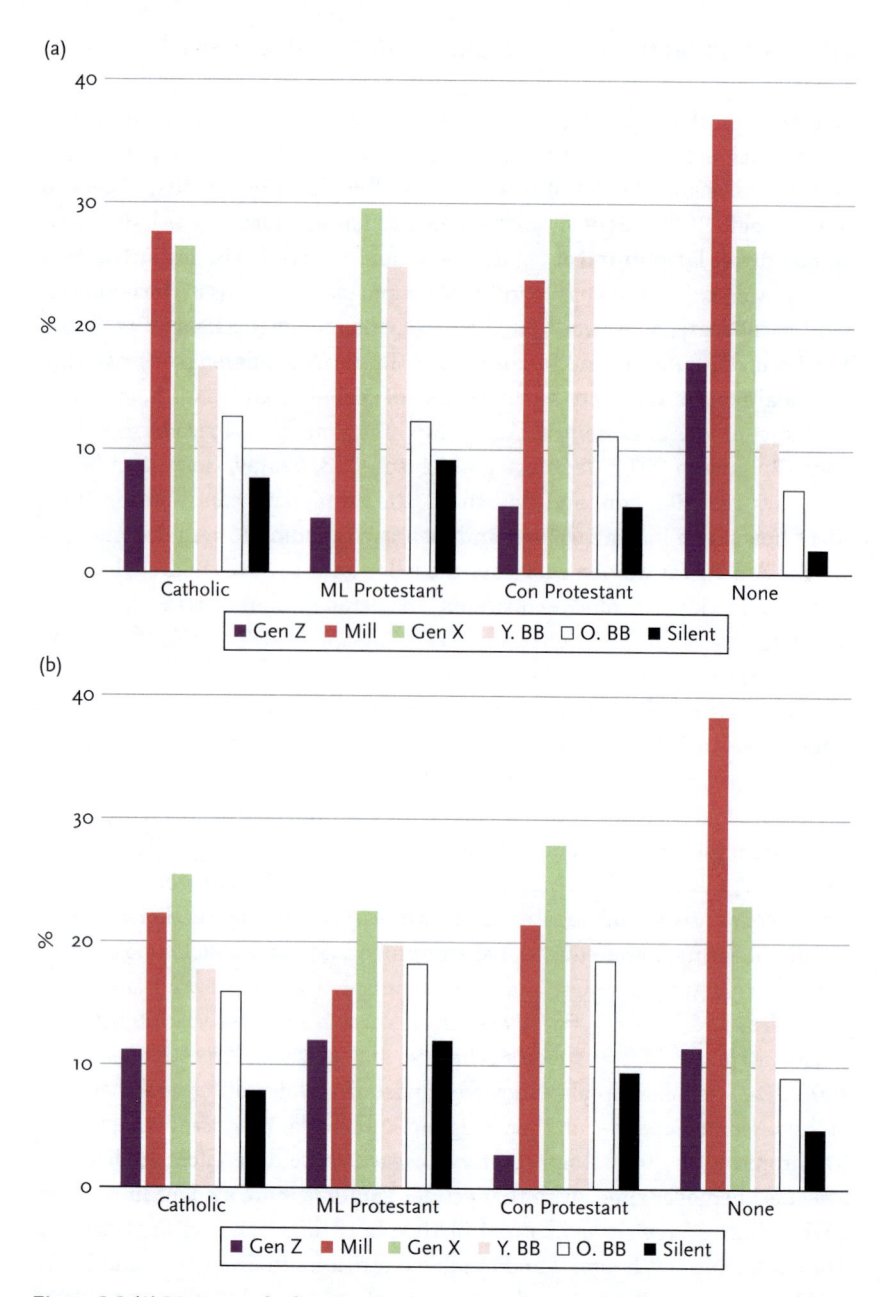

Figure 2.2 (A) Women and religious tradition. (B) Men and religious tradition

(17%, 17%), older Baby Boomers (13%, 16%), and Silent Generation (8%, 8%). The one notable difference that emerges is for Millennials: of female Catholics, 28% are Millennials; but of male Catholics, 22% are Millennials. Looking across Figure 2.2B suggests that these male Millennials are likely to

[22] *Catholics in America*

be religious nones. It is not possible to discern from Figure 2.2 whether this difference reflects religious switching over time, but I return to that question in Chapter 5.

There are also three notable differences between Catholics and people from other faith traditions in the distribution of birth cohorts and gender among their members. First, Catholic women are somewhat younger than either mainline or conservative Protestant women: of Catholic women, 37% are either Generation Z or Millennials. By contrast, Generation Z and Millennials account for smaller portions of mainline (24%) and conservative Protestants (28%). Second, the cohort distribution for Catholic men is similar to that of mainline Protestant men, but Catholic and mainline Protestant men are somewhat younger than conservative Protestant men. For example, about 33% of Catholic and 28% of mainline Protestant men are either Generation Z or Millennials, whereas only 22% of conservative Protestant men are in one of these younger cohorts. Third, the most pronounced difference shown in these figures is consistent with patterns that have been emerging for decades: Catholics and all Protestants, regardless of gender, are all older than religious nones: 53% of women and 49% of men who are religious nones are either Generation Z or Millennials.

ANCESTRY, ETHNICITY AND RACE, AND IMMIGRATION: DIVERSITY IN FAMILY ORIGINS

Ancestry

Diversity in family of origin—across measures of ancestry, ethnicity and race, and immigration—is an important part of the story of American Catholics. Immigration, nativity, and ancestry have played a critical role in defining religious identification for Catholics and other Americans for centuries. Indeed, more than one-third of Catholic parishes identify with a particular ethnic or language ministry (Zech et al. 2017). The country from which one's ancestors originated is foundational for understanding Catholics because it affects most other behaviors and processes that define a person's life.[3] Ancestry affects marriage and family processes, educational pursuits and accomplishments, job outcomes, income and wealth, and religious and secular attitudes. There is also clear evidence that ancestry is associated with how people live out their religious faith, including the life decisions they deem important (e.g., attending college vs. joining the labor force), religious conversion and switching, and religious beliefs and practices (Ramos, Woodberry, and Ellison 2017; Sherkat 2014; Smith et al. 2014; Stark 2008).

One notable change in ancestry—the increasing presence of those with Latin American ancestry—is fundamental to understanding who Catholics

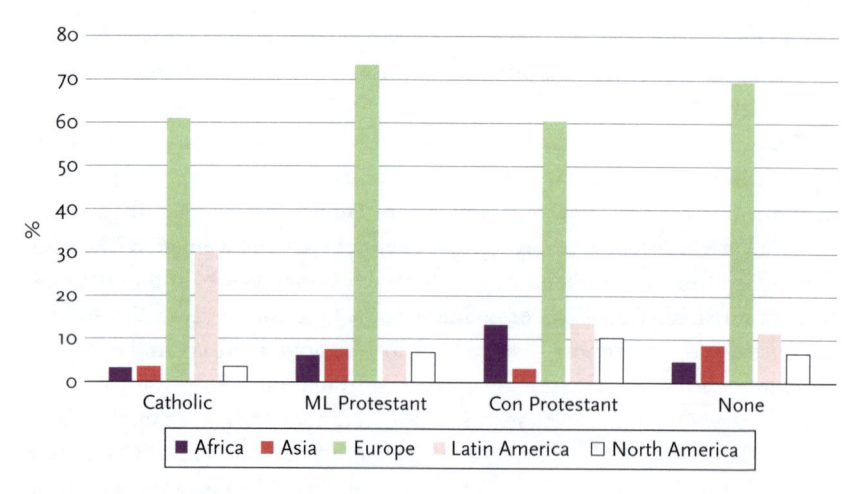

Figure 2.3 Ancestry and religious tradition

are today. The increasing presence of those with Latino ancestry, which had begun by the 1970s (Greeley 1977), is shown in Figure 2.3. Figure 1.2 provided details of the evolution of Catholic ancestry over time, and Figure 2.3 expands this by giving ancestry details in 2021. The bars in Figure 2.3 indicate the percentage of Catholics and those from other religious traditions who report having ancestors from Africa, Asia, Europe, Latin America, and North America. In the 1970s, about 80% of Catholics reported having European ancestry, but, by 2021, only about 60% of Catholics said their ancestors were European. Over the same time, the presence of Catholics with Latin American ancestry has grown: in the 1970s, only about 10% of Catholics had ancestors from Latin America, but nearly 30% of Catholics were descendants of those from Latin America in 2021; importantly, the percentage of Catholics with ancestors from Latin America (including Mexico) has remained at about 30% since the 1990s (time trend shown in Chapter 1). Descendants of people from Africa and Asia are an important part of the Catholic diversity story as well, although these groups are still rather small. Indeed, those with ancestors from African, Asia, and other parts of North America (e.g., Canada, Native Americans) account for only about 10% of all Catholics in 2021.

Catholics are also more diverse than those from other religious traditions, especially in the prominence of people with ancestors from Latin America. For example, Catholics have a notably different ancestry profile than mainline Protestants and religious nones (who are quite similar to each other): 61% of Catholics compared to 73% of mainline Protestants and 70% of religious nones have European ancestors. By contrast, 30% of Catholics and only 7% of mainline Protestants and 11% of religious nones have Latin American ancestors. Catholics are more similar to conservative Protestants in terms of those

[24] *Catholics in America*

with European ancestry; those with European ancestry make up about 60% of both groups. However, there are more Catholics than conservative Protestants with Latin American ancestors (30% vs. 14%). Conservative Protestants are unique in terms of people with African ancestry in part because this group includes a large number of black Protestants; indeed, more than 13% of conservative Protestants claim African ancestry compared to less than 6% for Catholics, mainline Protestants, and religious nones (see Appendix for details about data and variables).

Ethnicity and Race

The important presence of Latino Americans in the Church is also evident in the ethnicity and race of Catholics. Self-reported ethnic and racial identity are similar to—but distinct from—the origin of a person's ancestors that I described in the previous section. Ethnicity is considered a part of personal identity that reflects culture, language, and family history. Race is also a component of personal identity, and, although even experts differ in their definitions of race, it usually reflects both ancestry and physical characteristics such as skin color. Ethnicity, race, and ancestry are closely related; given this connection, patterns of ethnicity and race closely resemble patterns of ancestry for most people. I show both ancestry and ethnicity/race patterns for Catholics in this chapter to document these similarities, and I focus on ethnicity in subsequent chapters for simplicity. I follow most social science research and distinguish four ethnic groups: non-Latino white, non-Latino black, Latino, and other race (including Asian, Native American, and other races not specified here).

Catholics are, indeed, diverse in their ethnic self-identification. Figure 2.4 shows the percentage of respondents who identify with each of the four ethnicity/race categories by religious affiliation. The figure shows that ethnic identity patterns vary quite closely with the patterns of ancestry (shown in Figure 2.3): nearly 60% of Catholics identify as white, and 34% identify as Latino.

Figure 2.4 also underscores differences in ethnic identity between Catholics and other religious groups. Most notably, a much higher percentage of Catholics (34%) versus mainline Protestants (7%), conservative Protestants (10%), and religious nones (13%) are Latino. There are growing numbers of Latino Protestants in the United States, and some estimates suggest that this group will continue to grow (Mulder, Ramos, and Marti 2017). However, in 2021, as Figure 2.4 shows, very few Latinos are members of any Protestant denomination. Similarly, more than (76%) of mainline Protestants and more than 62% of conservative Protestants are white, though there are also many Protestants who identify as black. This is particularly true of conservative

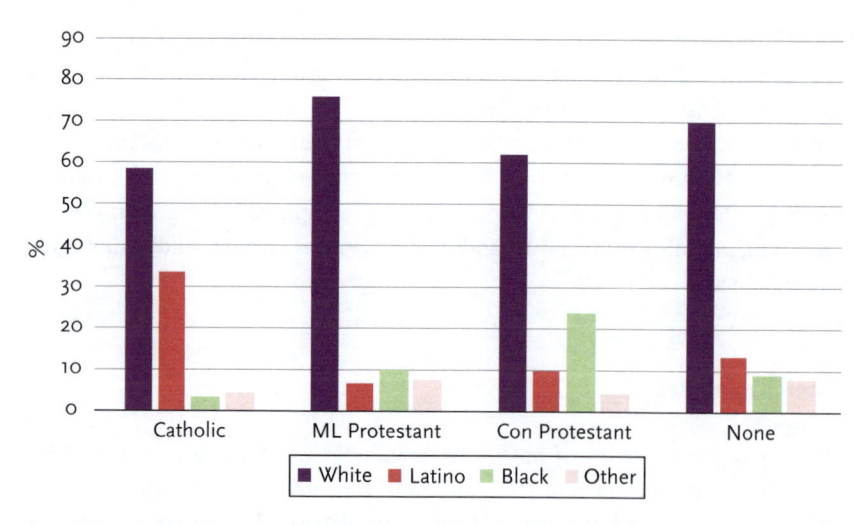

Figure 2.4 Race-ethnicity and religious tradition

Protestants, reflecting the important presence of black Protestant churches in the United States.

A unique set of issues is relevant to understanding four ethnic and racial groups in the Catholic Church: white, Latino, Asian, and black Catholics.

White Catholics

White Americans are still the dominant Catholic ethnic group, even though they now comprise a smaller portion of the Church than they did in previous decades. Compared with Catholics of previous generations (Greeley 1977, 1989; Zech et al. 2017), white Catholics are mostly non-immigrants and, to a lesser extent, second-generation immigrants.

Catholic population growth underscores this important transformation: Catholic membership has been changing unevenly across the United States, increasing in the South and West (i.e., in places where Latino populations are large) and shrinking in the Northeast and Midwest (i.e., where white populations are still dominant) (Wiggins, Gautier, and Gaunt 2021).

Catholic diversity highlights the degree to which prominent white Catholics—such as President Biden, members of Congress, and Supreme Court justices—represent just a segment of Catholics today. Previous academic research has shown that white Catholics have been upwardly mobile on many measures of social and economic attainment such as education, income, and wealth. It is likely that this pattern has continued and explains the increase in Catholics in prominent leadership positions, as I explore in Chapter 4.

Latino Catholics

Latinos have been a large portion of the U.S. population since the founding of the country (Jones et al. 2021). However, Latino immigration to the United States increased dramatically after 1965, when exclusionary immigration laws based explicitly on race were changed (Xie and Goyette 2012; Zhou 2009). Attention to the U.S. Latino population has grown recently as population expansion of the Latino community outpaced that of other ethnic groups by a considerable margin between the most recent census counts: the Latino population grew more than 23% between 2010 and 2020, while population growth for non-Latinos was slightly more than 4% in that same time frame (Jones et al. 2021). The strong association between religion and Latino ancestry is also well-documented (Alba, Raboteau, and DeWind 2009; Hondagneu-Sotelo 2008; Portes and Rumbaut 2006).

Political and social attitudes (Chapters 8 and 9) are important to understanding how Catholics, generally, influence the social politics of / social fabric of ? United States, and patterns of Latino population growth are an important part of this story. Latino population growth was strong in all 50 states, but it has been particularly notable in the Southwest—in states like California, Nevada, and Texas—for nearly 20 years and in states that are likely to be decisive in political contests—such as Florida and Arizona—in coming years (Igielnik and Budiman 2020; Masci and Smith 2018; Passel, Lopez, and Cohn 2022). In these political battleground states, it is particularly notable that large portions of the voting adult population are Latino. For example, in Florida, more than 20% of eligible voters are Latino, and in Arizona, about 25% are Latino (Igielnik and Budiman 2020). There have also been notable changes in the nativity of eligible voters in battleground states such as Florida. Increasing numbers of Florida voters are of Mexican or Puerto Rican descent, rather than Cuban descent, and Mexican and Puerto Rican Americans are more likely to register as Democrats or lean toward the Democratic party, whereas Cuban Americans are more likely to register as Republicans or lean toward the Republican party (Igielnik and Budiman 2020). In Texas, 32% of voters are Latino (Natarajan and Im 2022), and, particularly in South Texas, Latino voters were historically left-leaning but have recently begun to shift to the right, raising questions about the future of Texas and national elections (Sanchez October 15, 2022).

Most Latinos were once Catholic, but Catholic affiliation has declined for Latinos over the past 15 years. Indeed, in 2006, nearly 70% of Latinos were Catholic, but only 50% were Catholic in 2021 (author's estimates from the GSS). Latinos who leave the Catholic Church have tended to remain affiliated with other Christian denominations including both mainline and conservative Protestant churches. However, more Latinos have joined conservative Protestant denominations (Mulder et al. 2017). There are still very few older

Latinos who are religious nones or affiliated with a non-Christian religious group, but Millennial and Generation Z Latinos are more inclined than their older counterparts to disaffiliate with religion.

Although Latino Protestants are a growing and potentially important group, there are still relatively few of them in the United States and in the GSS data. In the remainder of this chapter, I continue to show descriptive statistics for Latinos who are mainline and conservative Protestant, and I include reminders that these are small groups. In the remainder of this book, I use regression models to control for the various processes that interact with religion to produce the outcomes I study. These models require larger sample sizes than the GSS includes for Latino Protestants. For this reason, in Chapter 3 and beyond, I pool Latino mainline and conservative Protestants into a single Latino Protestant category. I am also unable to show estimates for Latinos—Catholic or Protestant—by nativity. It is unfortunate to have to speak broadly about Latinos rather than to look more closely at Mexican, Salvadoran, Cuban, Dominican, and other Latino groups. Again, however, sample sizes make it impossible for me to provide more detailed estimates.

Asian Catholics

Catholic ethnic diversity is also evident in the important—and potentially growing—presence of Asian Americans in the Church. Only about 3% of Catholics are Asian (Figure 2.3), but Asian immigration to the United States is increasing and potentially bringing with it a rise in the percentage of Asian Catholics.

Asian immigration to the United States—like Latino immigration—has a long history dating to the mid-1800s. Asian immigration also increased dramatically after 1965 (Xie and Goyette 2012; Zhou 2009), but a recent influx has attracted renewed attention to Asian immigrants: in 2009, Asian immigrants surpassed Latino immigrants as the fastest-growing segment of the foreign-born U.S. population (Hoeffel et al. 2012; Pew Research Center 2012b). Much of this change can be attributed to a growth in Chinese immigration: Chinese Americans are the largest Asian subgroup, at 23.2%, and 76% of Chinese Americans are foreign-born (Hoeffel et al. 2012; Pew Research Center 2012b; Rumbaut 2008; Walters and Trevelyan 2011). However, there are also sizable Filipino, Vietnamese, Korean, Indian, and Japanese American populations, particularly in large metropolitan areas such as Los Angeles, New York, and Washington, DC (Gray, Gautier, and Gaunt 2014).

Christianity, including Catholicism, is becoming more common among Asian immigrants. In a now somewhat dated but still important nationwide survey of Asian Americans, the Pew Research Center found that Christianity (42%) was the largest religious group for Asian adults in the United States

(Pew Research Center 2012a). This same survey showed that similar percentages of Asian adults were Catholic (19%) and Protestant (22%) (Pew Research Center 2012a). Of the Asian subgroups, it is notable that Catholicism is growing among the large Chinese American population and that the majority of American Filipinos are Catholic (Gray et al. 2014).

These changes are significant for both the future demographics of U.S. population and for the Catholic Church. However, I do not provide additional details about Asian Catholics in the remainder of this book because there are far too few respondents in the GSS and most other representative datasets to make reliable statistical inferences about their family and SES traits, religious beliefs, and social and political attitudes.

Black Catholics

Black Catholics are another important part of the Catholic Church, as a Pew Research Center study shows (Diamant, Mohamed, and Alvarado 2022). There are approximately 3 million black Catholics in the United States, making this a sizable group with a notable presence in many Catholic churches. Unfortunately, however, it is difficult to study black Catholics using most data because only about 6% of black adults are Catholic, and only about 3% of Catholic adults have African ancestry (Figure 2.3) or self-identify as non-Latino black (Figure 2.4). The large group of black Catholics includes both African Americans (i.e., people with African ancestry who have lived in the United States, in many cases, their entire lives) and possibly recent immigrants (first- or second-generation immigrants). The Pew research showed that black Catholics have interesting and unique experiences that differ in important ways from those of white and Latino Catholics. For example, only about 25% of black Catholics attend Mass at predominantly black parishes, whereas the majority (80%) of white Catholics attend Mass at predominantly white parishes and about 67% of Latinos attend Mass at parishes that are predominantly Latino (Diamant et al. 2022). Black Protestants—the majority of black Christians in the United States—are more like white and Latino Catholics in this way: approximately 68% of black Protestants attend services at churches where most other attendees are also black (Diamant et al. 2022).

Black Catholics are also interesting in terms of their movement into and out of the faith and their identities as Catholics. The Pew survey finds that *more* black Catholics (about 16%) than white or Latino were raised in other faith traditions and converted to Catholicism; the survey also shows that, compared to white and Latino Catholics, fewer black Catholics (about 54%) who were raised Catholic are still members of the Church (Diamant et al. 2022). Given that there is diversity in when a person or their ancestors immigrated to the United States, there is also likely to be considerable diversity in experience among black Catholics. Related research shows that most black Catholics do not feel marginalized in the Church and have strong identities as Catholics, particularly compared to white Catholics (Davis and Pope-Davis 2017). Although black Catholics are interesting and potentially unique in many ways, I am unable to study them in depth in the remainder of this book because there are too few of them in my data.

Immigration

Immigrants have always been an important part of the American Catholic story, and they remain central to understanding who is Catholic today. Consistent with changes in the U.S. population, however, the country of birth of Catholic immigrants is now skewed heavily toward Mexico and other Latin American countries, although there has been some growth in Asian immigration as well. There are also important differences across immigrant generation, with both white and Latino Catholics more likely to be second-generation immigrants (born in the United States to immigrant parents) than first-generation immigrants (born in another country and migrated to the United States as an adult). The most pronounced difference among Catholics in immigration is between white and Latino Catholics (Figures 2.5A and 2.5B): white Catholics are now much more likely to be non-immigrants (62%) than first- or second-generation immigrants (5% and 32%, respectively). By contrast, nearly equal portions of Latino Catholics are non-immigrants (39%) and second-generation immigrants (38%). An additional 23% of Latino Catholics are first-generation immigrants.

White Catholics are much more likely than other white Americans to be immigrants, particularly second-generation immigrants, consistent with historic evidence that Catholics were once very likely to be European immigrants: whereas 62% of white Catholics are non-immigrants, 82% of mainline Protestants, 86% of conservative Protestants, and 77% of religious nones are non-immigrants. Similarly, there are few differences in terms of first-generation immigrants between white Catholics and other white Americans: between 4% and 6% of all white religious groups shown in Figure 2.5B are first-generation immigrants. However, there are large differences between white Catholics and other white Americans in the present of second-generation immigrants: about 32% of Catholics are second-generation immigrants compared to only 14% of mainline Protestants, 10% of conservative Protestants, and 17% of religious nones. There is little difference between Catholics and other Americans in first-generation immigrant membership: 5% of Catholics, 4% of Protestants, 6% of religious nones, and 7% of those of other faiths are first-generation immigrants.

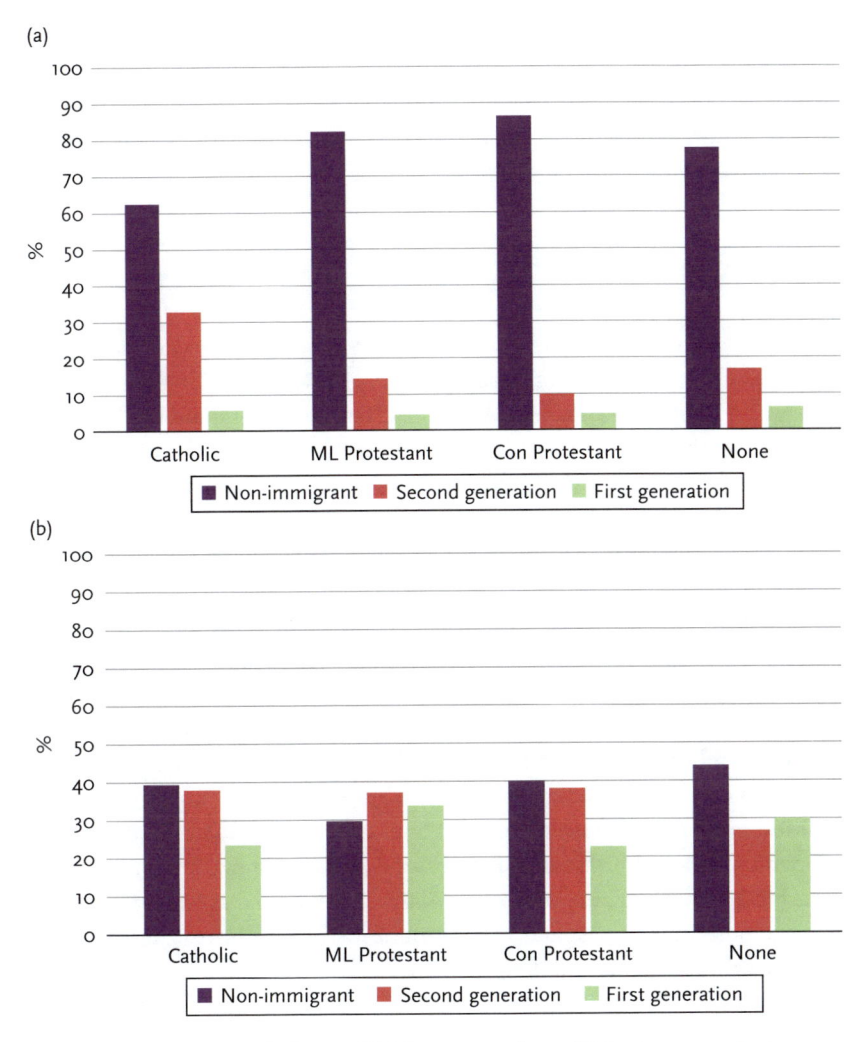

Figure 2.5 Immigrants and religion. (A) White respondents. (B) Latino respondents

CLASS BACKGROUND

Catholics also come from diverse class and family backgrounds, and this is vital to understanding their adult family behaviors and outcomes, achievements, and beliefs. Family income, parental education, and the geographic space in which a person grows up are all useful indicators of the conditions in which a person was raised. Parents' social status is important because it indicates whether they can provide resources (e.g., educational resources such as private school, after-school training, test prep) for their children and what parents expect for their children's own educational and work outcomes. Parental education and income are also highly correlated with other indicators of family well-being, such as family size and parents' marital status, that have independent effects on life trajectories. The geographic space in which an individual is raised also indicates the contextual resources and influences that work with parents' status to shape the trajectory on which individuals enter into—and navigate through—adulthood.

Parents' Social Status

Parents' social status is, indeed, a critical factor influencing most adult outcomes, and Catholics are remarkably diverse in the status of their families of origin. I found remarkable diversity in class background among Catholics on multiple dimensions; I describe patterns in the highest level of education completed by the father of GSS respondents to illustrate this diversity.[4]

Among Catholics, ethnic diversity in parents' social status is particularly salient. For white Catholics (Figure 2.6A), more than one-half (56%) of fathers completed high school or have an associate's degree, and 23% of fathers completed a bachelor's degree. Only 21% of the fathers of white Catholic respondents had less than a high school education. By contrast, more than 58% of the fathers of Latino Catholic respondents (Figure 2.6B) had less than a high school education. Yet there are sizable portions of Latino Catholics who report fathers with high school diplomas or associate degrees (31%) or bachelor's degrees (11%). These patterns for Latino Catholics reflect three interrelated realities. First, a large percentage of Latino Americans are second-generation immigrants or non-immigrants. Figures 2.5A and 2.5B show immigration patterns for GSS respondents, but there are large portions of respondents' parents who are non-immigrants, and these Americans had access to the American educational system. Second, first-generation Latino immigrants, particularly Mexican immigrants, tend to be selected on education: that is, documented Mexican immigrants to the United States tend to have higher levels of educational attainment than Mexicans who do not immigrate (Feliciano 2005, 2006). Third, Latino (again, particularly Mexican) immigrants who spend sufficient time in the United States ultimately attain notable levels of education and other measures of SES (Agius Vallejo 2012; Alba and Nee 2003; Keister, Agius Vallejo, and Borelli 2014).

Notably, white Catholics now look much more like white mainline Protestants in terms of family background than they did in the past. I return to the issue of status differences—and changes in these differences over time—between white Catholics and white mainline Protestants in Chapter 4. However, it is important to note here that white Catholics and white mainline Protestants are nearly identical in their background SES. By contrast, white conservative Protestants report slightly lower SES and religious nones report significantly higher SES than Catholics and mainline Protestants (Figure 2.6A).

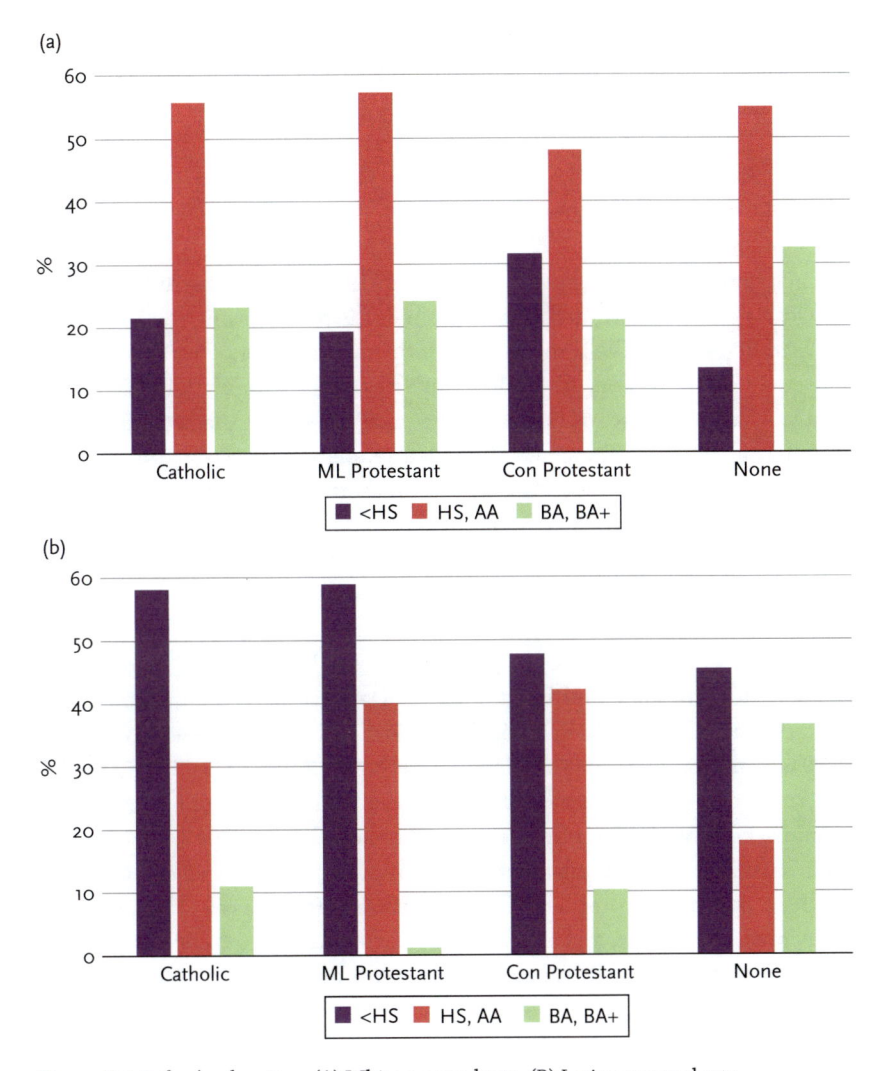

Figure 2.6 Father's education: (A) White respondents. (B) Latino respondents

The percentage of each of these groups whose father had less than a high school degree illustrates this point well: among white respondents, 21% of Catholics and 19% of mainline Protestants report that their fathers had less than a high school degree. By contrast, more than 31% of conservative Protestants and only 14% of religious nones had fathers with less than a high school degree.

Background SES patterns are slightly different for Latinos: similar percentages (58%) of Latino Catholics and Latino mainline Protestants had fathers who had less than a high school degree, but a significantly higher percentage of Latino Catholics (11%) compared to Latino mainline Protestants (1%) had

SOCIAL ORIGINS [33]

fathers with less than a high school degree. Importantly, there are relatively few Latino Protestants, as Figure 2.4 showed, suggesting that these estimates need to be interpreted carefully.

Urban–Rural Differences

The places where people grow up—rural, urban, or something in between—are closely associated with class background: the place in which an individual is raised determines the resources and influences that shape their early lives and entry in adulthood, in tandem with characteristics of the individual's family. As a result, place of birth affects a great deal about the paths individuals follow during their lives, including their families, SES, and attitudes. In recent decades, jobs have moved from rural areas to metropolitan centers where financial, technical, and other employers are located (Probst et al. 2011). Rural areas and small towns are also considerably slower to recover from recessions and economic downturns compared to urban areas, which has created widening economic gaps among geographic regions (Fry 2013).

Growing up in a rural area creates particular challenges that affect the paths people follow through adulthood. First, educational opportunities are more limited in rural areas (Biddle and Mette 2017; Economic Research Service 2019a; Hamilton et al. 2008; Keister, Moody, and Wolff 2021). High rates of poverty and low population density mean that funding for rural schools lags behind school funding in other regions (Biddle and Mette 2017; Carlson and Goss 2016). The result is dilapidated buildings, less experienced and qualified teachers, and limits to other resources such as after-school programs, athletics, music education, and other extracurricular activities (Biddle and Mette 2017; Carlson and Goss 2016; Lichter, Roscigno, and Condron 2003). Because of resource constraints in school and at home, rural students' access to the internet tends to be low, and, as a result, rural children have lower rates of adoption of new technologies that might contribute to educational achievement (Biddle and Mette 2017; Carlson and Goss 2016). Moreover, as rural populations declined in recent decades, rural schools consolidated, requiring students to spend more time on buses and thus reducing time available for educational and extracurricular activities, socializing with friends and family, and doing homework (MacTavis and Salamon 2003).

Resource and other constraints in rural areas have clear implications for both short- and long-term educational outcomes for youth. In particular, growing up in a rural area is associated with lower educational and occupational aspirations (Biddle and Mette 2017; Cobb, McIntire, and Pratt 1989; McLaughlin, Shoff, and Demi 2014), increased dropout rates, reduced preparation for postsecondary education, and, ultimately, lower lifelong educational achievement (Lichter et al. 2003). Youth who stay in rural areas are less likely to complete college degrees or professional training (Economic Research Service 2019a; Hamilton et al. 2008). Those who migrate to other areas in search of educational and occupational opportunities (often the most talented youth) contribute to the acute outmigration problem that faces many rural communities and that further lowers educational levels in rural areas (Carr and Kefalas 2009; Gibbs and Cromartie 1994; Johnson 2012; Sherman and Sage 2011). Rates of return to rural communities are notably low despite the draw of ties to family and friends (Hamilton et al. 2008) because employment opportunities are limited (von Reichert, Cromartie, and Arthun 2011).

Educational challenges in rural areas reduce job opportunities and income, further suppressing other professional opportunities. Agriculture, low-skilled manufacturing, and natural resource industries have been replaced with lower-paying jobs in the service industry in many rural areas (Hamilton et al. 2008). As a result, many rural communities that already lagged behind other geographic regions struggled to recover from the Great Recession, leading to even larger economic gaps among geographic regions (Fry 2013). Declines in federal investment in infrastructure for rural communities exacerbated these problems, and, although not all rural communities are the same (Hamilton et al. 2008), the broad trend has been toward high and rising levels of unemployment (Duncan 2015; Economic Research Service 2019b) and few opportunities for self-employment (Tsvetkova, Partridge, and Betz 2017). Consistent with increasing unemployment, incomes are comparatively low, and poverty—including child poverty—is high in rural areas (Duncan 2015; Economic Research Service 2019b). Recent evidence also suggests that poverty risk is high and increasing even for those who are employed in rural areas, that the rate of working poverty is higher in rural areas than in other geographic areas (Thiede, Lichter, and Slack 2018), and that poverty is persistent across generations (Lichter and Graefe 2011; Lichter and Schafft 2016; Thiede, Kim, and Slack 2017). Evidence that low-income children who grow up in rural commuting zones tend to be more upwardly mobile than their rural counterparts may, in reality, reflect lower starting points for rural children rather than a particularly propitious pattern (Chetty et al. 2014).

Like most Americans, both white and Latino Catholics largely grew up in towns (i.e., mid-sized cities) and, to a slightly lesser extent, in larger urban areas. Figures 2.7A and 2.7B compare the geographic regions where GSS respondents grew up, dividing the regions into three groups. The GSS defines rural areas as both farms and non-farm spaces in the country, towns are small cities with populations under 250,000, and urban areas are suburbs or cities with populations greater than 250,000. About 50% of all GSS respondents—including about 50% of white Catholics and 52% of Latino Catholics—grew

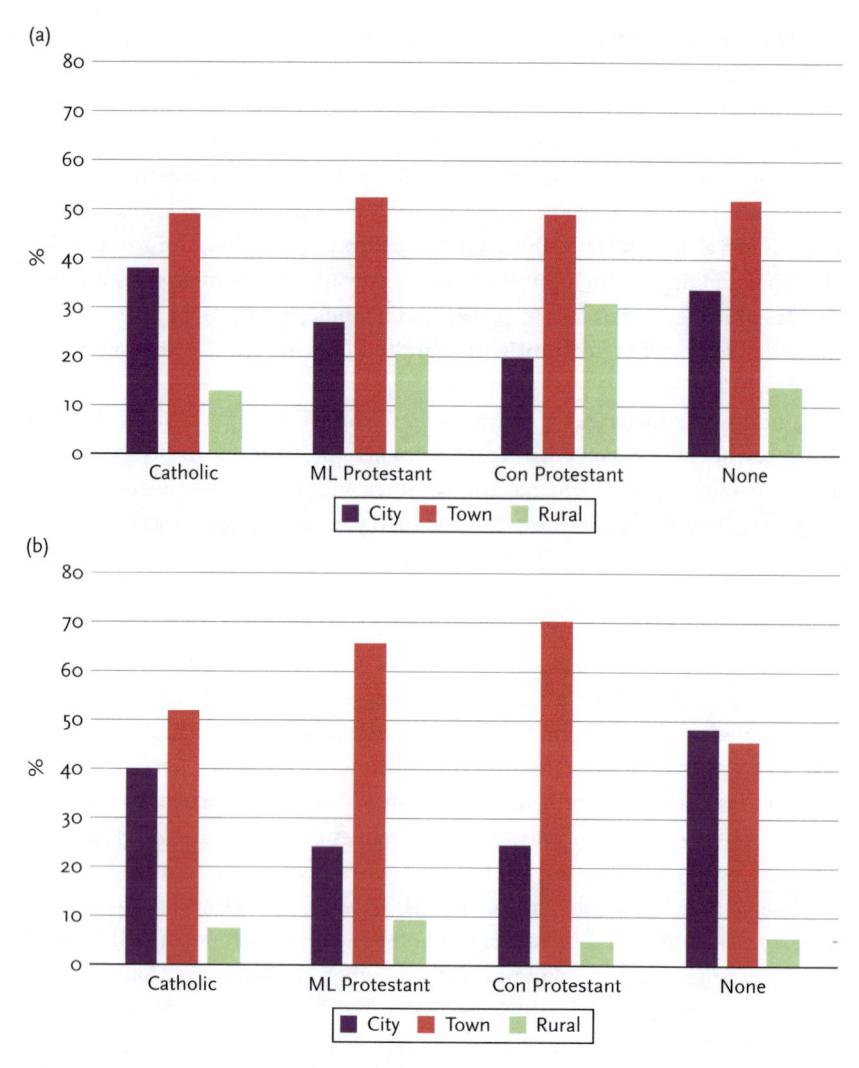

Figure 2.7 Growing up urban versus rural: (A) White respondents. (B) Latino respondents

up in towns. Another large portion of both white (38%) and Latino (40%) Catholics grew up in urban areas.

There is significant diversity among Catholics on geographic background, particularly whether they grew up in a rural area. Given the challenges associated with growing up rural, this factor is likely to become important as I explore differences across American faith groups in other outcomes such as education, income, and wealth accumulation. In particular, Figures 2.7A and 2.7B show that white Catholics were more likely than Latino Catholics to grow up rural: more than 13% of white Catholics grew up rural, compared to only 7% of Latino Catholics. However, compared to other white Americans, white Catholics were considerably *less* likely to be raised in rural areas. Indeed, whereas 13% of white Catholics were raised in rural areas, more than 20% of mainline Protestants and 31% of conservative Protestants were raised in rural areas. White Catholics are most comparable to religious nones (11% grew up rural) on this dimension.

THE INTERDEPENDENCE OF SOCIAL ORIGIN TRAITS

Although I have been discussing the various components of social origins separately, these traits are not isolated and do not affect other outcomes independently of each other. Rather, each of the individual and family traits I have been discussing is interdependent and they interact in nuanced ways in the lives of real people to affect their behaviors, accomplishments, and attitudes. The lives of two respondents from the American Voices Project (AVP) illustrate the interplay of birth cohort, ancestry and ethnicity, immigration, family background, and urban–rural background differences.

"Antonio" was born in Mexico City during the 1960s, making him a member of Generation X. He finished high school in two years and completed two years of normal school (teacher training). However, he had to work during school to support his family because his parents had no formal education, and the family's income was very low. Antonio's boss—at a textile factory—thought Antonio's homework was interfering with his work and gave him an ultimatum: quit school or be fired. Antonio had to quit school. He ultimately married and had two children while still in Mexico; he and his wife immigrated to the United States and had three more children. Despite his dream to become a teacher, he has worked as an employee of a landscape company since immigrating. He works more than 50 hours per week and earned just about $30,000 per year in 2019–2020. Antonio is Catholic, and he and his family attend Mass regularly. He admits that his finances are challenging, but he has a positive outlook: his wife is able to stay at home with their youngest children, the family takes regular time together to enjoy activities like going to a local swimming pool, and he is optimistic that his children will complete more education and have higher standards of living than he has.

"Ignatia" is a Millennial who, like Antonio, considers herself Latino and Catholic. Also like Antonio, Ignatia immigrated to the southern United States in early adulthood. However, the lives of these two immigrants are strikingly different. Ignatia immigrated from Cuba with her Cuban father and Chinese mother. Her parents both have professional occupations: her father is a civil engineer, and her mother is an accountant. Their family income is above average, and her parents have been able to assist her in financing an education and also helped her sister financially so that she was able to graduate from medical school. Ignatia has had a comparably comfortable life, but she has also faced challenges. She completed a bachelor's degree in Cuba, but the credits from that degree did not transfer to the United States, thus requiring her to start a new bachelor's degree. Fortunately, her parents are able to pay for this degree as well. Ignatia also works in the research department of a midsized engineering company, which gives her a source of income and funds a relatively comfortable life for her and her boyfriend. Although Ignatia considers herself Catholic, she says that she is "culturally Catholic" and "doesn't go to church or anything like that." Ignatia is unmarried and does not have children, but she is cohabiting with her boyfriend. Like Antonio, Ignatia is also optimistic about the future, but because she is still young and childless, her focus is on her own potential future success.

As I explore in the remainder of this book, these case studies of two Catholic immigrants have clear demographic similarities, but the realities of their lives are radically different because of where they came from and how their origins play out in their adult lives. That is, the differences between Antonio and Ignatia reflect their social origins—including the resources their parents were able to devote to their educations—and have influenced the trajectories on which their adult lives are moving. The two lives also underscore the interdependence of social origins and other behaviors and processes, an interdependence that will be critical to understanding the various differences—and similarities—both among Catholics and between Catholics and other Americans that I discuss in the remainder of this book. Perhaps most important, these two case studies document how Catholicism can play a very different role in the lives of Catholics, even Catholics who have other background traits in common. For Antonio, Catholicism is a central part of his life: he attends Mass regularly and donates to his church weekly even if it means cutting back on groceries to compensate. For Ignatia, Catholicism is part of her total identity, but it plays a much smaller role and is simply something she is aware of but that affects little about the rest of her life. These differences in the centrality of faith to the lives of Catholics are important for understanding what it means to be Catholic, and I will revisit them as I explore issues such as marriage, divorce, cohabitation, fertility, work, and charitable giving and how Catholic social teaching influences decisions about these processes.

CONCLUSION

Family background matters for most of what people accomplish, do, and believe during their lives. To provide an initial portrait of Catholics and a foundation for the remainder of the book, this chapter documented similarities and differences both among Catholics and between Catholics and other Americans in key elements of family background. In particular, I documented patterns in birth cohort, gender, ancestry, ethnicity and race, immigration, family SES, and the region in which people grew up. I showed that Catholics, overall, are relatively young, reflecting fertility differences between white and Latino Catholics (I return to this in Chapter 3) and the aging of the U.S. population. Because they are aging out of the population, there are relatively few members of the Silent Generation in any religious group, and religious nones stood out because they are relatively young.

Importantly, this chapter underscored the reality that differences between white and Latino Catholics are fundamental to understanding Catholics today; given that studying these two groups is empirically viable, I will focus on them in subsequent chapters. The Catholic Church includes nearly 30% Latinos by both ancestry and self-identified ethnicity. Asian, African, and black Catholics are also important, but much smaller, subgroups, making it difficult to study them with my data. Immigrants have always been an important part of the Catholic story in America, but Catholics today are much more likely to be from Latin America than Europe, as they were in the past. I concluded the chapter with an exploration of family background, comparing white and Latino Catholics and documenting differences between Catholics and other Americans. Findings in this section showed, for example, that white Catholics came from higher-SES families than Latino Catholics and were slightly more likely than Latino Catholics to be raised in rural areas. This section underscored the importance of these two broad comparisons and foreshadows the comparisons I make in the remaining chapters of this book.

NOTES

1. Details about Generation Z are particularly subject to change. I define this generation as those born 1997–2012 to be consistent with current practice (Dimock 2019). Practically, however, because the youngest GSS respondent is 18 years old, those born in 2003 are the youngest members of Generation Z included in my analyses.
2. I do not include people who identify as having a nonbinary gender or who identify as transgender because there are too few respondents in the GSS to accurately document patterns for these individuals. Given that members of younger cohorts are considerably more likely than people from older cohorts to have a nonbinary gender identity, future research may be able to explore issues related to religion and nonbinary or transgender issues.
3. The GSS asked "From what country or countries did your ancestors come?" If respondents offered more than one country, they were asked "Which one of these countries do you feel closer to?" I grouped the responses by world region. The GSS did not specify how far back in their family history respondents should consider when answering this question.

4. I use father's education to measure family background to be consistent with a long history of sociological research that focuses on father's education, training, and jobs. I could have included mother's education and various measures of occupational standing (occupational prestige), but these are highly correlated with father's education and family income (see homogamy section in Chapter 3); I omit these additional measures to save space.

CHAPTER 3

Family

Marriage, Divorce, and Fertility

Overall high marriage rates, low divorce rates, and shrinking fertility are hallmarks of today's Catholic family. However, today's white and Latino Catholic families look different from each other, with white Catholics resembling mainline Protestants more than in the past.

Family is a fundamental building block of all societies: much of what people do over their lives happens with members of their families, and family processes and events such as getting married and having a child do not happen in a vacuum. Rather, these family processes reflect the elements of social origins that were the subject of Chapter 2, including birth cohort, ethnicity, and family background. That is, there are critical differences in the occurrence and timing of many family processes that result from race/ethnicity, when and where people were born, and traits of the families they were born into. In turn, family processes create individuals' life trajectories, providing structure to many other events and outcomes that define their lives. As a result, family processes affect other social outcomes, including work, income, wealth and poverty, gender roles in and out of the home, and other behaviors, processes, and attitudes. There are feedback processes among these various events and outcomes that are beyond the scope of my discussion here (e.g., Does marriage affect education or vice versa?). However, family events and processes are an integral part of all life trajectories and family events are critical to understanding a wide range of behaviors, outcomes, and attitudes, including those that define who is Catholic.

In Catholic social teaching, the family is the center of social and religious life. The importance of the family is clear in the Catechism of the Catholic

Church, which calls the family "the original cell of social life" (CCC 2207). It is the place where future generations are created, raised, and instilled with moral values and spiritual heritage: "authority, stability, and a life of relationships within the family constitute the foundations for freedom, security, and fraternity within society. The family is the community in which, from childhood, one can learn moral values, begin to honor God, and make good use of freedom. Family life is an initiation into life in society." The family is also the place where children learn to pray, worship, take care of others, and live out their faith in other ways outside the home (Konieczny 2013). Thus, the Catechism describes the family as having a fundamental role in caring for those who cannot care for themselves: "the family should live in such a way that its members learn to care and take responsibility for the young, the old, the sick, the handicapped, and the poor. There are many families who are at times incapable of providing this help. It devolves then on other persons, other families, and, in a subsidiary way, society to provide for their needs" (CCC 2208).

The importance of the family in Catholic teaching also is clear in the writings of notable Catholics, such as Pope John Paul II. John Paul's series of lectures now known as the *Theology of the Body*, for example, teaches that people are made to live together in communion and that they will find happiness when they live in loving, self-giving relationships (Pope John Paul II 2006). Such documents include statements of the Church's doctrine celebrating openness to life and prohibiting extramarital sex, divorce, the use of birth control, abortion, and same-sex unions. These teachings are recorded in considerable detail and widely known—albeit in a cursory way—even to many who are not affiliated with the Catholic Church. In a widely cited homily, given in Perth Australia, Pope John Paul II noted that the

> family is the domestic church. It is not surprising that the Church has given much thought and attention in recent times to questions affecting family life and marriage. Nor is it surprising that governments and public organizations are constantly involved in matters which directly or indirectly affect the institutional well-being of marriage and the family. And it is everyone's experience that healthy relationships in marriage and the family are of the greatest importance in the development and well-being of the human person. . . . As the family goes, so goes the nation, and so goes the whole world in which we live. (Pope John Paul II November 30, 1986)

Of course, many Catholics do not conform absolutely to Church doctrine, and it is useful to consider how and when people conform or not. To illustrate this process, consider Michele Dillon's work on Catholics selectively embracing Church doctrine. In *Catholic Identity: Balancing Reason, Faith, and Power*, Dillon notes that "Catholics tend to be Catholic on their own terms, choosing

Box 3.1 COMPARING CATHOLICS AND OTHER RELIGIOUS–ETHNIC GROUPS

In subsequent analyses, I present results for six religious–ethnic groups: white Catholics, Latino Catholics, white mainline Protestants, white conservative Protestants, Latino Protestants, and white religious nones. Focusing on these groups has three advantages. First, these groups allow me to compare the two main Catholic ethnic groups: (non-Latino) white and Latino Catholics. Second, white mainline Protestants and white conservative Protestants are the two largest U.S. Protestant religious–ethnic groups, and white Catholics have converged with them on many of the traits I study. Isolating these groups allows me to compare Catholics with them. Third, given that religious nones are a large and growing group, understanding how Catholics (and other Americans) compare with them will situate my findings within the broader U.S. religious landscape. My data do not contain sufficient numbers of black Catholics or black nones to produce reliable estimates. I omit black Protestants because sample sizes are small for them and to be consistent with my exclusion of black Catholics. The Appendix includes additional details.

to remain Catholic while selectively embracing official church doctrine" (Dillon 1999: preamble). She provides a detailed exploration of how and why pro-change (i.e., institutionally marginalized) Catholics remain Catholic despite disagreeing with official Church doctrine (Dillon 1999). Her study focuses on Catholics who are gay or lesbian, advocates of women's ordination, or pro-choice regarding abortion and how these people negotiate their lack of conformity with their faith; however, her conclusions are relevant to all Catholics who disagree with Church teachings and remain Catholic. Dillon shows that pro-change Catholics recognize—although not necessarily consciously—that authority is diffuse and that Church doctrine is socially constructed. That is, authority is not the sole purview of Church leaders but is more democratic and grounded in the lived experiences of ordinary Catholics. People respond to formal, codified Church doctrine (formal institutions), but they also respond to the socially constructed norms that emerge from the behaviors of others around them. Together, the formal and informal constraints (similar to Dillon's ideas about the diffuse sense of authority) allow pro-change Catholics to interpret Church teachings autonomously and in a way that incorporates and makes sense given their unique experiences. Dillon's work highlights the considerable variation that exists among Catholic families and says a great deal about who Catholics are and how they engage with the Church and the rest of society.

I have three objectives in this chapter. First, I describe the current state of the Catholic family, situating it within historic trends. I describe marriage, cohabitation, and divorce patterns. I also discuss patterns in homogamy—marrying between people with the same religion or education—because it is closely related to marriage and divorce patterns and indicates the degree to which groups intermingle with each other. I also describe trends and patterns related to children, including ideal and actual fertility, the age at the birth of the first child, and remaining childless. Second, I explore how family and relationship states and processes differ among Catholics, focusing on differences between white and Latino Catholics. Finally, I document whether Catholics and other religious groups differ on key family behaviors and processes. In each section, I document both over-time trends and cotemporary states, considering how key demographic factors (such as differences in birth cohort among Catholics) intersect with religion to produce the patterns I present.

THE FAMILY AND ITS STRUCTURE

Family structure—the relationships among people who live in the same household and call themselves a family—is essential for understanding Catholics and how they compare with other Americans. Social scientists define family structure according to the marital status of the adults in the household. That is, a family is usually defined as married or cohabiting couples and never-married, divorced, or widowed people. Any of these family types may include children, but childless couples and individuals are also considered families. Coupled families have become less homogenous than they were historically. Newer arrangements, such as same-sex marriage, constitute a growing part of the U.S. family landscape but, because they remain a small population and are thus not well represented in General Social Survey (GSS) statistical analyses, in this chapter the discussion is restricted to opposite-sex couples.

Family structure affects many other outcomes and has varied across religious groups through most of the past century. Marriage, cohabitation, and divorce are particularly important for understanding Catholics because these family structures are associated with social and economic status (the subject of Chapter 4), religious beliefs and practices (Chapters 6 and 7), and attitudes regarding secular issues (Chapters 8 and 9). Religious factors have historically played a critical role in family structure, affecting entry into marriage, marital satisfaction, marital stability and divorce, and other family behaviors, such as childbearing and child-rearing decisions (Mahoney et al. 2008; Perry 2015; Perry and Schleifer 2019; Sherkat 2000, 2014).

Marriage

Getting married is a critical turning point in a person's life that affects much of what happens from that point on. Marriage increases income and wealth; improves physical health, mental health, and longevity; and can affect religious behaviors, political attitudes and behaviors, and attitudes regarding other secular issues (Simon 2002; Waite 1995; Waite and Lehrer 2004; Zagorsky 2005). Children raised by their own married parents generally have improved health, cognitive, and educational outcomes, which translate to improved later-life outcomes including health, income, saving, and wealth ownership (Cooksey 1997; Waite and Lehrer 2004). Marriage is also seen as a sign of achievement and prestige, particularly if a couple marries after having achieved other important milestones such as finishing education and paying off debt (for an excellent review of literature on marriage as a sign of prestige, see Kuperberg 2019).

Married-couple households are the most common family type in the United States, and most Americans will be married at some point in their lives. However, marriage rates have been declining dramatically since the 1950s and 1960s, including among Catholics. In 1950, 77% of people had ever been married, but that number fell to 68% by 2018. Among individuals aged 18–34—the age at which marriage typically occurs—only 29% had ever been married as of 2018 (Sassler and Lichter 2020). The age at which people marry has also been increasing: in the early 1960s, both women and men married in their early 20s, but women now postpone marriage until nearly age 28 and men until they are more than 30 years old (Manning, Brown, and Payne 2014; Sassler and Lichter 2020; Stone and Wilcox 2021).

Several factors contributed to changing marriage rates and the age at which people marry. Rising education levels are particularly relevant. Both women and men are now completing more education than at any other point in U.S. history, and the changes in educational outcomes have been particularly large for women. These changes were clear in my Chapter 2 discussion of differences in education and career opportunities that characterize recent U.S. birth cohorts. Rising education levels have combined with changes in the U.S. economy (away from manufacturing and toward service and white-collar occupations) to create unprecedented career opportunities for younger cohorts, particularly for the women in these cohorts. As their educational and occupational opportunities expanded, women have become less financially dependent on men and better able to support themselves outside marriage. Further, the wide availability of the birth control pill and other forms of contraception was accompanied by legal and normative changes in the acceptability and availability of cohabitation and divorce (Kuperberg 2019).

Declining marriage rates for Catholics have been particularly extreme. Catholics were historically known for having high marriage rates, but Catholic marriage rates began to decline following World War II (Center for Applied Research in the Apostate [CARA] 2023) and have converged with those of mainline Protestants (Stone and Wilcox 2021). Marriage is fundamental to Catholicism. Although a complete discussion of Catholic approaches to marriage is beyond the scope of this book, it is useful to note that the Catechism states that the "intimate community of life and love which constitutes the married state has been established by the Creator and endowed by him with its own proper laws. . . . God himself is the author of marriage" (CCC 1603). Exposure to such doctrine can affect evaluations of the costs and benefits of marriage, the types of partners considered acceptable, and decisions about whether to cohabit before marriage (Kuperberg 2019; Lehrer 2004; Perry 2015). However, Catholics have been susceptible to the secular changes and influences that have reduced marriage for all groups. Moreover, looking at Catholics as a monolith is no longer sensible, given the growing ethnic diversity in the Catholic Church. Evidence also suggests that Latinos have distinctive family patterns but that Latino and white marriage rates might be converging (Ellison, Wolfinger, and Ramos-Wada 2013; Landale and Oropesa 2007).

Figure 3.1 documents marriage rates for the six religious–ethnic groups (see Box 3.1, "Comparing Catholics to Other Religious–Ethnic Groups"). The figure shows the predicted probability that a respondent has ever been married, broken down by religious affiliation and ethnicity (see Box 3.2, "Interpreting Predicted Probabilities").

Box 3.2 PREDICTED PROBABILITIES

Predicted probabilities are an efficient way to summarize a large amount of information about complex patterns. A predicted probability is the likelihood that a certain type of respondent has a trait that we care about (e.g., a white Catholic is married). The probability is similar to a percentage, but it allows me to show results for joint characteristics (e.g., ethnicity and religion) and to hold other factors constant (e.g., age).

In my predicted probability figures, the *point* on each bar is the average probability for that group (e.g., white Catholics) based on a logistic regression model that includes only religion and ethnicity. For example, Figure 3.1 shows that a randomly selected white Catholic has a .83 chance of having ever been married.

The *bar* represents the 95% confidence interval, and the *asterisks* indicate that other groups differ statistically from white Catholics on the trait. See Appendix for details.

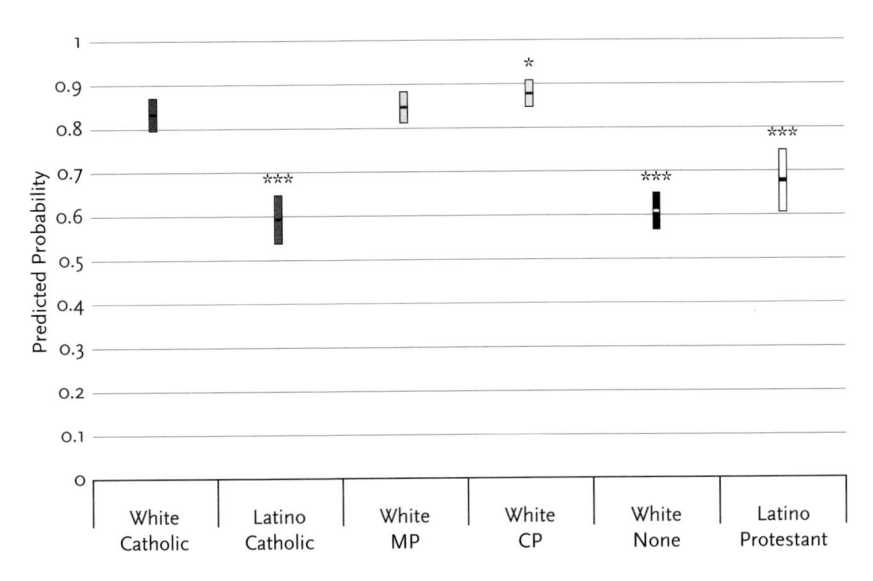

Figure 3.1 Marriage: High for white Catholics, lower for Latino Catholics

Three noteworthy patterns are evident in Figure 3.1. First, Latino Catholics are less likely than white Catholics to have ever married. Notably, however, this difference between white and Latino Catholics is entirely explained by birth cohort differences between Latino and white Catholics. Figure 3.1 shows that the predicted probability of ever having been married is statistically significantly lower for Latino Catholics than for white Catholics. The regression models that produce this figure are included in the Appendix: the base regression model includes only religion and ethnicity and shows a significant difference between Latino and white Catholic marriage rates. However, in a second regression model that holds birth cohort constant, Latino and white Catholic marriage rates do not significantly differ.

Although Latino Catholics are, on average, less likely than white Catholics to have ever been married, this difference is entirely demographic: it reflects Latino Catholics' average younger age relative to white Catholics. This finding differs from other research that found that young Latino women are *more* likely than other ethnic minorities and as likely as white Americans to marry (despite Latinos' lower socioeconomic status [SES], which might predict *lower* marriage rates) (Landale and Oropesa 2007). GSS sample sizes prevent me from examining small groups more closely. However, the patterns I show here are consistent across male and female respondents, with patterns in other more recent GSS data waves, and with Latino Catholics' younger ages and relatively lower SES family backgrounds (see Chapter 2).

The difference in approaches to marriage across birth cohorts is critical to understanding the difference in marriage rates between white and Latino

FAMILY [47]

Catholics. Figure 3.1 illustrates the difference statistically, and the way these differences play out in real lives is exemplified in the lives two American Voice Project (AVP) respondents I introduced in Chapter 1: Antonio and Ignatia. Antonio, a Generation X immigrant from Mexico, has been married to the same woman since he was in his 20s and did not cohabit before marriage. For Antonio, cohabitation would have been unthinkable, and he expressed hope that his children would marry without cohabiting. By contrast, Ignatia, a Millennial Catholic who immigrated from Cuba, was cohabiting with her boyfriend when she was interviewed for the AVP. For Ignatia, cohabiting seemed natural, and although her commitment to Catholicism was weak, she saw no contradiction between being Catholic and living with her boyfriend before marriage. Because Antonio and Ignatia are both Latino, their lives do not speak to differences—or lack of differences—between Latino and white Catholics. However, their stories are common for AVP respondents in their cohorts: those from Generation X and older rarely speak about cohabiting but rather describe entry into marriage without mentioning cohabiting. By contrast, Millennial AVP respondents are more likely than other respondents to be cohabiting currently and talk about living with their unmarried partners as a natural part of the unfolding of intimate relationships.

The second important pattern shown in Figure 3.1 is that marriage rates do not significantly differ between white Catholics and white mainline Protestants—a finding that is consistent with recent evidence that marriage rates have converged for these two groups (Stone and Wilcox 2021). Perhaps more surprising is the finding that white conservative Protestants are only slightly more likely than white Catholics and white mainline Protestants to marry, a relatively new pattern consistent with evidence of convergence among Protestants on fertility (see the second half of this chapter).

The third notable pattern in Figure 3.1 is that white religious nones are significantly less likely than white Catholics, white mainline Protestants, and white conservative Protestants to have ever married. The difference is statistically significant, indicating a real difference between religious nones and white Catholics. This difference remains in models that control for birth cohort, indicating that the difference between religious nones and other religious groups in marriage rates may reflect something other than the predominance of young people among the nones. One likely explanation is more widespread changes in attitudes toward marriage, cohabitation, and extramarital sex. Most Christian religious groups encourage marriage and have at least some admonitions against extramarital sex. Patterns of cohabitation, the subject of the next section, are similar to those shown in Figure 3.1 and suggest that religious nones are more likely to live with intimate partners without getting married.

Cohabitation

As marriage rates have declined and the age at first marriage has increased, cohabitation rates have increased significantly. In the early 1960s, about 5% of marriages were preceded by cohabitation. By the 2010s, nearly 70% of newly married couples had lived together before marrying (Kuperberg 2019; Sassler and Lichter 2020; Stone and Wilcox 2021), and the majority (66%) of all young adults had cohabited by 2014 at some point (Manning et al. 2014).

Cohabitation has become so common that many people, including social scientists, treat it as equivalent to marriage. However, Catholic teaching regarding marriage includes a prohibition against extramarital sex, effectively prohibiting cohabitation (assuming sex is involved). This prohibition remains despite open conversations the Church has had—including at the 2014 Synod on the Family led by Pope Francis—about issues on which Church teaching is at odds with secular norms and practices (Dillon 2018). Many Protestant denominations also discourage cohabitation, although these denominations vary considerably in their approaches to marriage, premarital sex, and cohabitation. Nevertheless, evidence suggests that adults who were *raised* as Catholic, mainline Protestant, or conservative Protestant have cohabitation rates that are similar to each other and lower than those of adults not raised in a religious tradition (Stone and Wilcox 2021).

As with marriage rates, Catholics' cohabitation rates are, indeed, more similar now to other American religious groups than they were historically. Figure 3.2 displays the predicted probability that an individual from each of the six

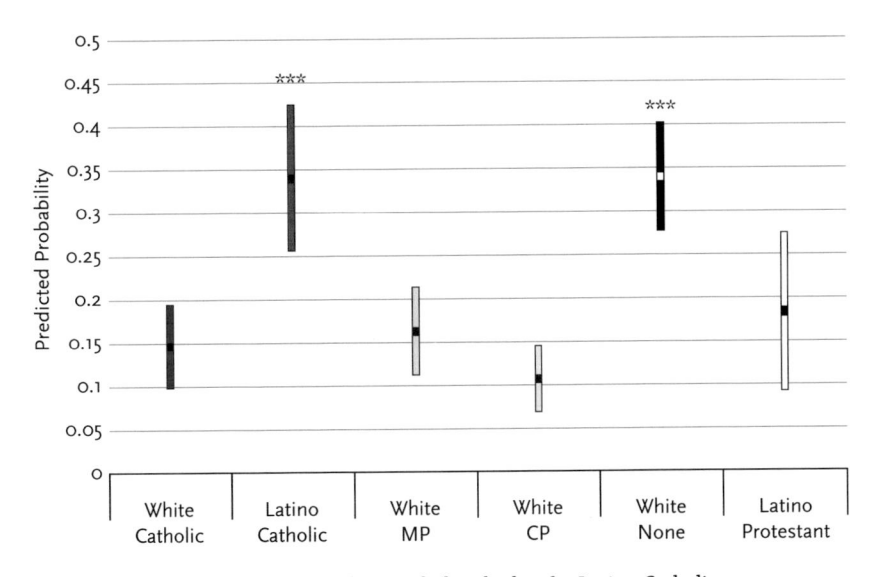

Figure 3.2 Cohabitation: Low for white Catholics, higher for Latino Catholics

religion–ethnic groups is cohabiting. Three patterns that are similar to those shown in Figure 3.1 regarding marriage emerge.

First, Latino Catholics are more likely than white Catholics to cohabit, but the difference between these two Catholic groups is explained by birth cohort: Latino Catholics are, on average, younger than white Catholics. These differences are unsurprising, given that members of younger birth cohorts are more likely to cohabit than members of older birth cohorts. Notably, however, the difference in cohabitation rates disappears when birth cohort is held constant (results not shown in a figure). This finding suggests a high level of internal consistency among Catholics despite differences in ethnicity—a pattern with important implications for understanding religious practices and beliefs and attitudes toward secular issues (discussed in the second half of this book).

The second pattern that is clear in Figure 3.2 is that cohabitation rates for white Catholics and mainline Protestants are similar to each other. However, white conservative Protestants are less likely than white Catholics and white mainline Protestants to cohabit.

The third pattern shown in the figure is that white religious nones are significantly more likely than white Catholics, white mainline Protestants, and white conservative Protestants to cohabit. This difference is highly statistically significant, and both patterns move in similar but opposite directions to the marriage patterns described earlier and shown in Figure 3.1.

As others have noted, cohabitation is a complicated issue for Latinos (Ellison et al. 2013). Approval of cohabitation is high among Latinos more broadly, particularly for stable cohabiting relationships that include children (Manning 2004) and consistent with the approval of consensual unions in parts of Latin America (Ellison et al. 2013; Landale and Oropesa 2007; Manning 2004). However, religion and ethnicity interact for Latinos on this issue. Catholic teaching effectively prohibits cohabitation, and many conservative Protestant denominations (many with large Latino membership) strongly discourage it. Despite the consistency in religious teachings, evangelical Protestant Latinos tend to have more conservative attitudes toward cohabitation than do Catholic Latinos (Ellison et al. 2013). The difference between Latino Catholics and Latino Protestants shown in Figure 3.2 reflects these complicated issues: both Latino Catholics and Latino Protestants are statistically similar to white Catholics in their likelihood of cohabiting[1]; however, Latino Catholics are more likely than Latino Protestants to cohabit, and these patterns persist even when factoring in birth cohort and gender differences (results not shown in a figure).

Divorce

U.S. divorce rates also began to increase in the 1960s, reflecting many of the same factors that reduced marriage rates and increased cohabitation rates: growing educational and occupational opportunities, especially for women; changing norms about marriage and divorce; and a loosening of legal hurdles to marriage dissolution (Kuperberg 2019). Although some researchers speculated that divorce rates had begun to stabilize in the 1980s, more recent evidence finds that age-standardized divorce has increased rapidly since 1990 (Kennedy and Ruggles 2014). However, this overall increase masks differences in divorce by age: between 1990 and 2008, divorce rates doubled for people over age 35 but were stable or declining for younger people (Kennedy and Ruggles 2014). One particularly noteworthy finding is that divorce has remained high for people over age 50 (Kennedy and Ruggles 2014; Wright, Brown, and Manning 2021). As Kennedy and Ruggles (2014: 595) noted, these patterns suggest a cohort effect, with Baby Boomers responsible for high divorce rates in the 1980s and 1990s and still displaying high levels of marital instability in later life.

A long history of research documents clear associations between religious factors and divorce. Religious affiliation, practice, and belief are all strongly associated with marital expectations, relationship commitment, conflict, infidelity, attitudes toward divorce, and the risk of marital dissolution (Ellison et al. 2013; Lehrer and Chiswick 1993; Stokes and Ellison 2010; Vaaler, Ellison, and Powers 2009). Conditional on marrying, individuals raised in religious families or affiliated with a Christian religion in adulthood appear to have a slightly reduced chance of divorcing (Stone and Wilcox 2021). Conservative Protestants and others with conservative theological beliefs tend to have particularly traditional approaches to various family issues, including divorce (Ellison et al. 2013).

Despite changing cultural norms, Catholic doctrine regarding marriage has remained constant: marriage is a sacramental bond between a baptized woman and man that is sealed by God and cannot be dissolved (CCC, article 7). The Catholic Church's prohibition on divorce is well known, but details regarding Church doctrine are less well understood. Again, a complete discussion of Catholic approaches to divorce are beyond the scope of this book, but it is useful to note that the Catechism states that the "unity, indissolubility, and openness to fertility are essential to marriage. . . . Divorce separates what God has joined together" (CCC 1664). Divorce granted through a state's courts legally dissolves a valid marriage and declares the spouses to be single according to the secular legal system. However, the Church still considers legally divorced Catholics to be married unless their marriage has been declared null by the Church (i.e., they have been granted an annulment). Legally divorced or separated Catholics whose marriage has not been declared null are not in full communion with the Church and cannot participate completely in the Church (e.g., cannot receive communion). If a divorced or separated Catholic remarries without going through the annulment process, they will be excommunicated. The Church will declare a marriage null through a well-defined

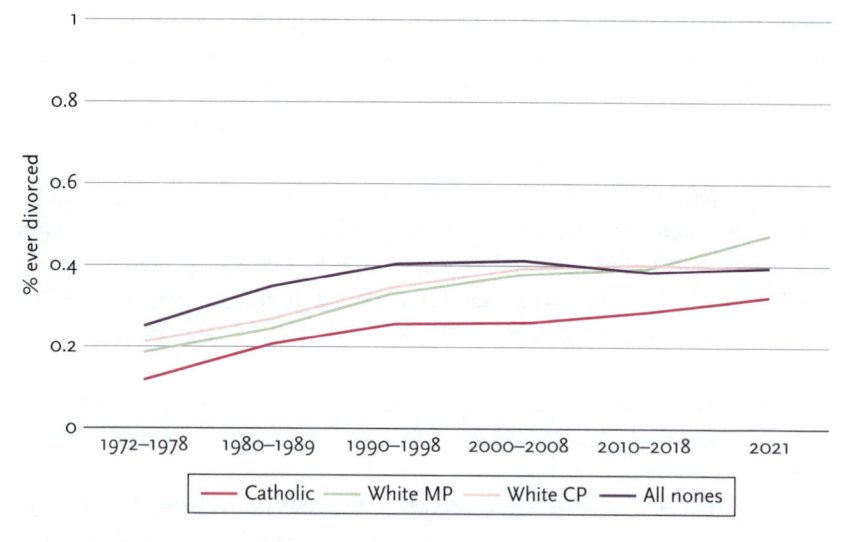

Figure 3.3 Rising divorce rates

process that occurs in the individual's local diocese if it declares that—for a list of well-defined reasons—the marriage was not valid on the day it was performed. Valid reasons include that one or both spouses did not freely consent to the marriage or were not open to having children. The growing number of divorced Catholics has motivated the Church to expand access to annulments and to soften its language about marital dissolution (Wilde 2001), but official doctrine has remained unchanged.

Despite Church teaching, many Catholics end their marriages through the secular, legal divorce process. Figure 3.3 shows that divorce rates for Catholics have increased over time just as they have for members of other religious groups. The figure shows the percentage of GSS respondents by religion and ethnicity who have ever divorced over time; in this figure, I do not distinguish white from Latino Catholics because the GSS does not contain information on Latino ethnicity for all past data waves. Nonetheless, the figure shows that although the percentage of Catholics who have ever divorced remains lower than the percentage for all other groups, divorce has increased for Catholics as well: in the 1970s, about 12% of Catholics had ever been divorced, but that percentage had increased to more than 30% by 2021.

However, patterns in divorce rates among Catholics distinguish contemporary Catholics from members of other religious traditions. Figure 3.4 shows the predicted probability that a respondent has ever been divorced—regardless of their current marital status—as a function of religious affiliation and ethnicity. I use "ever divorced" to fully capture a person's marriage history rather than modeling the current prevalence of divorce for consistency with other research on divorce (Kennedy and Ruggles 2014).

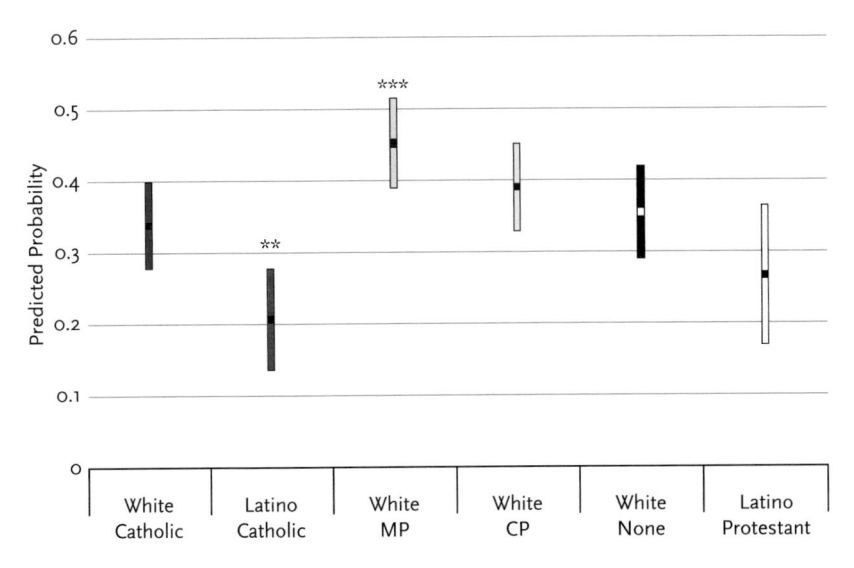

Figure 3.4 Divorce: Low for white Catholics, lower for Latino Catholics

Figure 3.4 displays three patterns that parallel those shown earlier for marriage and cohabitation rates. First, Latino Catholics are less likely than white Catholics to have ever divorced, but the difference is explained by birth cohort (results not shown in a figure). Also noteworthy is that divorce rates for Latino Protestants are similar to those of white and Latino Catholics. This pattern is consistent with evidence that Latino Protestants tend to be affiliated with conservative Protestant churches, and these churches are relatively traditional in their approaches toward marriage and divorce (Ellison et al. 2013; Stokes and Ellison 2010).

Second, white Catholics are significantly less likely than white mainline Protestants and *slightly* less likely than white conservative Protestants to have divorced. The difference between white Catholics and white mainline Protestants is particularly large and significant—a finding that differs from other work that shows high similarity between white Catholics and white mainline Protestants (Stone and Wilcox 2021). My finding holds in models that control birth cohort and gender as well (results not shown in a figure), which suggests that the difference is not in these other factors that are also associated with divorce. A more likely explanation is a difference in the measure of divorce I use. Whereas I model *ever* divorced, previous research has often measured whether a person is *currently* divorced. Of course, there may also be differences across datasets, including in sampling.

Catholics' relatively low divorce rates are consistent with Church teaching, which many Catholics have certainly internalized. Eduardo, an AVP respondent, expressed how deeply his long-time Catholic faith affected his decision to end his marriage. Eduardo is a 64-year-old Latino Catholic immigrant who grew up

FAMILY [53]

in a poor, rural area of Mexico and works as a ranch hand in the United States. Eduardo's parents did not finish elementary school, but he considers himself fortunate to have graduated from high school and to have attended some college. Eduardo married young, but he and his wife divorced several years ago. They share custody of their 16-year-old daughter. Eduardo's regret about his divorce is palpable in his interview and clearly connected to his Catholic faith and upbringing. Indeed, he appears to feel that he disappointed his parents and his Church in having a failed marriage. He lingers on the reasons for the divorce, even attributing some of the blame to the Church: his wife spent too much time, in his estimation, volunteering for the church and otherwise engaged in church activities. Eduardo stays in close touch with his ex-wife, continuing to help her financially and with manual labor at her house, tasks that he describes as akin to penance for failing her in marriage. He has a girlfriend and expresses that it was important for him that his new partner is also Catholic, a reality that appears to compensate—in his mind—for the divorce.

The third evident pattern in Figure 3.4 is that white Catholics are less likely than white religious nones to have ever divorced. However, the predicted probability is less distinct for these groups than the model results (reflected in the significance level), reflecting the inclusion of birth cohort in the calculation of the predicted probability. In this case, the predicted probability reflects the fact that religious nones are younger than white Catholics, on average and that by virtue of their youth, have not had less time in which to experience divorce.

Homogamy

The selection of a marriage partner is closely related to family structure and can be helpful for understanding Catholics and how they compare with other Americans. A well-documented pattern is that individuals choose intimate partners who are similar to themselves on several dimensions, including religion and SES. Marrying or partnering among people with the same traits, referred to as *homogamy*, is a specific form of *homophily*, the tendency of people to flock together with similar others. Homogamy occurs between individuals with similar values, priorities, and life experiences. Once people are partnered, homogamy can reinforce the similarity of their values and priorities and contribute to even greater similarity in future experiences and behaviors. A common pattern that occurs in many cultures is that women have strong preferences to marry men with education levels that are comparable to or higher than their own (Curtis and Ellison 2002; Myers 2006; Qian 2018; Sherkat 2004).

A long history of research in the social sciences shows that homogamy has important—and usually unintended—consequences for individuals, families, and societies. For example, homogamy can increase marital satisfaction and stability, reduce the likelihood of divorce, and increase material well-being—including income, saving, and wealth ownership—by creating shared goals, such as having children and owning a home. Homogamy is also associated with negative outcomes: the more similar two partners are, the less they are exposed to new ideas, values, and people. This contributes to increasing in-group focus and possibly increases inequality over time as high- and low-SES individuals mate with similar others rather than mixing with dissimilar others (Kalmijn 1991; Marcum 1986; Qian 2018; Sherkat and Ellison 1999).

Religion and SES are two measures that are commonly used to study homogamy. Religious homogamy captures similarities in values, religious affiliation, and sometimes ethnicity. Educational similarity is a common measure of SES homogamy used to capture both ascribed traits (e.g., gender, ethnicity, birth cohort, family background) and personal achievement. Homogamy results from two broad sources. First, social structure constrains the types of others with whom individuals interact, creating opportunities to interact with similar others and restricting opportunities to mix with dissimilar others. For example, neighborhoods tend to be relatively homogenous in terms of education levels, income, and ethnicity. Interactions among people in the same neighborhoods tend to be relatively high, a pattern that contributes to people interacting with similar others. Second, personal preferences which result from norms and individual tastes operate within social structures to further increase homogamy. Within the same neighborhood, then, individuals are more likely to interact with similar others because of personal preferences and normative pressures than with dissimilar others.

There are important and significant differences among Catholics as well as more subtle differences between Catholics and other Americans on homogamy. First, Latino Catholics are much more likely than white Catholics to marry someone of the same religion and education level; on this measure, Latino Catholics resemble white conservative Protestants more than they do white Catholics. Figure 3.5 shows the predicted probability that an individual is married to someone of the same religious faith, and Figure 3.6 shows the predicted probability that both marriage partners are college graduates. I focus on college graduation as the SES measure because graduating from college is increasingly common in the United States, including among both white and Latino Catholics, and other education measures are less informative. These differences likely reflect both personal preference and structural constraints. The structural component is certainly relevant: relatively few American Latinos are not Catholic, and college graduation is high but not ubiquitous among American Latinos. Regardless of the source of the homogamy, the results—both positive and negative—are the same.

By contrast, white Catholics, white mainline Protestants, and white religious nones have nearly comparable levels of religious homogamy. Religious

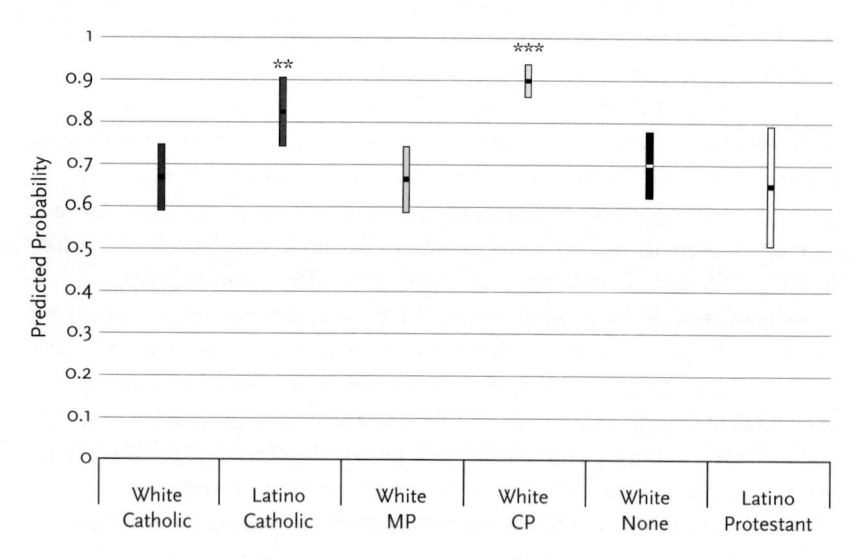

Figure 3.5 In-group preference: Religious homogamy

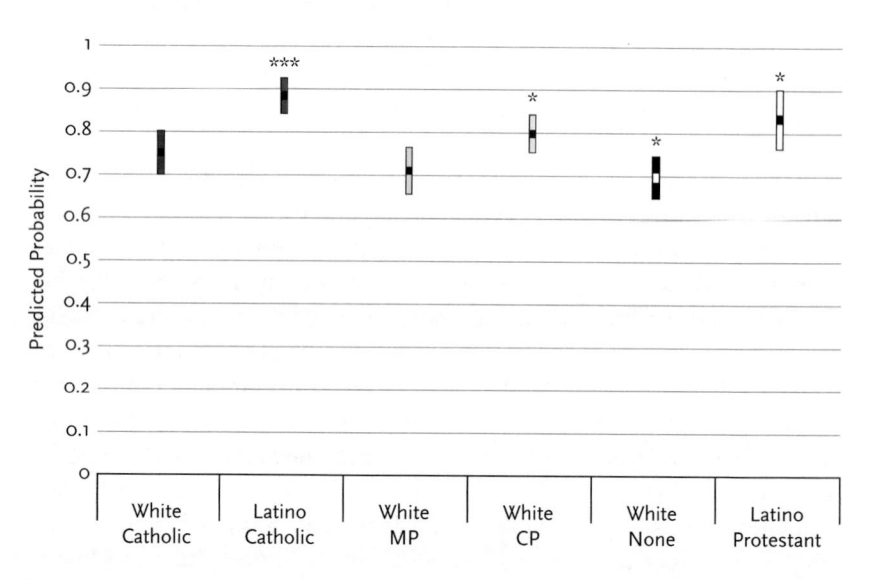

Figure 3.6 In-group preference: Educational homogamy

nones have slightly lower levels of educational homogamy than white Catholics and white mainline Protestants, but the difference is minimal. To be clear, homogamy is still high for these groups, but it is lower than for Latino Catholics and white conservative Protestants. Again, these patterns certainly reflect personal preference, but an element of structural constraint is at play as well. These groups differ from many others in the U.S. population on

[56] *Catholics in America*

religious affiliation but are similar to them on other dimensions, including educational attainment. As Latino and white conservative Protestant SES continues to increase (see Chapter 4 on changes in education levels) and as more Latino Catholics and conservative Protestants disaffiliate with their current religious groups (assuming current trends; see Chapter 5), homogamy among the groups depicted in these figures is likely to converge.

CHILDREN AND FERTILITY

Perhaps no issue captures the complexity of behaviors, outcomes, identities and attitudes, and issues related to compliance to religious teaching more completely than those surrounding children and fertility. When social scientists study children, they tend to think in terms of fertility rates, or the number of children that people have. A long history of sociological and demographic research shows that fertility reflects several personal and background traits that interact with one another over the life course and that include the traits I studied in Chapter 2: birth cohort, ethnicity, family SES, and place of birth. Fertility rates also vary with environmental factors, such as the economic conditions during an individual's childbearing years. Fertility, in turn, affects an individual's life course and other outcomes, such as education, income, wealth, and a wide range of behaviors and attitudes. Birth rate differences across major groups might also create differences in these other outcomes between groups and may affect the well-being of individuals, families, and societies.

Yet fertility rates also reflect a complex set of other factors that are more difficult to quantify but equally important for understanding fertility. In particular, the number of children a person has reveals a considerable amount about personal attitudes toward religious, political, and social issues, including willingness to comply with the teachings of a person's faith tradition, social norms about children and families, and the availability and social acceptability of birth control and abortion. Complex legal and political factors also affect individual behaviors as they did in the politics of birth control that occurred in the twentieth century. As Melissa Wilde shows in her historic account, the history of Christian churches in the United States promoting and discouraging access to and the use of birth control is complex and closely intertwined with the politics of race, class, and gender. Over much of the twentieth century, churches played a central role in supporting and disavowing eugenics, and these dynamics ultimately led to the wide-ranging set of views on birth control evident across Protestants denominations today (Wilde 2020). Coupled with this political and racially motivated wrangling was an altruistic motive to provide birth control to poor women, including poor Catholic women.

The Catholic Church and Fertility

The Catholic Church's official stance on birth control has changed little over time. Official Church teaching, reaffirmed in the twentieth and again in the twenty-first centuries, specifies that sex is intended to be open to procreation and this openness should not be intentionally interrupted by artificial contraception except under extreme circumstances and, even then, only natural family planning is acceptable. Natural family planning/fertility awareness methods are not considered the same as artificial contraception by the Church. Artificial contraception is never permitted, whereas periodic abstinence can be used when there are medical or other reasons for a couple to avoid pregnancy. Catholic women are permitted to take hormonal birth control for medical reasons, although it is ordinarily discouraged. For example, there are questions about whether some forms of hormonal birth control might be abortifacients, and there is limited evidence regarding the efficacy of hormonal birth control for some medical conditions for which women take hormones. Details on the Catholic approach to birth control are documented in "Humane Vitae," written by Pope Paul VI in 1968.[2]

Despite relative constancy in Church teaching regarding birth control, the behaviors of individual members of the Catholic Church have changed dramatically since the 1960s. This disconnect between official teaching and individual behavior highlights diversity in attitudes and beliefs among Catholics and their relationship to the official teachings of the Church. Some estimates indicate that 99% of U.S. Catholics have used birth control (Jones 2020). The Catholic Church has made efforts to incorporate secular expectations and realities through various efforts at institutional renewal, including Church stances on the family (Dillon 2018). Dillon's account of postsecular Catholicism credits Pope Francis, in particular, for his accessible vision of the Church, its teachings, and its relationship to ordinary Catholics as potentially bridging the gap between doctrine and people's lived experiences (Dillon 2018). Dillon's companion work (described in the introduction to this chapter) describes why pro-change Catholics (e.g., LGBTQ+, issues advocates of women's ordination, or a pro-choice stance regarding abortion) remain Church members by acknowledging that authority is diffuse and that Church doctrine is socially constructed. The same logic likely underlies the behavior of Catholics who use birth control despite Church teaching. Notably, a similar but reverse logic may also explain the small number of Catholics who continue to have large families despite social pressure to limit family size.

Fertility Trends

Within the complex religious and political environment that characterized the twentieth and early twenty-first centuries, fertility rates have changed dramatically, leading to changes in Catholic fertility and in how Catholics compare with other Americans in family size. Historically, U.S. fertility rates have been high relative to those of other developed countries, at least in part because Americans tend to be comparatively more religious than citizens of other countries (Adserà 2015; Perry and Schleifer 2019). Indeed, some of the earliest sociological and demographic research on U.S. fertility found significant differences in birth rates by religious tradition, and Catholics figured prominently in this research. In the 1950s and 1960s, American Catholics had the highest fertility rates of all U.S. religious groups, Protestants had the second highest rates, and Jews had the lowest (Freedman, Whelpton, and Smit 1959; Freedman, Whelpton, and Smit 1961). Research at that time tended to consider all Protestants together rather than distinguishing mainline from conservative Protestants, and Catholic fertility rates exceeded those of this large group of Protestants by a significant margin.

Catholic fertility rates declined through the 1970s and 1980s as Catholics became increasingly willing to use birth control despite continued Church prohibitions against it (Mosher, Hendershot, and Johnson 1992). By the 1970s and 1980s, researchers had begun to take seriously differences between mainline and conservative Protestants and showed that Catholic fertility rates had become similar to those of mainline Protestants. By contrast, conservative Protestant fertility rates were high in this period, exceeding those of both Catholics and mainline Protestants. Some speculate that high fertility among conservative Protestants reflected subcultural ideologies more than religious beliefs, but this research is complicated by the realities that cultural ideologies and religious beliefs are related to each other and that it is difficult to document the motivations that lead people to have children (Hout, Greeley, and Wilde 2001).

Conservative Protestant fertility remained higher than that of Catholics and mainline Protestants until recently. It appears that this fertility gap may be declining (Figure 3.7). Indeed, declines in fertility—including conservative Protestant fertility—have been rapid and significant across time and birth cohort, potentially leading to convergence between conservative Protestants and other U.S. religious groups and a corresponding decline in the predominance of conservative Protestants in the U.S. population overall in the future (Hout et al. 2001; Perry and Schleifer 2019; Skirbekk, Kaufmann, and Goujon 2010). Figure 3.7 illustrates the number of children born for those with at least one child and shows that overall changes appear modest: for example, Catholics had about 3 children on average in the 1970s and about 2.5 children in 2021. In the academic study of demographic change, this is a large difference.

In addition to varying by religious tradition, ideal and actual fertility reflect individuals' commitment to their faith and their frequency of exposure to religious messages regarding children, family, and related teaching on birth

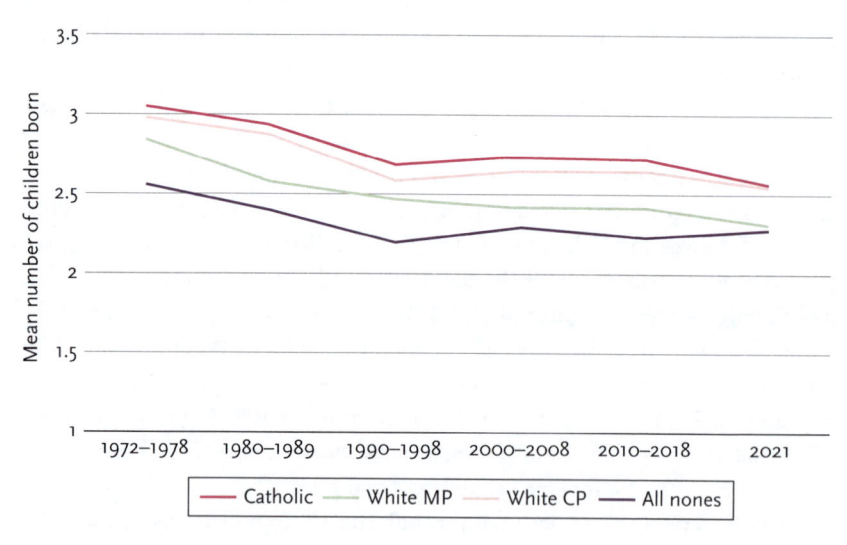

Figure 3.7 Declining and converging fertility rates

control and abortion. Researchers frequently measure religious commitment by frequency of attending religious services and literal Bible interpretation (Sherkat 2014). Both factors have historically been associated with higher fertility for all U.S. religious groups, and recent evidence shows that religious commitment is associated with slower than average declines in fertility for all groups (Perry 2022). However, the association between religious commitment and fertility is stronger for Catholics and mainline Protestants than for conservative Protestants (Perry 2022). Indeed, religious commitment appears to be associated with higher fertility for Catholics and mainline Protestants but to have no association with fertility for conservative Protestants (Perry 2022).

Four fertility measures capture who Catholics are today and underscore ways in which Catholics compare with other Americans: ideal number of children, actual number of children, age at first birth, and remaining childless.

Ideal Number of Children. An individual's stated ideal family size (i.e., the number of children they would like to have) reflects their aspirations about children, thereby reflecting their religious and other values. Ideal number of children also varies with other social traits, such as age, ethnicity, gender, family background, current family structure (including the individual's actual number of children), and SES. Moreover, ideal family size has declined considerably in recent years—from approximately four in the 1970s to closer to two today—reflecting changes in norms about family and children. In addition, social groups differ in their perceptions of an optimum number of children (Gao 2015). This important measure might also capture remaining differences between Catholics and other Americans and could illuminate how Catholic preferences for children align with Church teaching regarding "openness to life".

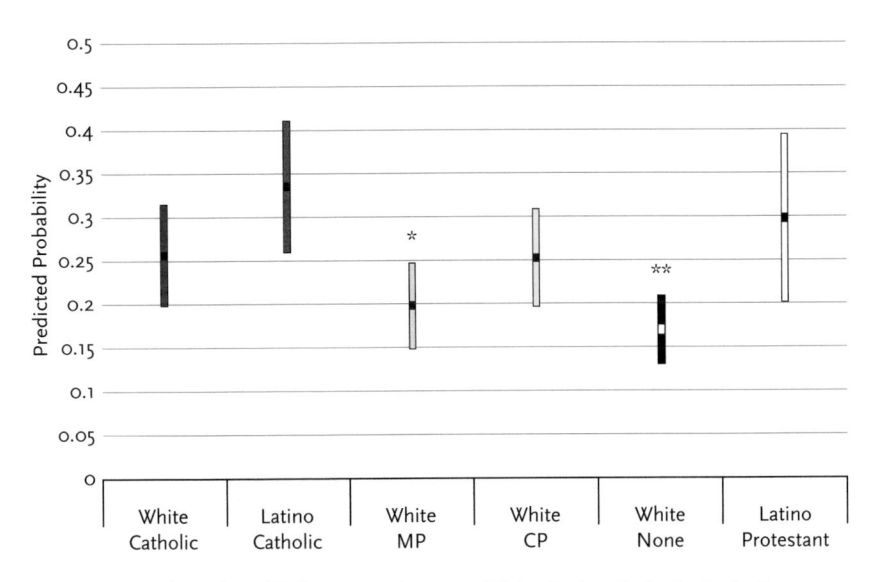

Figure 3.8 Ideal number of kids is more than two: White–Latino Catholic similarity

White Catholics, Latino Catholics, white conservative Protestants, and Latino Protestants are equally likely to say that more than two children is ideal. Figure 3.8 shows the predicted probability that respondents express an ideal number of children greater than two (with birth cohort and gender held constant). I examine this particular ideal number of children to capture the likelihood that GSS respondents want a large family or more children than the typical American wants. The figure shows that Latino Catholics are slightly more likely than white Catholics to say that more than two children is ideal, but this difference is not statistically significant. Similarly, the figure reveals no difference in the predicted probability for white conservative Protestants and Latino Protestants.

The two groups who are less likely than white or Latino Catholics to want more than two children are white mainline Protestant and white religious nones. These differences are important for at least two reasons. First, white Catholics and mainline Protestants have converged in the actual number of children as historically high Catholic fertility rates began to decline in the 1960s. However, white and Latino Catholics continue to be more likely than white mainline Protestants to think large families are ideal. Very few GSS respondents, including Catholics, say they want large families (i.e., more than four children). Still, as Figure 3.8 illustrates, white Catholics prefer slightly larger families than their mainline Protestant counterparts. Second, white religious nones are less likely than any of the other religious groups pictured in Figure 3.8 to say that more than two children is ideal. This finding is particularly noteworthy because these predicted probabilities hold birth cohort

FAMILY [61]

constant, indicating that the difference in ideal number of children between white Catholics and white nones is not explained by an age difference between these two groups. Although the GSS data cannot be used to explain this difference with certainty, the pattern is consistent with white Catholics adhering to Church doctrine and tradition regarding family size.

Actual Number of Children. White and Latino Catholics are similar in the number of children they consider ideal (Figure 3.8) and in the actual number of children they have (Figure 3.9). As large error bars (the red bars around the Latino Catholic estimate) suggest, there is more variation among Latino Catholics than white Catholics in fertility, leading to less confidence in the statistical estimates of the number of children they have. By contrast, mainline Protestants and religious nones have significantly fewer children than white Catholics, and white conservative Protestants and white Catholics do not differ significantly in their actual number of children. Importantly, however, the differences across religious–ethnic groups in individuals' actual number of children are only modestly significant. As Figure 3.8 showed, fertility among Catholics and Protestants began to converge as early as the 1970s, leading to near identical fertility rates for these groups in 2021. Figure 3.10 shows that Latino Catholic fertility has also converged to that of these other groups.

Age at First Birth. The age at which people start having children captures a great deal about their backgrounds and current situations, including birth cohort, ethnicity, SES, and social and economic context. The bars of the histogram in Figure 3.11 represent the percentage of individuals in each of the six religious–ethnic groups who had their first child at ages 18–25, 26–30, 36–40,

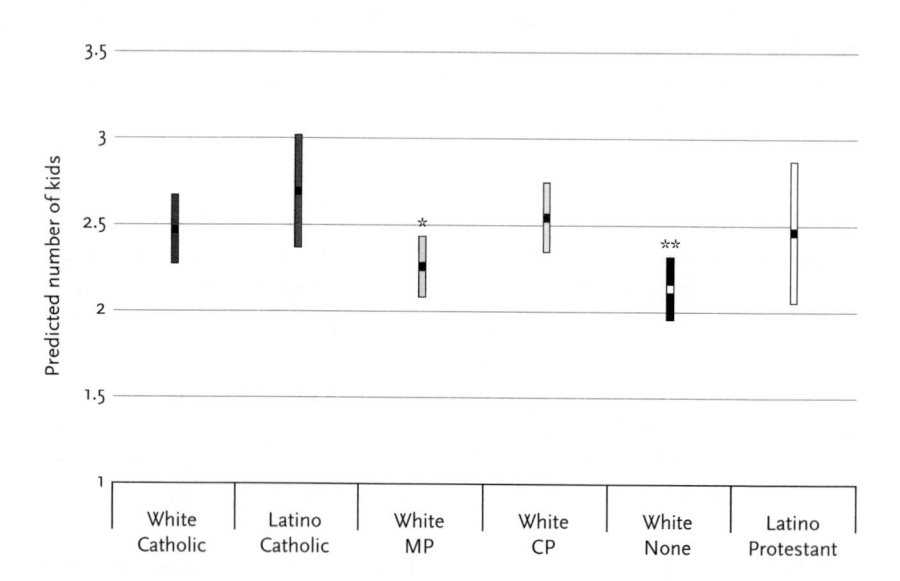

Figure 3.9 Actual number of kids: White–Latino Catholic similarity

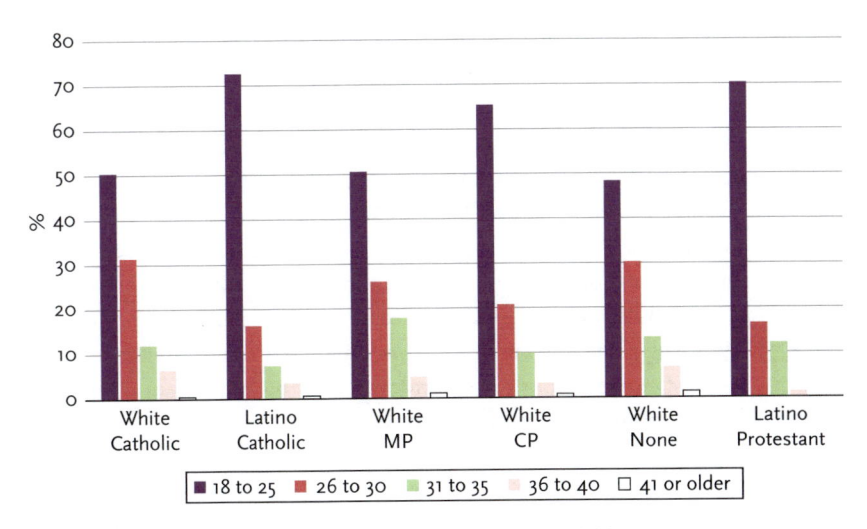

Figure 3.10 Age at birth of first child: Latino Catholics have children young

or 41 and older. For example, 50% of white Catholics had their first child between ages 18 and 25.

Figure 3.10 shows that Catholics differ in their age at first birth. The most pronounced difference is that most (72%) Latino Catholics have their first child by age 25, compared with a large but notably smaller percentage of white Catholics (50%). By contrast, white Catholics are more likely than Latino Catholics to have their first child after age 25: 31% of white Catholics and only 16% of Latino Catholics have their first child at ages 26–39, and nearly 20% of white Catholics and only 11% of Latino Catholics have their first child at age 31 or later. The figure also reveals no significant difference in the age at first birth between Latino Catholics and Latino Protestants.

White Catholics, white mainline Protestants, and white religious nones have their first child at nearly identical ages. By contrast, white conservative Protestants have their first child at slightly younger ages than do white Catholics, although this difference is fairly small and consistent with evidence of convergence in the fertility of these groups (Perry and Schleifer 2019). Approximately 50% of white Catholics, white mainline Protestants, and white religious nones have their first child by age 25, and the other 50% of each group waits until age 26 or later to have a child. White conservative Protestants are unique among the groups shown in the figure: white conservative Protestants (65%) are less likely than Latino Catholics (72%) and Latino Protestants (70%) to have their first child by age 25, but they more likely to do so than white Catholics, white mainline Protestants, and white religious nones.

FAMILY [63]

Remaining Childless. Americans are increasingly forgoing childbearing, and Catholics are no different. Childlessness is an important social indicator, but it is not a new phenomenon. In fact, remaining childless was widespread in the nineteenth century for reasons including nonmarriage, delayed marriage, fertility control, and gender imbalances as populations grew in previously unsettled areas of the United States (Morgan 1991; Smith 2020). Childlessness became rare starting in the early 1900s, remained unusual through the Baby Boom years, and then began to rise starting in the late 1960s. As these patterns suggest, childlessness trends are closely related to delays in marriage and fertility, rising rates of cohabitation and divorce, the availability of birth control, changing norms about family and women's role in the family, and educational and economic opportunities for women.

However, remaining childless is an informative social metric apart from its connection to other marriage and fertility indicators. On the one hand, childless people have more time and resources to focus on their own goals and therefore have more financial resources. They are better able than those with children to meet educational and occupational objectives, build lifetime income, save assets, and pay off debts. Not all the benefits of remaining childless are self-centered; in fact, childless people also volunteer more and make higher charitable contributions than do those with children. Yet childlessness also has disadvantages for individuals: children can provide economic and social support throughout life, particularly later in life.

Childlessness early in adulthood reflects changing social trends (e.g., delayed marriage, increased cohabitation) and predicts later-life childlessness. However, *completed fertility*, or childlessness after the age when most people have children is the strongest predictor of the social and economic costs and benefits that not having children creates. Demographers define early and later fertility differently, and gender differences in the biological ability to have children matter for this definition. However, it is common to consider a person childless if they have had no children by age 50. For this reason, Figure 3.11 compares the predicted probability of remaining childlessness for those older than 50.

For Catholics, childlessness is complex. The openness to life doctrine compels Catholics to be willing to have children if they are sexually active (and sexual activity should occur only in marriage). Yet, as we saw above, delays in marriage and fertility and increases in cohabitation and divorce for Catholics suggest that Catholics might be more likely to remain childless than they were historically.

A comparison of white and Latino Catholics underscore the complexity of childlessness for Catholics. Figure 3.11 reveals no significant difference between white and Latino Catholics in the probability of childlessness at age 50 and older. Because Latino Catholics are younger, on average, than white Catholics, it might be tempting to assume that this similarity

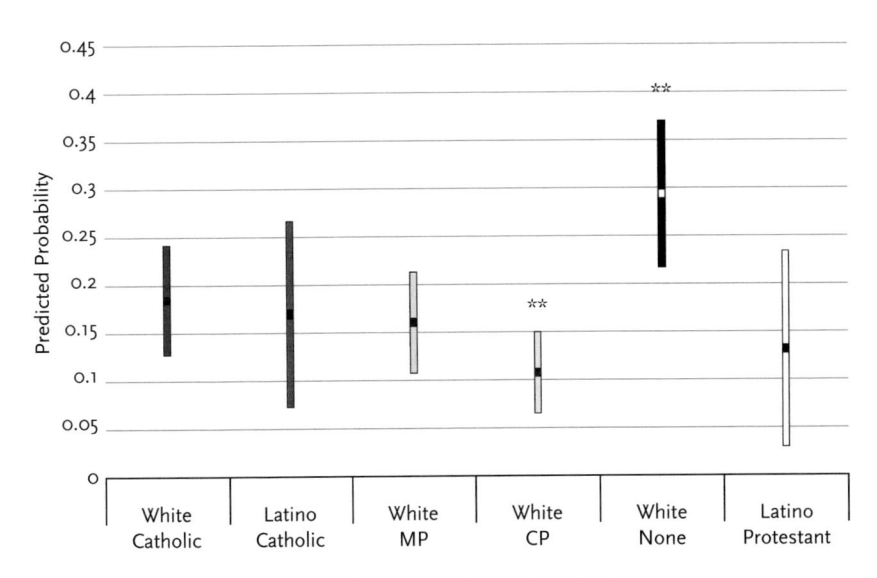

Figure 3.11 Remaining childless: White–Latino Catholic similarity

reflects age differences. However, the inclusion of birth cohort in the model that produced these estimates does not change the relationship. It is more likely that the similarity in the probability of remaining childless reflects two issues, one substantive and one demographic. Substantively, Catholics may take seriously the issue of openness to life and may be affected by related norms among Catholics regarding the advantages of large families. However, a demographic issue is also likely at play: because Latino Catholics are comparatively young and because the GSS is a cross-sectional dataset, relatively few Latino Catholics are older than 50. The large confidence interval surrounding the Latino Catholic estimate (the large red bar around the estimate) indicates that confidence in the Latino Catholic estimate is weak.

Comparing Catholics and other religious groups underscores other family patterns shown earlier in this chapter. First, white Catholics and white mainline Protestants are equally likely to be childless at age 50 and older, consistent with similarities in their marriage, cohabitation, and fertility patterns. Second, white conservative Protestants are less likely than white Catholics to remain childless. Overall, fertility has begun to converge for white conservative Protestants, white Catholics, and white mainline Protestants (Perry and Schleifer 2019). However, documented cohort differences in remaining childless (Morgan 1991; Smith 2020) do not explain this difference in childlessness. Third, white religious nones are much more likely than white Catholics to remain childless. Again, this difference does not reflect a difference in cohort behavior but at least suggests that Catholics and religious nones differ substantively in their approaches to family and children, as shown in Figure 3.11.

CONCLUSION

Family processes and events create the trajectories and turning points that define people's lives, and family events are critical to understanding who is Catholic. In this chapter, I documented important differences among Catholics in marriage, cohabitation, divorce, and fertility trends. I also situated the current state of the Catholic family within historic trends and compared Catholics with other Americans on key family states and processes. I showed sizable family differences between white and Latino Catholics, and I also documented relative similarities between white Catholics and white mainline Protestants. For example, I showed that Latino Catholics are less likely to marry, more likely to cohabit, and less likely to divorce than white Catholics. However, I also showed that these differences are explained by age differences between Latino and white Catholics. In addition, I demonstrated that marriage and cohabitation rates are similar for white Catholics and white mainline Protestants, but that white Catholics are less likely than white mainline Protestants to have ever divorced. By contrast, white Catholics are less likely than white conservative Protestants to marry, equally likely to cohabit, and *slightly* less likely to have divorced. Some of the starkest family structure differences are between Catholics and religious nones: relative to white religious nones, white Catholics are more likely to marry, less likely to cohabit, and less likely to divorce, even when age and gender are held constant.

I also documented differences in fertility among Catholics and between Catholics and other Americans. In particular, white Catholics, Latino Catholics, and white conservative Protestants are equally likely to state an ideal family size is one with more than two children, whereas white mainline Protestants and white religious nones are less likely than white or Latino Catholics to want more than two children. Although there are few differences among Catholics in their ideal number of children, there are important differences in their actual number of children. White Catholics and white mainline Protestants have nearly identical overall fertility rates, have their first child at roughly the same age, and are equally likely to remain childless. By contrast, Latino Catholics and white conservative Protestants, on average, have more children and have their first child at a younger age than white Catholics.

As we will see in the next chapter, each of these differences in family and relationships builds on social origins (Chapter 2) to create a host of SES outcomes, such as work and career patterns, income, wealth, and the gendered division of labor.

NOTES

1. Most of the Latino Protestants in the GSS sample (65%) are members of conservative (rather than mainline) Protestant churches.
2. There was significant backlash to "Humane Vitae" when it was issued that has continued until today. Many Catholics expected the Church to change its stance on birth control, consistent with a birth control commission that suggested a change; other Catholics praised (and continue to praise) the Pope's adherence to the Church's traditional stance. A full discussion of "Humanae Vitae," its origins, and the ensuing fallout is beyond the scope of this book but well-documented elsewhere (Catholics for Choice 2023; Hahn 2001; Winters 2018).

CHAPTER 4

Achievements

Education, Work, Income, and Wealth

Catholics were historically some of the poorest families in America, but they are now among the country's highest-achieving religious groups. However, Latino Catholics lag behind white Catholics on most measures of socioeconomic status (SES), whereas white Catholics are notably similar to white mainline Protestants on these outcomes.

Education, work, income, and wealth—the four basic measures of SES—are essential for understanding who Catholics are, how they have changed over time, and how they compare with other Americans. Because these four components of SES simultaneously convey information about past, present, and future well-being, they are essential to understanding many other aspects of people's lives. Ascribed traits (e.g., birth cohort, gender, ancestry) and family background (e.g., parents' SES) interact with each other to shape educational goals and attainment. Education has indisputable benefits of its own (e.g., improved critical thinking, confidence, interpersonal skills) and is one of the strongest predictors of work and career outcomes, income, and wealth accumulation. Of course, work, income, and wealth also have advantages: they allow people to purchase the goods and services necessary to live safe, healthy, and pleasant lives; provide social status and prestige; and can be transferred to future generations (e.g., through inheritance) to extend these benefits indefinitely. In addition, education, work and career, income, and wealth interact with each other—and with marriage and family traits—to affect the behaviors and attitudes that are the subject of the second half of this book.

Religion is one of the strongest predictors of SES. More than a century of research has documented—and debated—the nature of that relationship, and Catholics have been central to much of the discussion in this literature. Early theorists observed important correlations between religion and SES and found evidence of a relatively stable rank ordering of religious groups on many measures of status through much of the twentieth century (Durkheim 1912/1954; Featherman 1971; Greeley 1969; Lenski 1961; Roof 1979; Weber 1930). The exact rank order of religious traditions has shifted over time, but the U.S. religious stratification structure was largely unchanged for many decades: mainline Protestants and Jews ranked relatively high on most measures of achievement, Catholics ranked in the middle, and conservative Protestants and black Protestants ranked at the low end of the distributions.

In the second half of the twentieth century, however, American religion underwent a major restructuring that happened in tandem with—and because of—the major changes in technology, demographics, education, and politics that occurred following World War II. Among other changes, existing religious organizations adapted their programs and priorities, new religious organizations emerged, and individuals changed their religious beliefs, practices, and affiliations (Wuthnow 1990). As a result of these and other social and economic changes, the religious stratification order began a transition (Featherman 1971; Glenn and Hyland 1967; Lenski 1961; Stryker 1981; Wuthnow 1990). There was some evidence of SES convergence between Catholics and mainline Protestants as early as the 1960s. However, the degree to which these groups were converging proved difficult to disentangle because data representing the U.S. population were limited (Glenn and Hyland 1967; Greeley 1977; Lenski 1961; Roof and McKinney 1987) and, perhaps, because the relationship was changing even as researchers were studying it.

Researchers continued to identify clear and consistent associations between religion and SES through roughly the mid-2010s. However, this work paid less attention to a rank ordering of religious groups than to documenting detailed patterns between religion and SES outcomes. Research in this area showed that religion is associated with education, including orientations toward education, the type of education people pursue, high school and college graduation rates, the number of years of schooling completed, and other measures of academic success (Horwitz et al. 2022; Keister and Sherkat 2013; Muller and Ellison 2012; Regnerus 2003). Religion is also associated with various work and employment measures, such as wages, the gendered division of household responsibilities, decision-making about material pursuits within marriage, and saving, wealth, and the types of assets owned by particular religious groups (Denton 2004; Keister 2011; Schnabel et al. 2022; Smith and Faris 2005).

Research on religion and SES has slowed somewhat since about the mid-2010s, even as changes to the American religious and economic landscapes suggest that different religious groups are now relevant and the association between religion and SES may be different now than it was 10 years ago.[1]

Changes in religion have been profound, including a restructuring of the religious and secular orientations of some Protestant groups (Greeley and Hout 2006; Smith 1998, 2000; Wuthnow 1990), an increased presence of religious nones (Burge 2021; Levin et al. 2022; Smith et al. 2014), changes in the beliefs and practices of non-Protestant religious traditions (Burton 2022; Stark 2008), and a growing importance of new immigrant groups with unique religious practices and identities (Amin and Sherkat 2013; Ellison, Wolfinger, and Ramos-Wada 2013; Keister and Borelli 2013). In addition, the American economy is in transition. Service, gig, and other nontraditional occupations are increasingly common (Baber 2023; Bergmann 2011; Keister and Southgate 2022), postsecondary education is now a requirement for more careers than was the case historically (Biddle and Mette 2017; Fry and Parker 2018), and dual-earner couples are the norm despite stalled progress toward gender equality (England, Levine, and Mishel 2020; Yavorsky et al. 2023). Rising student debt, housing shortages, and increasing housing costs have made homeownership—a way of accumulating assets that previous generations took for granted—largely out of reach for many Millennials (Beckert 2022; Rodriguez 2023).

My goal in this chapter is to offer a contemporary SES portrait of Catholics and other religious groups. I first document objective patterns of education, work, income, and wealth. I then compare Catholics to other Americans on their subjective sense of class position and financial well-being. I also use data in this chapter that I did not use in previous chapters. I continue to use the General Social Survey (GSS) for most estimates because it provides excellent detail on education, work, income, and homeownership (one component of wealth). However, the GSS does not contain other information about wealth ownership or inheritance. To provide estimates for these important SES components, I also use the Panel Study of Income Dynamics (PSID). The Appendix describes the PSID in additional detail.

EDUCATION

Education is a long-standing priority of the Catholic Church; however, Catholic schools have not always been accepted as part of the broader U.S. educational system. Greeley's (1977) social portrait of Catholics underscores how controversial Catholic schools once were. He noted that "Catholic schools have always been offensive to many non-Catholics. They were prime targets for nativist bigotry; long ago, in some cities, schools were burned to the ground" (p. 164). The hatred of Catholic schools was part of the larger disdain for Catholics that was evident as early as colonial times and that strengthened—often following waves of Catholic immigration—during the nineteenth century and into the mid-twentieth century (Davis 2010; Zeitz 2015). This disdain was reinforced in public schools where "anti-Catholic venom was part of the typical American school day, along with Bible readings" (Davis 2010). Much of the hatred of Catholic schools centered on the perception that they prevented immigrants from assimilating and that they were "'un-American,' no one knew what went on in them, their teachers were not adequately trained, and subject matter taught was not academically sound" (Greeley 1977: 164). These nativist claims led to related accusations that—because Catholic schools did not strictly adhere to the curricular guidelines used in public schools—Catholic school students must be receiving an inferior education.

Such claims did not deter the Catholic education system, and, despite steep enrollment declines, school closures, and other challenges (Dolan 2018), the system is still a vital part of American education. In 2022, the Catholic Church operated more than 4,700 elementary schools, 1,100 secondary schools, and 220 colleges and universities. These schools were educating 1.2 million elementary school students, nearly 528,000 secondary school students, and more than 717,000 college-aged students. An additional 2 million elementary and secondary school children were participating in Catholic religious education programs (Center for Applied Research in the Apostolate [CARA] 2023).

Moreover, not long after Greeley wrote about the disdain for Catholic schools, education scholars began to recognize advantages to a Catholic education, which are similar to those of other private schools: Catholic schools tend to have smaller class sizes, more focused attention to students facing academic difficulties and other challenges, and stricter discipline than public schools. Catholic schools are also better able than public schools to select high-potential students and suspend or expel students with less potential or demonstrated disciplinary or academic problems. Therefore, Catholic schools create an environment with fewer distractions for students and teachers that can better facilitate learning. In addition, Catholic schools are diverse in terms of both race/ethnicity and social class—like the Church overall—exposing students to a variety of viewpoints and cultural backgrounds. Finally, Catholics schools have the added advantage of emphasizing moral and other education that is focused on character development (Brooks 2015; Bryk, Lee, and Hollan 1993; Hallinan and Kubitschek 2010).

In the 1990s, academic research began to explore whether there are benefits to attending Catholic schools. This work found evidence that Catholic middle and high school students had higher test scores, a higher probability of completing high school and attending college, increased rates of college graduation, and higher adult salaries and wages than their counterparts in public schools (Bryk et al. 1993; Evans and Schwab 1995; Neal 1997; Sander 1996). However, recent research offers more modest evidence of a Catholic educational advantage (Carbonaro and Covay 2010; Dallavis et al. 2021; Hallinan and Kubitschek 2010). Although researchers acknowledge that there may be a Catholic school advantage, they also agree that it is extremely difficult to determine whether Catholic school quality is superior to public education, whether there has been a change in school quality (Catholic or public) over time, or whether research methods and data have changed over time. The weaker recent findings may also reflect the reality that it is difficult to disentangle the advantages of a particular school or school sector from the other factors (e.g., urban location, parental involvement in children's lives, peer influence, parents' SES) that contribute to educational outcomes.

A related body of research has explored changing Catholic education levels and shows that Catholic education levels have risen over time. Catholic education levels were at the national average and increasing by the late 1970s (Greeley 1977; Roof 1979). However, rising Catholic education levels occurred alongside an overall increase in American education levels and changing demographics of the Catholic Church (i.e., the proportion of Latino Catholics was growing) (Wuthnow 1990). As a result, empirical evidence regarding educational parity with mainline Protestants was conflicting as recently as 2013. Some research showed that Catholic education levels still lagged slightly behind that of Jewish and mainline Protestant Americans, even when ethnicity was controlled (i.e., when educational differences between Latino and white Catholics were considered) (Massengill 2013). Others found parity between white, U.S.-born Catholics and mainline Protestants but emphasized the increasing importance of considering new immigrants' education levels when comparing education levels across religious groups (Amin and Sherkat 2013; Keister 2011). In addition, as Massengill (2013) speculated, educational differences across religious groups, including the comparably low education levels of Catholics relative to mainline Protestants, might reflect cohort changes: younger Catholics are likely to be more upwardly mobile than older Catholics.

My analyses of GSS data show that—as of 2021—white Catholics continue to have educational levels equivalent to white mainline Protestants, but Latino Catholics and white conservative Protestants lag behind both white Catholics and white mainline Protestants. Figure 4.1 depicts educational differences—the probability that respondents have a bachelor's degree or more education—by religion and ethnicity. I use "attaining a bachelor's degree or more" as my education measure in this figure to compare education levels for white Catholics and white mainline Protestants at the upper end of the education distribution; this measure provides a stricter test of educational convergence given that completing lower levels of education (e.g., high school) is fairly common in the United States. However, the patterns represented in Figure 4.1 are the same when I use other measures of education, such as total years of education or completion of other educational milestones (e.g., high school completion, completing an associate's degree).

Figure 4.1 shows that white Catholics, white mainline Protestants, and white religious nones have nearly identical probabilities of having completed a

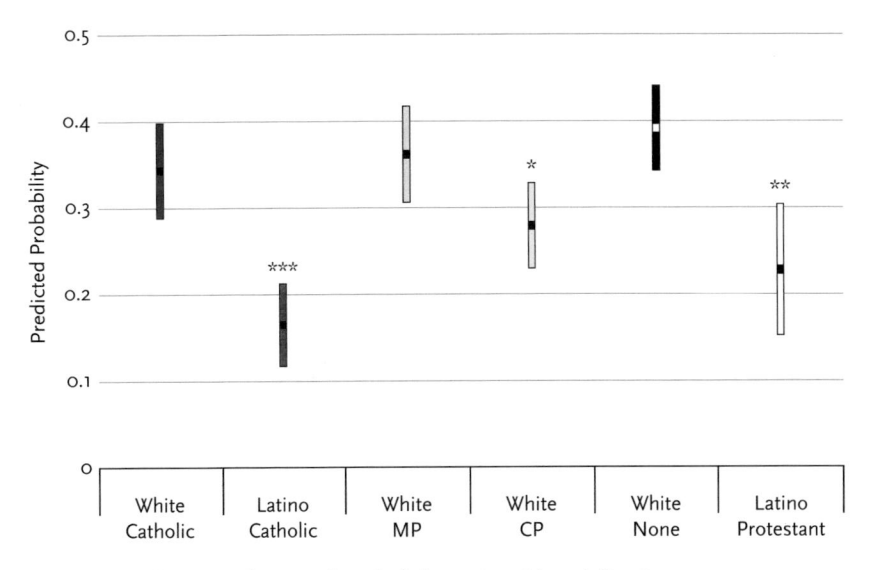

Figure 4.1 College completion: White Catholic parity with mainline Protestants

bachelor's degree or more education. By contrast, Latino Catholics and Latino Protestants are less likely to have completed college than white Catholics. Similarly, white conservative Protestants are less likely than white Catholics to have completed college, but this difference is small, suggesting that educational attainment for these groups is converging. All these differences remain when I control birth cohort and gender, suggesting that the patterns are not reflective of these ascribed traits.

"Julia," an American Voices Project (AVP) respondent, offers some insight into Catholic education, including its advantages and disadvantages. Julia is, in many ways, typical of high-SES white Catholics. She is 50 years old, was born in a large city in the Northeast, married (never divorced), and has two sons ages 15 and 17 (making her 33 and 35 years old, respectively, when she had her children). Julia was raised in a lower middle-class home. Her father was a bus driver, and her mother stayed at home until Julia and her siblings were in high school. Her mother then worked as a secretary. Julia was upwardly mobile: she has two master's degrees and is a school principal. Her husband has a bachelor's degree and is a professional at a large retail chain. Their total household income is in the top 20% of income earners, and their wealth is in the top 20% of wealth owners.

Julia and her husband both went to Catholic schools, and she credits the small classes and individualized attention of their schools with their upward mobility. Her sons attend Catholic high schools, after having attended public elementary schools, because she was frustrated with the public school system. Notably, Julia has worked her entire career in a public school—first as a teacher and now as a principal. She appears to appreciate the irony: after all, she is in a position to change some of what frustrates her about the public school system. However, she feels helpless—even as a leader in a public school—to improve her own school, including such issues as large class sizes, which make individualized attention difficult. She works hard to find ways to improve teacher quality in her school through hiring, training, mentoring, and selective firing; however, she acknowledges that she cannot single-handedly address all the challenges associated with public education. She also acknowledges that Catholic schools are imperfect: she values the religious education component but realizes that not all parents want this for their children. She is also aware that Catholic schools are expensive, even for someone with her income.

Julia and her husband are also excellent examples of the problems of studying Catholic education. Although the schools her sons attend probably have some advantages, Julia and her husband are very involved in their children's education, assisting with homework, extracurriculars, and other school events. They restrict their children's use of video games and watching television to weekends, making them use extra time on weekday evenings to study, read, or do homework. Their children have jobs, and Julia and her husband prioritize teaching them to save and to make charitable contributions with their earnings. Their deep involvement in their children's education is typical of high-SES parents—a pattern that is well-known to complicate data on educational outcomes.

WORK

Like education, work is essential to individuals, families, and societies. Having a job provides purpose, financial resources, and long-term social and economic stability to individual workers and their families. In addition, some jobs provide opportunities for workers to develop the experience and skills needed to successfully participate in social, economic, and civic activities beyond the workplace. Work also matters outside the individual and family: societies and economies depend on individuals participating in the labor force to supply the goods and services necessary for the survival and well-being of all members of society.

Full-Time Work

Full-time participation in the labor force—regardless of an individual's occupation—is among the most basic and informative measures of work status. Both full-time work and other forms of work (part-time, temporary, gig) are informative about an individual's engagement in the labor force, but working a standard American 40-hour workweek is particularly instructive. Working full time indicates that an individual is committed to a job, may be moving along a career path, and is receiving wages or a salary. For example, full-time work may have tangible advantages—such as medical benefits, a retirement plan, and paid time off—that are not typically associated with less than full-time employment. Full-time work also has intangible benefits, signaling commitment to a job and potential career mobility. Full-time work may also indicate that the employed person has a degree of long-term financial security that is less likely available to individuals in other forms of work.

Full-time work says a great deal about who Catholics are today, how they have changed over time, and how they compare with other Americans. Figure 4.2 shows the probability that a GSS respondent was working full time or more in the past week. The figure shows that white Catholics and white mainline Protestants are equally likely to be working full time, a pattern that underscores the change in SES that white Catholics have undergone since the 1960s and that is consistent with evidence of convergence between white Catholic and white Protestant family patterns (i.e., marriage, cohabitation, divorce, fertility) shown in Chapter 3. Figure 4.2 also shows that white conservative Protestants are converging with white Catholics and white mainline Protestants. The figure shows that white conservative Protestants are less likely than white Catholics and white mainline Protestants to work full time, but this difference is small and not statistically significant.

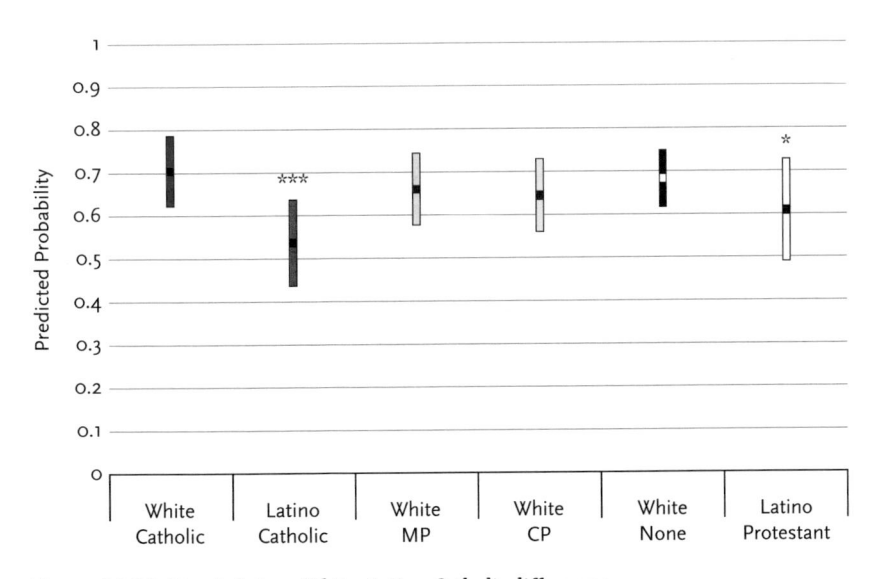

Figure 4.2 Working full time: White–Latino Catholic differences

The most pronounced pattern depicted in Figure 4.2 is that Latinos—both Catholic and Protestant—are less likely than white Catholics to be working full time. The difference between white and Latino respondents remains when birth cohort and gender are held constant; however, controlling for being a first- or second-generation immigrant reduces the difference slightly (results not shown in a figure). In other words, U.S.-born white and Latino respondents are more similar in their work behavior although differences remain that might reflect discrimination in hiring and termination of workers by ethnicity. This finding is also consistent with research demonstrating that it takes new immigrants time to find full-time work and that educational deficits, skills mismatches, and discrimination hamper immigrants' efforts to be fully engaged in the labor force (Alba 2009; Rumbaut and Portes 2014; Zhou et al. 2008).

Self-Employment

Self-employment says a great deal about both individual achievement and the functioning of societies and economies. For the individual, self-employment can be a marker of innovation, creativity, motivation, and resourcefulness. If it involves starting a new business, self-employment can also lead to high income, wealth accumulation, and upward social and economic mobility beyond what is possible as an employee (Kim, Aldrich, and Keister 2003). Of course, there are risks associated with entrepreneurship, and not all entrepreneurs earn high incomes or build great fortunes. In addition, not all those who are self-employed are entrepreneurs (Gohmann 2012). Yet self-employment provides unique insights into many other individual and family traits and resources. It is an important indicator of personal resources, such as home equity and access to resources from banks and other sources (Harding and Rosenthal 2017). Self-employment is also a marker of individual-level work strategies and work ethic, social resources provided by family and other networks, and cultural and institutional constraints on work and related behaviors (Aldrich, Renzulli, and Langton 1998; Kim et al. 2003; Renzulli, Aldrich, and Moody 2000; Rietveld and Hoogendoorn 2022). When self-employment involves new business formation, it can also shape social and economic stratification in an economy and may be a vehicle for economic growth and technological evolution and revolutions (Bodrožić and Adler 2018; Crosa, Keister, and Aldrich 2001).

Given the enormous amount of information that self-employment provides, it is useful for understanding who Catholics are and how they compare with other Americans. Current understanding of the role of religion in self-employment is limited because of the limited availability of data on the topic. As a result, research on religion and self-employment largely continues

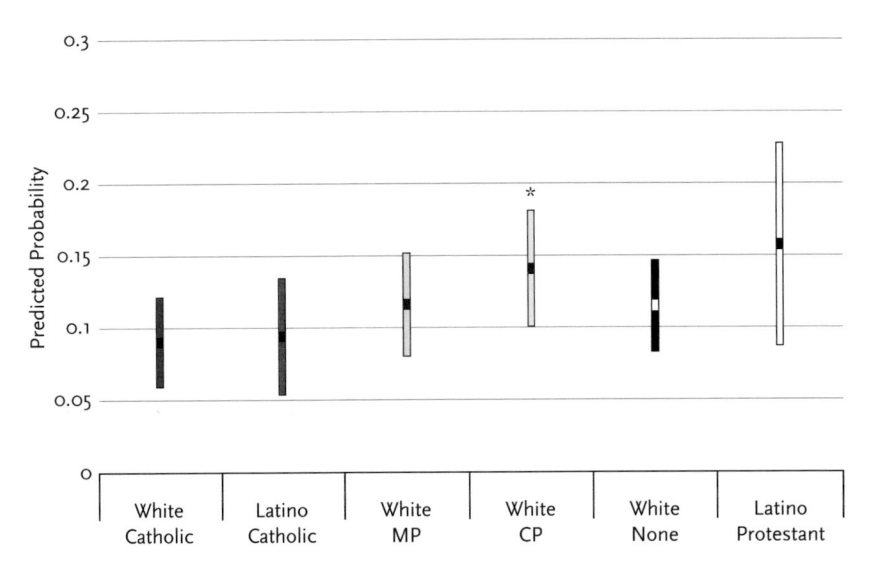

Figure 4.3 Self-employment: White–Latino Catholic similarity

Weber's well-known focus on entire economic systems, largely exploring whether religion affects economic activity and growth by encouraging entrepreneurship (Seabright 2016; Weber 1930). Moreover, much of the research in this tradition focuses on Protestants, again in line with Weber's original thesis regarding the Protestant ethic. However, some notable and relatively recent exceptions document the association between individual religious affiliation and beliefs and entry into self-employment (Dougherty et al. 2013; Rietveld and Hoogendoorn 2022). This research is dated and does not separate white from Latino Catholics, but it does provide useful preliminary evidence that Catholics are entrepreneurial (e.g., that Catholics' likelihood of ever starting or currently starting a business is higher than that of religious nones and similar to that of mainline Protestants) (Dougherty et al. 2013).

Self-employment is a rare SES characteristic on which white and Latino Catholics are similar. My evidence from the GSS shows that white and Latino Catholics who are working are equally likely to be self-employed (Figure 4.3) despite differences in overall patterns of full-time work between these groups (Figure 4.2) and evidence that self-employment varies by ethnicity as well as by other ascribed traits, such as gender and nativity (Saurav, Goltz, and Buche 2013; Valdez 2011; Zhou 2007). Ideally, the GSS would include questions about whether respondents have ever started a business or are currently starting a business, but the GSS asks respondents only whether they are self-employed. Figure 4.3 uses the self-employment question to show that the probability of being self-employed is relatively low for all respondents, consistent with prior evidence (Tsvetkova, Partridge, and Betz 2017). Latino

Catholics, white Catholics, and white mainline Protestants are equally likely to be self-employed, whereas white conservative Protestants are more likely than white Catholics to be self-employed. These patterns remain when birth cohort and gender are held constant and when immigrant status (being a first- or second-generation immigrant) is controlled.

Household Division of Labor

Because the household division of labor in and out of the home is closely related to work and career outcomes, it is often studied alongside other work-related issues, such as work in the paid labor force. Couples negotiate—albeit not always explicitly—how they will divide their paid and unpaid (i.e., household work and childcare) labor. The way that couples divide their labor affects many outcomes within and outside the family, including parents' involvement in their children's education and other activities, the careers of each member of the couple, and the household's financial resources. The division of household labor can also affect the way a society is arranged and functions. There is evidence, for example, that in the United States, high-income and high-wealth households have a more traditional division of household labor than lower-income and lower-wealth households. This pattern can exacerbate inequalities over the generations by allowing higher SES households to devote resources to their children, increasing their educational and occupational achievements (Yavorsky et al. 2023).

Three interdependent factors influence how most couples divide their labor, and these factors might vary across religious groups. First, exchange theories in sociology and related bargaining theories in economics propose that relative status influences how couples negotiate their division of paid and unpaid labor. Women, on average, earn less than men in the paid labor force, giving them less bargaining power in their relationships. This inequality in earnings also means that, if a couple is going to have one person stay out of the paid labor force, it will most often make financial sense for the woman to stay home.

Second, gender roles within and outside the family follow closely from family structure (Lehrer 1995; Thébaud and Halcomb 2019). For example, a woman in an opposite-sex marriage may find it financially and socially easier to decide to stay out of the workforce to raise children than a never-married or divorced but otherwise equivalent woman. An increasing number of married or cohabiting men also choose to stay out of the workforce, particularly if the family has young children, although stay-at-home fathers are still quite rare (Lachance-Grzela and Bouchard 2010; Yavorsky et al. 2023). Given the religious differences in family structure discussed in Chapter 3, both power differences and family structure differences by religion will lead to religious differences in the division of labor. Indeed, some evidence points to an association between religious affiliation and the household division of labor (Ellison and Bartkowski 2002).

Third, social and cultural norms affect the division of household labor. In the contemporary United States, norms encourage women—rather than men—to stay home when a couple decides to forgo one income. Notably, these norms appear to be at least as strong, if not stronger, among highly paid professional women and men (England et al. 2016; Killewald and Gough 2010). Similarly, workplace and school practices and policies often make it difficult for women to stay in the paid labor force particularly when they have young children. Many professional occupations, for example, assume that workers will be available for long hours, including traveling, working evenings and weekends, and foregoing vacations and other time away from the workplace (Padavic, Ely, and Reid 2020). Yet schools are often in session only a fraction of the time that professionals are expected to be at work; similarly, if a child is sick, a parent needs to be able to pick the child up from school with little notice and take care of the child for an unpredictable amount of time. Given gender differences in income, again it usually makes more financial sense for women to take primary responsibility for childcare under these circumstances (Thébaud and Halcomb 2019; Yavorsky et al. 2023).

Catholic teaching about gender roles is complex and perhaps less well-known—including by many Catholics—than teaching on other family issues such as divorce and birth control. A complete discussion of Catholic approaches to gender is beyond the scope of this book, but it is worth noting that Catholic doctrine promotes the dignity of all people regardless of gender. Indeed, the Catechism states that "men and women have been created in perfect equality as human persons" (CCC paragraphs 369–73) and that the "equality of men rests essentially on their dignity as persons and the rights that flow from it: every form of social or cultural discrimination in fundamental personal rights on the grounds of sex, race, color, social conditions, language, or religion must be curbed and eradicated as incompatible with God's design" (CCC paragraph 1935).

Pope John Paul II reiterated the importance of gender equality in a summary of the teaching of a 1987 synod of bishops on the laity's role in the Church: "[T]he Synod Fathers gave special attention to the status and role of women, with two purposes in mind: to themselves acknowledge and to invite all others to once again acknowledge the indispensable contribution of women to the building up of the Church and the development of society. . . . [T]he Synod Fathers, when confronted with the various forms of discrimination and marginalization to which women are subjected simply because they are women, time and time again strongly affirmed the urgency to defend and to promote the *personal dignity of woman*, and consequently, her equality with man." He added that the Church must actively oppose gender discrimination by noting that "Vigorous and incisive pastoral action must be taken by all to overcome completely these forms of discrimination so that the image of God that shines in all human beings without exception may be fully respected" (Pope John Paul II 1988).

Yet many of the Church's doctrines can make gender equality challenging, at least in the way that equality is defined by secular society. For example, doctrine related to an openness to life in marriage and the prohibition of birth control—when followed closely—can lead to large families. Large families, in turn, can make it difficult for couples to have dual careers, an issue which usually affects women's—rather than men's—decisions to work out of the home. Of course, women often play essential roles in the family, as they do in other organizations, that may be less visible (but often equally important) than men's roles (Keister, Thebaud, and Yavorsky 2022; Ostrander 1984; Padavic et al. 2020).

Despite these competing religious influences, white Catholics are quite similar to other Americans in their propensity to have dual-earner marriages. Moreover, consistent with patterns on other SES measures, white Catholics are more similar to mainline Protestants whereas Latino Catholics are different: in this case, Latino Catholics are less likely than white Catholics to have two incomes. Figure 4.4 shows the probability that both members of a married couple are employed full time outside the home. In other analyses (not shown), I explored patterns by religion and ethnicity on other division and labor measures such as having a traditional division of labor (man works out of the home, woman does not) or a progressive division of labor

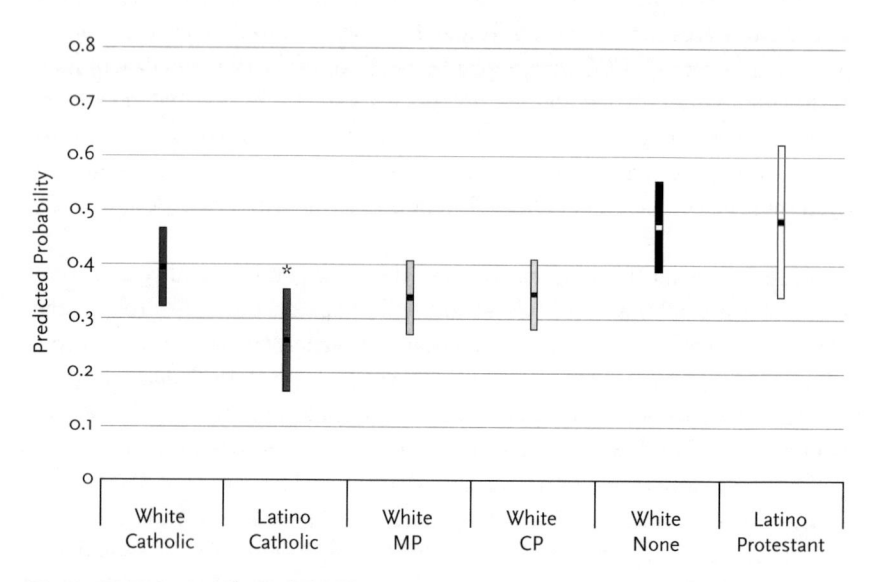

Figure 4.4 Division of household labor: Dual-Income families are more common for white Catholics than Latino Catholics

(woman works out of the home, man does not). The patterns in these other analyses were substantively similar to those I report in Figure 4.4: the probability is high for all couples—more than one-half of most couples are now dual-earners—and there is no significant difference between white Catholics and white mainline Protestants. Notably, there is also no difference between white conservative Protestants and white Catholics, indicating an important convergence among all white Catholics and white Protestants.

Julia and her husband, the AVP respondents I described earlier in the education section of this chapter, are typical of today's Catholics in terms of their work behavior and the division of labor in their marriage. Both Julia and her husband work full time, and, in her AVP interview, she took for granted that working a full-time job was normal for a woman of her generation (Generation X). Yet she was also aware that women in her mother's generation faced different norms and, on average, worked differently than Julia and her peers. Typical of other women of her generation (Silent Generation), her mother only worked out of the home after her four children were in high school. These generational differences exemplify generational differences between white Catholics in Generation X and the Silent Generation that contributed to changing income and wealth across these generations, as the next sections of this chapter describe.

INCOME

Income—perhaps the most commonly used measure of social and financial well-being—is vital to understanding who Catholics are. Income is the flow of financial resources into a household, and it is necessary to purchase goods and services including both necessities (e.g., food, shelter, clothing, utilities, transportation, medical care) and luxuries (e.g., vacations, entertainment, dining out, jewelry, art, some types of clothing). Income can also facilitate saving and wealth accumulation, which creates a financial cushion that can be used for spending in the event that a breadwinner's income is interrupted or stops entirely for a period of time. In addition to these tangible benefits, income—and the goods and services purchased with income—can be used to signal social and economic standing, occupational success, and social mobility. Income comes from a range of sources that can be informative about the social and economic status and well-being of the recipient. For example, most households receive income from wages or salaries earned from work. However, lower-income families might receive income from government transfer payments including social security, disability, unemployment, Supplemental Nutrition Assistance Payments (i.e., SNAP or food stamps), or Temporary Assistance for Needy Families (TANF). By contrast, higher-income or retired families may receive income from investments in the form of interest, dividends, or payments from pension savings.

Low Income

Poverty, one of the most common measures of low income, underscores SES differences between white and Latino Catholics. In the United States, poverty is usually measured as income poverty (IP) and calculated by comparing household income—adjusted for family size—to federally defined poverty thresholds. In 2021, nearly 12% of families, or 38 million people, were in poverty in the United States (United States Census Bureau 2021). Figure 4.5 shows that Latinos—both Catholic and Protestant—are much more likely than white Catholics to have income below the poverty line, consistent with other SES differences between these two groups shown elsewhere in this chapter (e.g., education, work, dual income). Similarly, white conservative Protestants and religious nones are more likely than Catholics to be poor. This figure also shows that white Catholics and white mainline Protestants are both highly unlikely to be in poverty, and, notably, white mainline Protestants are slightly more likely than white Catholics to have income below the poverty threshold. These patterns are particularly relevant given the history of Catholics as poor.

High Income and Investment Income

In stark contrast to those living in poverty, some households have particularly high incomes. Given that the income distribution is highly skewed (i.e., there are relatively few households at the top), it is useful to start by looking at the

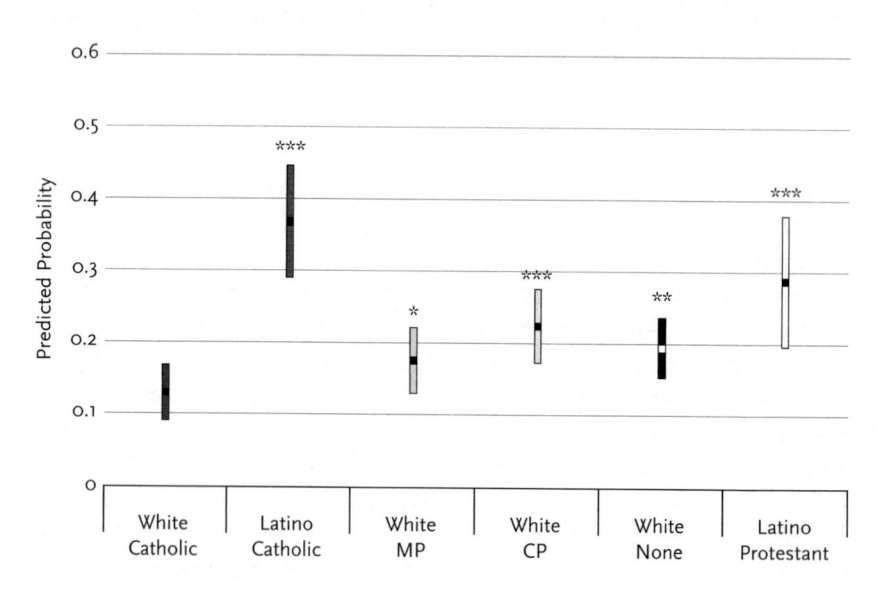

Figure 4.5 High poverty rates for Latino Catholics

probability that a household has income in the top of the distribution. Figure 4.6a uses GSS data to show which religious-ethnic groups have incomes in *the top half* of the income distribution. Admittedly, being in the top half of the income distribution is not the ideal measure of having high income; however, the GSS sample is too small and contains too few high-income respondents

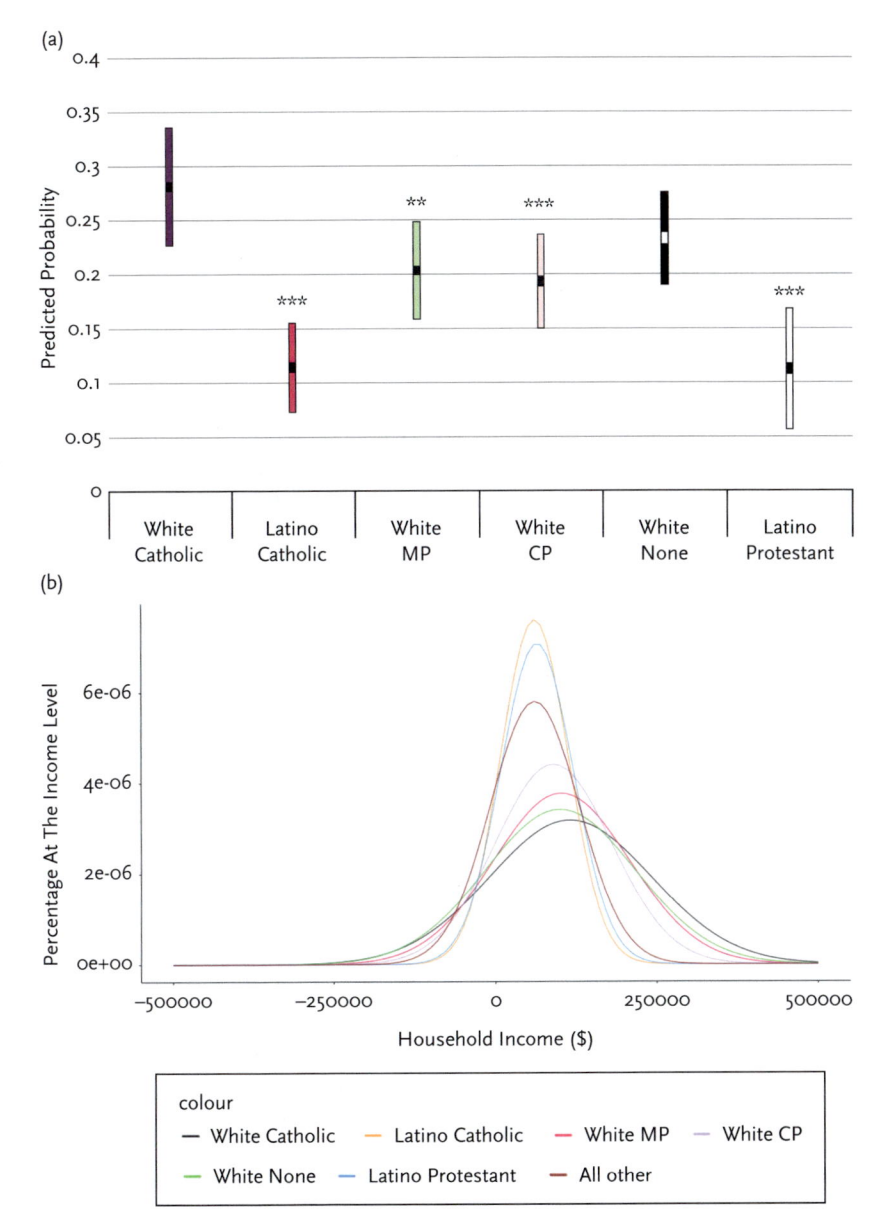

Figure 4.6 High income: (a) White Catholics have above-average income. (b) More white Catholics than white Protestants have high income

to compare religious-ethnic groups higher up the income distribution. I look more closely at differences between religious-ethnic groups in having high financial resources when I compare their wealth in the next section.

However, it is noteworthy that white Catholics (like Julia, the AVP respondent I described above) are more likely than nearly all other Americans to be in the top half of the income distribution (Figure 4.6A). The difference between Latinos—both Catholic and Protestant—and white Catholics is particularly large. White Catholics are also more likely than religious nones to be in the top half of the income distribution, although the difference between white Catholics and white religious nones is modest and not statistically significant. Perhaps most notable is that white Catholics are more likely than white Protestants—both mainline and conservative Protestants—to be in the top half of the income distribution. Figure 4.6B uses PSID data to show that the median income for white Catholics and white Protestants are quite similar, but there are slightly more white Catholics than white Protestants with high income. The difference between white Catholics and white mainline Protestants is modest but underscores the significant change that white Catholics have undergone in their financial profiles in recent decades. It is also significant that white conservative Protestants are less likely to be in the upper half of the income distribution but that the difference between white conservative Protestants and white Catholics is modest. Indeed, the income gap between white conservative Protestants and white Catholics is lower than it was as recently as 2011 (Keister 2011) suggesting income convergence between these groups.

The receipt of some forms of income is also useful for understanding social and economic status. For instance, investment income is a common measure of high status because it signals that a family has enough income to invest in financial assets such as stocks and bonds or tangible assets such as investment real estate. Figure 4.7 documents patterns in receipt of investment income among religious-ethnic groups. I use PSID data to illustrate differences in investment income receipt because the GSS does not include data on investment income or other income sources. Figure 4.7 shows that white Catholics are more likely than Latinos—both Catholic and Protestant—to receive investment income. White Catholics are also more likely than white conservative Protestants and religious nones to receive investment income and these differences remain when birth cohort is controlled.

Investment income differences between white Catholics and white mainline Protestants are potentially more indicative of future SES rankings than of income levels. Figure 4.7 shows that white Catholics and white mainline Protestants are equally likely to receive investment income. However, this pattern only holds *before* birth cohort is controlled. When birth cohort is entered into the model, white mainline Protestants are less likely than white Catholics to receive investment income. This difference reflects cohort differences in

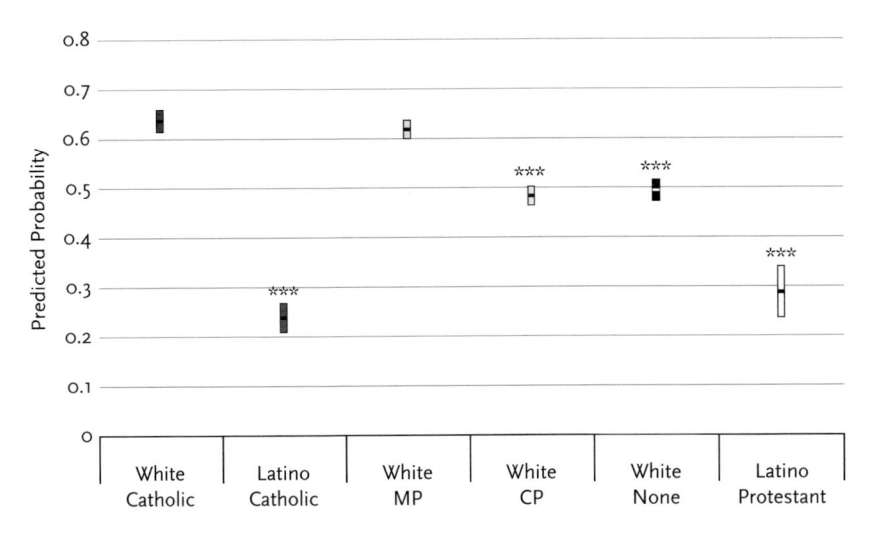

Figure 4.7 Investment income: White Catholics have income from investments

investments in income-producing assets such as stocks, bonds, and real estate, and all of these assets tend to appreciate over long stretches of time, a pattern that enhances wealth accumulation. These differences have the potential to lead to large differences between white Catholics and white mainline Protestants in coming decades.

WEALTH

Wealth is among the most important measures of social status and financial well-being because it is relatively enduring and related in some way to most other measures of achievement. Wealth—or net worth—is total household assets less total debts. Wealth and income are related to each other but are distinct concepts: income is a measure of the *flow* of money into a household over time, and wealth is a measure of the *stock* of money a household has at a single point in time. Although income certainly makes saving easier, the correlation between income and saved assets is surprisingly low: the correlation is about .50 across most ages, life stages (e.g., during the working years, in retirement), and family types (e.g., single, married, with or without children). That means that families save differently regardless of their income and other demographic traits.

For those who own it, wealth can enhance educational attainment, occupational opportunities, political influence, and social advantages. It provides a financial buffer against income interruptions, medical emergencies, and other crises such as accidents and natural disasters. Wealth can generate income in the form of interest and dividends, and it can create more wealth when it is reinvested. Wealth can also be passed to future generations to extend these benefits beyond those who initially accumulated it. Wealth ownership is highly concentrated—even more so than income—and wealth mobility is rare at least in part because assets can be transferred across generations. In 2019, the top one percent of U.S. households owned 37% of total wealth, and the next 9% of households owned another 39% of wealth; the remaining 90% of households owned just 24% of total wealth.

Religion is a strong predictor of household wealth, affecting asset ownership and the acquisition of debts through two mechanisms. First, religion affects wealth *indirectly*, through other demographic processes. Adult wealth ownership is a function of behaviors and strategies learned early in life that influence fertility, the timing and ordering of marriage, educational aspirations and attainment, job-related outcomes, and attitudes toward saving. Religion affects many of these behaviors and processes, including fertility, marriage, and divorce (see Chapter 3), education, female employment rates, and earnings (see previous sections of this chapter). Marriage increases wealth because two individuals combine their assets when they create a single household. It also creates common goals (e.g., homeownership, retirement objectives) that encourage couples to save. However, children increase expenses that reduce saving (Keister 2003a). By contrast, delayed fertility increases wealth because it facilitates educational attainment, career development, occupational advancement, and initial saving and investing that can contribute to life-long asset appreciation (Keister 2005, 2007). Likewise, there is evidence that saving increases initially with family size as couples save for the added expenses associated with having children, but wealth declines precipitously after approximately two children as expenses increase and saving becomes more difficult. Education, full-time work, and income are also among the strongest predictors of wealth ownership and accumulation over time (Keister 2005).

Second, religion may also affect household wealth *directly* by shaping saving behavior and portfolio composition. Children learn how to save from their families and other acquaintances, and religion can influence the financial lessons they learn. Religion shapes values and priorities and contributes to the set of competencies from which actions such as saving behavior is constructed (Fitzgerald and Glass 2013; Keister 2003b, 2011; Vaisey 2009). Nearly all religious groups offer some guidance for living, often including specific tips for money management such as household budgeting, spending, saving, and tithing. Together, these indirect and direct effects are likely to create a powerful influence of religion on wealth ownership. The lessons that Julia and her husband—the AVP respondents I described above—attempt to instill in their sons are examples of this connection between religion and saving. Julia attributes these values regarding money at least in part to a service ethic (i.e., those with personal resources should help those in need), a key precept of Catholic social teaching.

Four broad measures of wealth can help us understand who Catholics are: low wealth, high wealth, homeownership, and inheritance.

Low Wealth

Because wealth is so highly skewed, it is useful to look at a family's location in the wealth distribution to fully understand their social status and financial well-being. Net worth poverty (NWP) is a particularly useful measure of low wealth: NWP is an indicator that a family's wealth is insufficient to cover spending if their income is unpredictable or stops entirely, to pay costs associated with crises such as medical emergencies, or to recover from other unforeseen events such as natural disasters. The problems associated with NWP were evident during the COVID-19 pandemic when many households suddenly lost incomes and were unable to pay for necessities such as food and housing. NWP complements the more common income poverty measure—discussed in the previous section—by considering saved assets and expanding the conception of poverty to include a household's stock of resources. NWP is defined as household net worth (or wealth) that is less than one-fourth of the federal poverty line (Gibson-Davis, Keister, and Gennettian 2020)—less than $6,562 for a family of four in 2020. Notably, NWP has increased over the past 40 years even as IP has declined (Gibson-Davis et al. 2020).

NWP patterns across religious-ethnic groups are similar to the income patterns shown in the previous section: Figure 4.8 shows the probability of being net worth poor. The figure shows that Latinos—both Catholic and Protestant—are more likely than white Catholics to be net worth poor. Similarly, white conservative Protestants and white religious nones are more likely than white Catholics to be net worth poor. By contrast, white mainline Protestants and white Catholics are equally likely to be net worth poor. Again, the similarity in NWP for white mainline Protestants and white Catholics is most usefully understood in the historic context of these two groups. Although household wealth data are limited for decades prior to the 1980s, historic data show clearly that positions at the top of the wealth distribution were filled almost exclusively by mainline Protestants and that members of other religious groups held almost no assets (Keister 2005). If researchers had been able to calculate wealth deprivation through most of U.S. history, it is likely that Catholics would have been among the most asset-deprived Americans. Research from more than a decade ago showed that white Catholics had, indeed, begun to move up in the wealth distribution (Keister 2007). The evidence in Figure 4.8 shows that this trend has persisted: white Catholics have overcome some of the educational, work, income, and family size obstacles that reduced their wealth in previous decades.

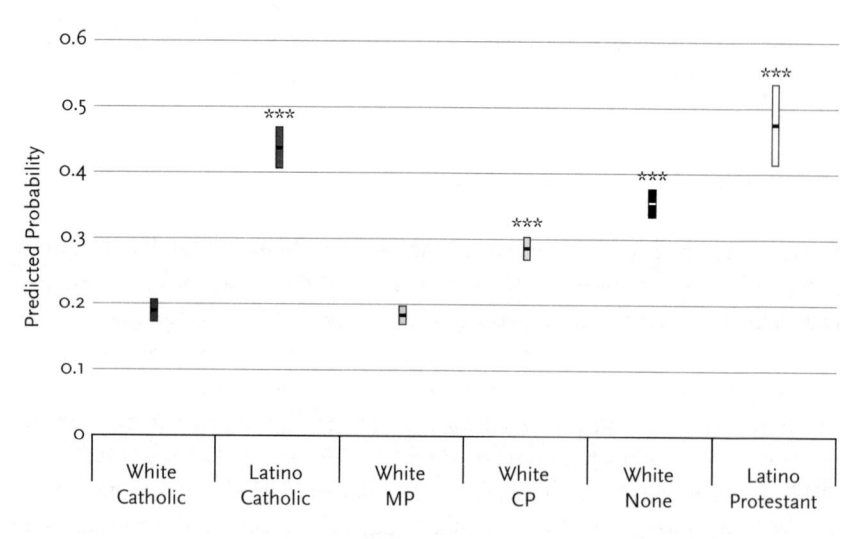

Figure 4.8 Net worth poverty: Latino Catholics have high net worth poverty rates

High Wealth

It is certainly important that the average white Catholic is no longer net worth poor (Figure 4.8), but if Catholics have been upwardly mobile, they should also be represented at the top end of the wealth distribution. Admittedly, being a top wealth owner is a high bar for indicating socioeconomic achievement: because wealth reproduces itself over generations (e.g., through inheritances and other wealth transfers, and educational and occupational advantages), the same families can occupy top wealth positions for many generations. Yet highly visible individuals such as President Biden and members of the Supreme Court suggest that at least some white Catholics have moved into the top of the wealth distribution. Indeed, Forbes estimates that Biden's net worth is about $8 million (Tindera 2021), a wealth level that puts him in the top one percent of wealth owners (Keister 2014).[2]

Given this anecdotal evidence, it is tempting to conclude that white Catholics—or at least many white Catholics—are wealthy and perhaps even to deduce that they have become America's new rich. These statements may be true, but data challenges make it difficult to conclude with certainty whether visible white Catholics are typical or outliers. Wealth data are difficult to collect because the United States does not keep official records of household wealth, and survey datasets easily miss high-wealth households unless their sampling procedures include active attempts to include top wealth holders (Keister 2014). The Survey of Consumer Finances (SCF) is the only U.S. survey that includes high-wealth households, making it the only source of representative data on top wealth holders. However, the SCF does not include information on religious affiliation. The Forbes ranking is an excellent

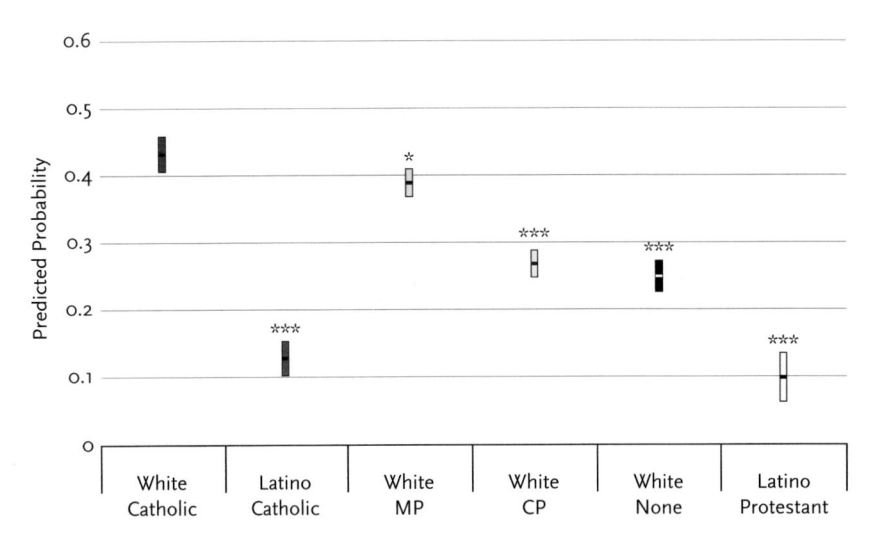

Figure 4.9 High wealth: White Catholics have above-average wealth

source of information on top wealth holders as well, but it is intended to identify only the billionaires at the very top of the wealth distribution rather than including the mere millionaires who occupy positions farther down the wealth distribution.

Despite these challenges, it is possible to estimate whether Catholics have relatively high wealth using the PSID. Figure 4.9 shows that white Catholics and white mainline Protestants are equally likely to be in the top half of the wealth distribution (with white Catholics having slightly more wealth), providing additional evidence that these two groups are still relatively equal on these key SES measures. By contrast, all other religious-ethnic groups shown in Figure 4.9 are less likely than white Catholics to have above-average wealth.

Homeownership

The assets and debts held by families can also be instructive about their social and financial well-being, and homeownership is particularly salient for Americans. The family home—or the primary residence—is a significant component of household wealth for many Americans, and, for this reason, it is often used by social scientists as a proxy for total wealth (Harding and Rosenthal 2017; Rugh 2020; Spilerman and Wolff 2012; Wainer and Zabel 2020). Homeownership is also considered fundamental to the American dream: the somewhat cliché—but very real—notion that no matter where you start, it is possible to be successful in the United States (Fry 2013; Grinstein-Weiss,

Michal, and Carrillo 2015; Rodriguez 2023). The family home is considered an important measure in this lore: it indicates achievement, financial stability, and financial independence (Goodman and Mayer 2018; Wainer and Zabel 2020). For immigrants, those raised in poor families, and others who consider themselves marginalized, homeownership is also considered part of being (or becoming) part of the American mainstream (Agius Vallejo and Lee 2009; Agius Vallejo 2012; Hao 2007; Myers, Megbolugbe, and Lee 1998). Of course, there are risks associated with homeownership, as the Great Recession demonstrated: during that economic crisis and subsequent recession, housing loss was extreme including for low- and middle-income households (Brainard 2016; Grinstein-Weiss et al. 2015; Qian 2013; Wolff, Owens, and Burak 2011). However, there are also real financial and social advantages to homeownership: a home can force its owner to save, it appreciates in value and builds wealth for its owner, it eliminates rent payments, and it becomes a source of income in retirement.

Homeownership also says a great deal about who Catholics are and how they compare to other Americans. In particular, Figure 4.10 shows that Latinos—both Catholic and Protestant—and religious nones are all less likely than white Catholics to be homeowners, consistent with their comparatively low achievement on other SES measures. This difference is another important SES pattern that indicates a broad gulf among Catholics; in the case of homeownership, the gulf has the potential to lead to long-term differences among Catholics because homeownership is a primary way that people build wealth in the United States. A large difference in homeownership is not a guarantee of future SES differences between white and Latino Catholics, but it is certainly a difference that will be challenging to overcome.

By contrast, Figure 4.10 also shows that white Catholics, white mainline Protestants, and white conservative Protestants are equally likely to be homeowners. This is striking for two reasons. First, the similarity between white Catholics and white mainline Protestants is consistent with evidence of their parity on other wealth measures shown above. This finding is also consistent with—somewhat dated—research that showed wealth convergence between these two groups in the early 2000s (Keister 2003b, 2011). The Catholic-mainline Protestant similarity that is evident in Figure 4.10 indicates that wealth parity between these two groups has persisted.

Second, the results shown in Figure 4.10 are significant because previous research showed that white conservative Protestants were less likely than white Catholics and white mainline Protestants to be homeowners (Keister 2003b, 2011). That research found some evidence of cohort differences in homeownership by religious affiliation: older conservative Protestants had begun to catch up with white Catholics and white mainline Protestants as they approached retirement, but they still lagged behind even in their later years. Cohort differences in homeownership—across all religious groups—have become more

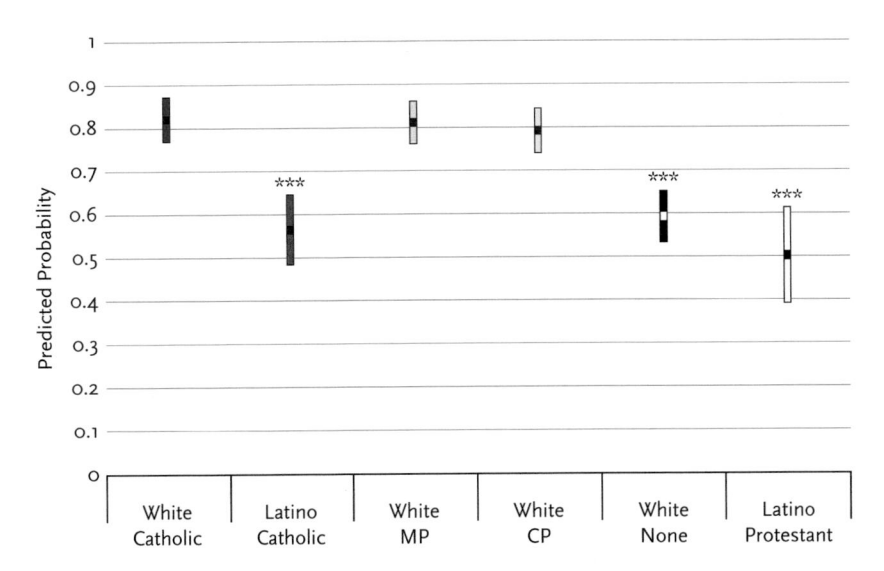

Figure 4.10 Homeownership: High for white Catholics, low for Latino Catholics

extreme since that research was published, largely as a result of rising home prices in some markets and increasing millennial debt which prevents many younger families from acquiring mortgages (Choi et al. 2018; Petersen 2019). However, Figure 4.10 shows that—despite these broad cohort differences—white conservative Protestant homeownership rates are now equivalent to those of white Catholics and white mainline Protestants. This pattern reflects the indirect (e.g., education, family size, region of residence) and direct (e.g., tithing) effects I described above and elsewhere (Keister 2005, 2008).

The figure shows that there is no significant difference in the likelihood of homeownership between Catholics and conservative Protestants in a baseline model, but, importantly, these patterns all hold when birth cohort is controlled.

Inheritance

Wealth is distinct from income because wealth can be passed across generations to extend the benefits of asset ownership indefinitely. Given this unique characteristic of wealth, inheritance and wealth mobility provide critical insight into a family's wealth status. Inheritance—or wealth transfers—are one of most basic ways that inequality is recreated across generations. The related concept of wealth mobility refers to whether individuals change their SES status over time; this can mean changing relative to their parents' SES (i.e., intergenerational mobility) or changing over their own lives (i.e., intragenerational mobility). Both intergenerational and intragenerational mobility

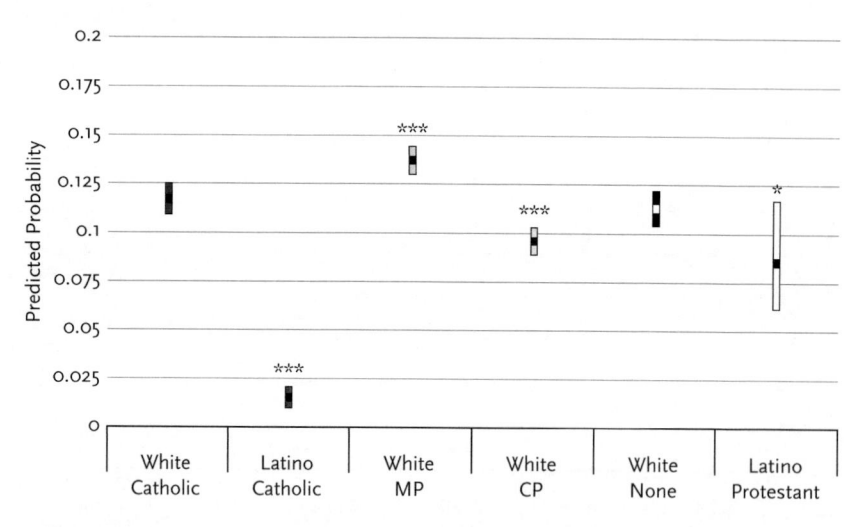

Figure 4.11 Inheriting: Low inheritance for white Catholics, lower for Latino Catholics

provide information about the ascribed and achieved characteristics in a person's own life and about equality of opportunity in a society. For example, if there are differences across birth cohorts (an ascribed trait) in access to educational opportunities (an example of equality of opportunity), these may affect whether members of the respective cohorts are able to accumulate more wealth than their parents over their lives.

Inheritance is a crucial measure for understanding who Catholics are and where they came from. Figure 4.11 shows that white Catholics and white mainline Protestants are equally likely to inherit any amount of money; however, in supplementary analyses (not shown), white Catholics were also less likely than white mainline Protestants to receive large inheritances. In other supplementary analyses using the PSID data (also not shown), white Catholics are more likely than the other religious groups to have more wealth than their parents at comparable ages. This pattern provides additional evidence that white Catholics have been upwardly mobile relative to white mainline Protestants. By contrast, the other groups shown in Figure 4.11 are less likely than white Catholics to have inherited.

SUBJECTIVE WELL-BEING

The measures I have looked at so far in this chapter are all *objective* indicators of SES, but an individual's self-assessment—their *subjective* sense—can be equally informative about their social and financial situations. Two measures are particularly useful: self-assessment of class position and self-assessment of how easy it is to make ends meet.

[92] *Catholics in America*

Class Position

The notion of social class is fundamental to understanding social status, financial security, and the structure of inequality. Debates are ongoing about how to define and measure social class, which social classes exist in the United States, and how much class consciousness Americans have. There also are debates about whether social class or other personal traits—such as race, ethnicity, and gender—matter more for determining well-being. Despite these debates, however, there is widespread agreement that social class is extremely important. Most people have a sense of what social class is, occasionally mention class in everyday conversations, and have a sense of who falls into particular class groups. Thinking in terms of class—or discrete status groups—is useful because people tend to group together on some traits. For example, there are a limited number of occupations, and people in those occupations generally have roughly the same education, income, and pattern of wealth ownership. In addition, class membership can be meaningful to the people who are members of a class.

Catholics vary on their class membership, both internally and compared to other Americans, as Figure 4.12 shows. To gauge personal assessment of class position, the GSS asks "If you were asked to use one of four names for your social class, which would you say you belong in: the lower class, the working class, the middle class, or the upper class?" Responses are gleaned from the standard classes identified over many decades of research by social scientists and include lower class, working class, middle class, upper class, and no class. Consistent with a long history of research on class that spans nearly six decades (Bendix and Lipset 1966; Keister and Southgate 2022; Rivera and

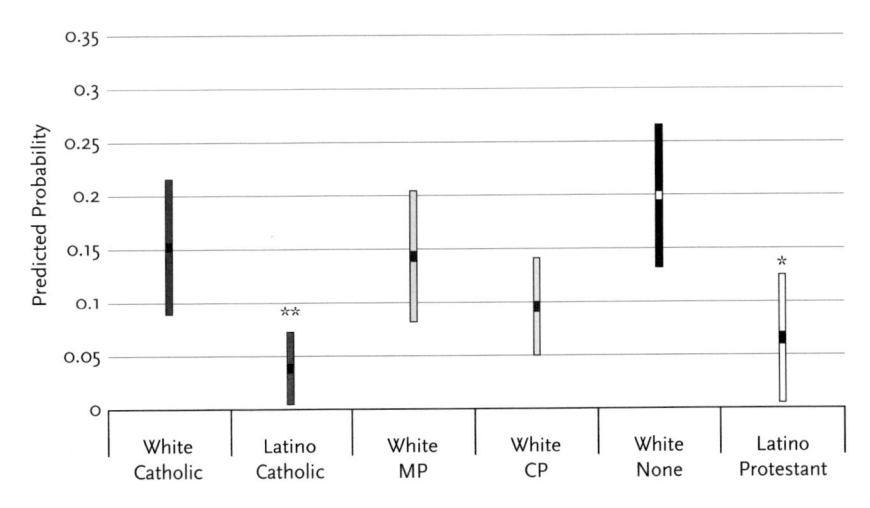

Figure 4.12 Self-reported class: White Catholics consider themselves upper class, Latino Catholics do not

Tilcsik 2016; Wright 1997), most GSS respondents evaluate their class as middle class (note shown). What is more interesting and insightful is whether respondents think of themselves as upper class: as Figure 4.12 shows, Latinos, regardless of religious affiliation and consistent with their actual SES, are less likely than white Catholics to consider themselves upper class. By contrast, and in spite of SES differences, there are no differences among white respondents in their self-evaluation of class.

Making Ends Meet

There are similar patterns among Catholics and between Catholics and other Americans in their abilities to make ends meet. To evaluate whether families think they have sufficient income, the GSS asks "Thinking of your household's total income, including all the sources of income of all the members who contribute to it, how difficult or easy is it currently for your household to make ends meet?" Possible answers include very difficult, fairly difficult, neither easy nor difficult, fairly easy, and very easy. Figure 4.13 highlights whether respondents find it fairly or very difficult to make ends meet. The most pronounced difference is that Latinos—both Catholic and Protestant—say that they have a harder time making ends meet than do white Catholics. This is consistent with the differences in education, income, and wealth between white and Latino respondents shown in previous sections of this chapter and documented in statistical evidence on American Latino SES (Pew Hispanic

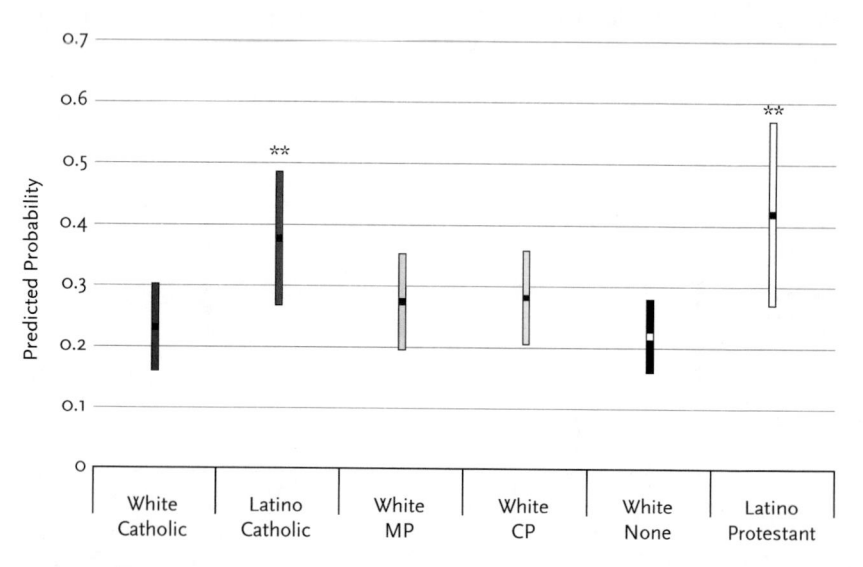

Figure 4.13 Making ends meet: Latino Catholics have a hard time making ends meet, white Catholics do not

Center 2011). Notably, all other groups evaluate their abilities to make ends meet similarly, a pattern that provides additional evidence of SES convergence among these groups.

CONCLUSION

Social and economic status convey important meaning about where people came from, who they are now, and what will happen to them in the future. In this chapter, I explored education, work, income, and wealth traits, comparing white and Latino Catholics and exploring how Catholics compare to other Americans.

I found dramatic and consistent SES differences between white and Latino Catholics. Latino Catholics—regardless of immigrant status—lag behind white Catholics on nearly all of the SES measures I studied: educational attainment, full-time work, having two incomes, income poverty, high income, investment income, net worth poverty, high net worth, homeownership, and inheritance. Latino Catholics were also less likely than white Catholics to evaluate themselves as upper class and were more likely to say they have a hard time making ends meet. Self-employment is the one exception to these differences among Catholics: white and Latino Catholics are equally likely to be self-employed. Importantly, however, there are signs from the data that the SES of Latino Catholics is changing. For example, differences between white and Latino Catholics on working full time and having two earners are minimal. Given similarities between white and Latino Catholics in self-employment and evidence of convergence on marriage and fertility (Chapter 3), it is possible that future research will find convergence among Catholics on other SES measures such as income and wealth.

Equally important, I found strong and consistent evidence of continued SES parity between white Catholics and white mainline Protestants. Indeed, the data showed suggestive evidence that white Catholics may be in the process of moving ahead of white mainline Protestants on some of the measures I studied. In particular, I found no difference between white Catholics and white mainline Protestants on most of my education, work, income, and wealth measures. However, white Catholics are slightly more likely to have high incomes and wealth than are white mainline Protestants. These finding underscore the upward mobility of white Catholics and, more significantly, suggest that white Catholics may be moving further up the income and wealth distributions than they were even in the relatively recent past. For example, my own work from 2003–2011 showed that white Catholics were upwardly mobile and had largely achieved SES parity with white mainline Protestants (Keister 2003b, 2007, 2011). Future research will want to explore whether white Catholic mobility on income continues, and, more importantly, whether they begin to surpass white mainline Protestants on other SES measures such as education and wealth.

Finally, I found some evidence of SES convergence between white Catholics and white conservative Protestants. White conservative Protestants lag behind white Catholics (and white mainline Protestants) on most SES measures, including education, work, income, and wealth. However, there were signs of convergence between white conservative Protestants, white Catholics, and white mainline Protestants on self-employment and homeownership. Future research should continue studying SES changes among these groups.

A final note is in order about the potential cause of the SES differences I document. Some of the differences are attributable to the demographic and cultural factors I described in Chapter 1 and in the introduction to this chapter. However, there might also be an effect of religious change on SES differences. For example, if lower-SES individuals are more likely to leave a faith group than are higher-SES individuals, the SES of the group will increase over time regardless of other demographic or cultural changes. The dramatic religious change that has been occurring in the United States in recent decades suggests that this possibility is critical to understanding who Catholics are and how (if) they have changed over time. The next chapter touches on this issue in the broader context of religious changes.

NOTES

1. There are some important exceptions to this slowdown including works that largely focused on religion and SES (Horwitz 2022; Konieczny 2013) and others that include sections related to SES (Burge 2021; D'Antonio, Dillon, and Gautier 2013; Smith et al. 2014). However, the overall volume of research on religion and SES has not kept pace with that of previous decades.
2. Although accumulating this level of wealth is certainly an accomplishment, it is insufficient to place President Biden in the Forbes list of the top 400 wealthiest families, which starts at $2.7 billion (Forbes 2023).

CHAPTER 5

Catholicism Evolving

Leaving, Joining, and Staying with the Church

Disaffiliation from religion has attracted considerable attention in recent decades, but how extensive have exits from Catholicism been? This chapter studies movement into and out of the Church and the reasons former Catholics give for disaffiliating.

Profound changes in religious affiliation have been a defining feature of American life for at least three decades (Glass, Sutton, and Fitzgerald 2015; Greeley 1989; Sherkat 2014; Smith et al. 2014). The United States is still home to more Christians than any other country (Diamant 2019). However, religious change among Americans has been substantial, including over relatively short and recent periods. Among these changes, the increasing prevalence of religious nones rightfully attracts the most attention from researchers, the popular press, and religious leaders because this increase could potentially affect the organization of U.S. religious groups for decades (Burge 2021; Newport 2022; Pew Research Center 2015; Smith et al. 2014). The growth in the religiously unaffiliated has, indeed, been remarkable: only 5% of Americans claimed no religious affiliation in the early 1970s, but more Americans were religious nones (28%) than Catholic (21%), mainline Protestant (24%), or conservative Protestant (20%) by 2021.

Disaffiliation has clearly dominated the religious landscape in recent decades, but other religious changes have also occurred. Religious adherents have been moving among faith traditions, and some previously unaffiliated individuals have joined faith groups. In addition, a core of adherents have remained affiliated with each of the major religious groups over long periods, often over their entire lives. Although those who remain members of a

Catholics in America. Lisa A. Keister, Oxford University Press. © Oxford University Press 2024.
DOI: 10.1093/oso/9780197753675.003.0005

religious group may not seem very exciting, their persistence in a faith tradition is notable amid high and growing social pressure to disavow religion. In addition, we can better understand who changes religion by contrasting disaffiliates' demographic characteristics and beliefs with those who remain affiliated with a religious tradition.

Naturally, changing religious affiliation—also called *religious mobility*—involves and affects Catholics and understanding who leaves, joins, and stays with Catholicism and other faith traditions is fundamental to understanding contemporary American Catholics. Clearly, Catholicism has lost a significant number of adherents in recent decades, and many of those who have left are young (Sherkat 2014; Smith et al. 2014). However, many of the other traits on which Catholics vary and that distinguish Catholics from other religious groups (e.g., ethnicity, family behaviors, and socioeconomic status [SES]) are also likely to be associated with who has left, joined, or stayed with the Church. In addition, those who leave, join, and stay with Catholicism might differ in important ways from those who leave, join, and stay with other faith groups.

A small body of research has explored religious mobility, including important general treatments of religious change (Greeley 1989; Pew Research Center 2015; Sherkat 1991, 2001, 2014; Wuthnow 1990) and more detailed explorations of the trajectories of members of particular faith traditions (Bullivant 2022; McCarty and Vitek 2018; Wuthnow 1999). The general treatments provide excellent overviews of the U.S. religious landscape and have been fundamental to shedding light on trends in disaffiliation and other religious changes. However, these general approaches have necessarily focused on broad issues and aimed to capture trends across all faith groups rather than paying particular attention to any single group such as Catholics. Other treatments of religious change have studied Catholics in more detail, with less attention to broader trends (D'Antonio, Dillon, and Gautier 2013; Smith et al. 2014). But most of these more focused treatments of religious change have not situated Catholics within the broader religious environment. Perhaps most important—given the continuing evolution of America's religious groups—most extant work on religious mobility is a bit dated, suggesting that a current exploration of patterns is warranted.

I have three goals in this chapter. First, I document contemporary American religious mobility patterns, using General Social Survey (GSS) data to provide an updated portrait of *how much* movement into and out of the Catholic Church has occurred. I describe how many people leave, join, and stay with the Church, and I explore how movement into and out of the Catholic Church compares to movement into and out of other faith traditions. Second, I explore *who* leaves, joins, and stays with the Catholic Church and other faith traditions. I explore differences by social origins (birth cohort, gender, ethnicity), family type (married, divorced, with children), and SES (education, work, income, wealth). I primarily rely on GSS data and define religious change as a difference in affiliation between childhood and adulthood. However, I also turn briefly to the Panel Study of Income Dynamics (PSID) data to look at changes in religious affiliation over the lives of the same individuals, including multiple religious changes where possible. Finally, I consider *why* people leave the Church. I harness responses to open-ended questions from American Voices Project (AVP) interviews to offer a glimpse into the reasons people offer for leaving Catholicism. Although these responses are not comprehensive of the motivations for disaffiliation from Catholicism, they provide important, contemporary detail that is only possible through qualitative interviews.

A PORTRAIT OF THE EXTENT OF RELIGIOUS CHANGE

The Big Picture: Aggregate-Level Religious Change

Aggregate estimates of the percentage of Americans affiliated with major religious groups provide a general overview of movement into and out of the faith traditions, highlighting broad patterns of affiliation and disaffiliation. Figure 1.1 (Chapter 1) used this approach and showed the dramatic changes in Americans' religious affiliations from the 1970s through 2021. Over the relatively short period between the 2000s and 2021, the portion of the U.S. population that was affiliated with a Christian church fell from 80% to 73%. In the 2000s, 27% of Americans were Catholic, 21% were mainline Protestant, and 32% were conservative Protestant (mainline and conservative Protestant details are not shown in Figure 1.1). By 2021, those percentages had fallen to 22%, 19%, and 23%, respectively. In that same period, the proportion of the population not affiliated with a religion (the religious nones) grew from 15% to 29%.

Over these decades, there was little change to the percentage of the population affiliated with other religious traditions (a change from 6% to just less than 7%); however, interpreting this pattern is challenging because the samples are small and the "other" religious category includes several religious groups with few similarities among them (e.g., Jewish, Hindu, and Buddhist groups are all included in this category).

The Details: Individual-Level Religious Change

Underlying aggregate patterns of religious change, individuals are opting to leave, join, or stay with religious groups. It is this level of change (or steadiness) that fuels aggregate-level patterns and is critical to understanding the broader religious transitions. To understand these behaviors, it is useful to compare childhood religious affiliation and adult religious affiliation for the same individuals. This comparison captures change over time, often over long stretches of time, particularly among older individuals. It also provides information about individuals' decision-making regarding religious affiliation: childhood religion is usually chosen by parents, whereas adult religion is typically self-determined. Comparing childhood and adult religious affiliation is also practical because it is relatively easy to collect data on religious change by asking adult survey respondents about their childhood religious affiliation and experiences.

To document individual-level religious change (Figure 5.1), I use two measures of religious affiliation from the 2021 GSS data: (1) the respondent's retrospective report of childhood religious affiliation and (2) the same respondent's 2021 religious affiliation. These individual-level measures succinctly document change—and likely capture information about key issues in the life stories—of a representative group of individuals who were adults in 2021. Yet, because respondents' ages vary, their childhood (i.e., age 16) religion refers to a wide range of years. For example, an 80-year-old respondent was 16 in 1957, whereas a 40-year-old respondent was 16 in 1997. Thus, patterns of individual-level religious change shown in Figure 5.1 differ from the aggregate patterns shown in Figure 1.1.

The lines in Figure 5.1 show individual respondents' origin and destination religions. For instance, the large line leading from "Catholic" to "none" indicates respondents who were Catholic in childhood (cradle Catholics) and religiously unaffiliated in 2021. However, the 22% of respondents who were Catholic in 2021 includes individuals who were Catholic in childhood as well

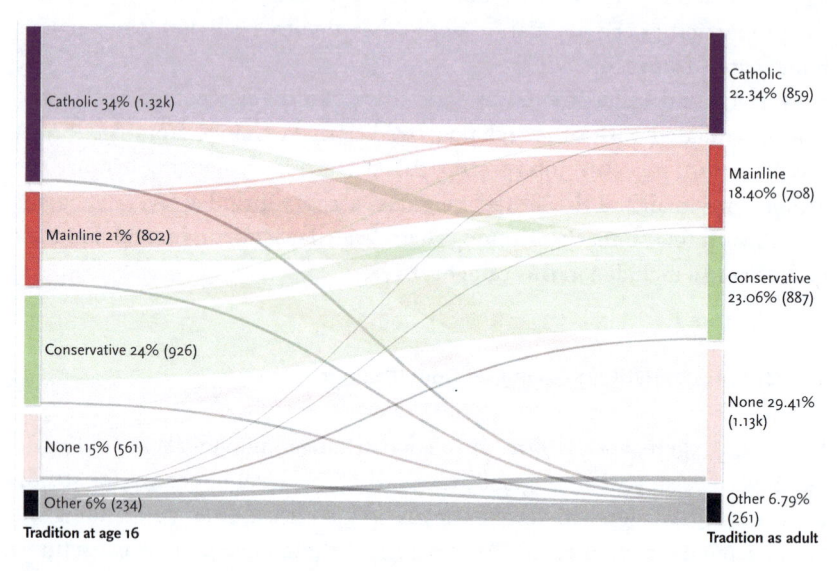

Figure 5.1 Movement among religious groups: Childhood to adult religion

[100]   *Catholics in America*

as individuals who joined the Catholic Church in adulthood. Figure 5.1 shows these individuals only as lines; it does not include a breakdown of the percentage of respondents who changed from one faith tradition to another versus those who stayed with a faith group. I look more closely at how many people change versus stay in the next section of this chapter.

Three significant patterns are clear in Figure 5.1. First, the figure underscores the magnitude of religious disaffiliation. For example, 34% of respondents in the 2021 GSS were Catholic in childhood, but only 22% were Catholic in 2021. Recall that the starting year (i.e., the year in which religion at age 16 is measured) in this figure is not the same for all respondents; rather each respondent has a starting year that reflects their age. However, the end year (i.e., the year in which adult religion is measured) is 2021 and is the same for all respondents. There was less change in the lives of individual Protestant respondents: 21% of respondents were mainline Protestants in childhood, compared with 18% in 2021; 24% were conservative Protestants in childhood, compared with 23% in 2021. Not surprisingly, the most vivid pattern emerging from Figure 5.1 is disaffiliation from all Christian faiths, including Catholicism. That is, if you look at the values on the left of the figure, sum them, and compare them with the "none" sum on the right, the values are substantial and underscore the remarkable amount of disaffiliation that has occurred. Visually, this is equivalent to following the lines that start on the left at the Christian groups and coalesce as religious nones on the right.

Second, notable numbers of individuals join the Church during their lives. The largest group of converts to Catholicism came from various Protestant denominations, with slightly more individuals converting from mainline than conservative Protestant churches. Small—and roughly equal—percentages of individuals also converted to Catholicism from other faith traditions and from having no religious affiliation to Catholicism and Protestantism. Larger percentages of respondents converted to both mainline and conservative Protestant denominations than to Catholicism, although the converts were also overshadowed by the exodus from Christian faith groups into the religious none category.

Third, amid the trends in disaffiliation shown in Figure 5.1, significant numbers of respondents remained Catholic—or left the Church and returned—over their lives. Indeed, the *largest, most pronounced lines in this figure are those who stayed with their childhood religion into adulthood.* This pattern also holds for other Christians, members of other faith traditions, and religious nones. Although those who stay affiliated with the same religion throughout their lives attract little attention, they are an important part of the story of religion in America. The figure does not disentangle movement among the various Protestant denominations but rather focuses on change among the three broad Christian groups (Catholic, mainline Protestant, and conservative Protestant) that are the focus of the rest of this book. Preliminary analyses

Table 5.1 CHANGING AFFILIATION: MOVEMENT BETWEEN CHILDHOOD AND ADULTHOOD

	Adult religion					
Youth religion	Catholic	Mainline	Conservative	None	Other	n
Catholic	803	71	90	336	26	1,323
Mainline Protestant	23	468	103	185	24	802
Conservative Protestant	15	113	599	176	23	926
None	18	50	78	388	28	561
Other	2	7	19	48	160	234
n	859	708	887	1,134	261	3,846

Notes: Data are from the 2021 General Social Survey (GSS). Cells are numbers of GSS respondents by religion in which they were raised ("youth religion") and adult religious affiliation ("adult religion"). Numbers may not match other GSS estimates and do not sum perfectly because they are weighted and rounded.

(not shown) suggested that the broad patterns I show in Figure 5.1 do not change if I break Protestant groups into their component denominations.

But what do these patterns say about the overall stability or change in the Catholic Church? Whereas Figure 5.1 shows the broad flows of membership into and out of each of the major Christian groups, Table 5.1 provides more detail about patterns of religious stability and change by showing the number of GSS respondents who stayed with a faith group or changed from one group to another between childhood and adulthood. Of the more than 3,800 GSS respondents included in this table, 1,323 were Catholics at age 16 ("young Catholics"). Of these young Catholics, about 60% (803 respondents) remained Catholic as adults (Table 5.1). Some of those who remained Catholic as adults may have left the Church at some point in the intervening years, but the GSS does not include details on multiple religious changes (see below for more on this topic). The remainder moved to other religious groups: 71 (about 5%) became mainline Protestants, 90 (about 7%) became conservative Protestants, 336 (about 25%) became religious nones, and 26 (about 2%) became some other religion. Meanwhile, 859 respondents were Catholic in adulthood (including the 803 who were young Catholics). In addition, a small number of respondents joined the Catholic Church after childhood: 23 (about 3%) had been mainline Protestant, 15 (about 2%) had been conservative Protestant, 18 (about 2%) had been religious nones, and 2 (0.2%) had been some other religion.

Table 5.2 shows the percentage of all respondents who left and joined each group. That is, 13.5% *of all GSS respondents* left the Catholic Church between childhood and adulthood, and only 1.5% of all respondents joined the Church. This table highlights how the leavers and joiners sum to the current adherents (i.e., the numbers add across the rows) and shows that the Catholic Church

Table 5.2 THE MAGNITUDE OF RELIGIOUS CHANGE

	Childhood religion %	Leaving group %	Entering group %	Current tradition %
Catholic	34.4	13.5	1.5	22.3
Mainline Protestant	24.1	8.2	6.2	18.4
Conservative Protestant	20.9	9.0	7.5	23.1
None	14.6	4.5	19.3	29.4
Other	6.1	1.9	2.6	6.8
	100.0			100.0

Notes: Data are from the 2021 General Social Survey (GSS). Mainline and conservative Protestant groups include members of historically black churches. Percentages are calculated using the total GSS sample as the denominator.

has seen somewhat greater membership losses and much smaller membership gains than other Christian groups. Mainline Protestant churches lost 8.7% and gained 6.2% of respondents; conservative Protestant churches lost 8.5% and gained 7.5% of respondents. Of course, there were comparatively small losses and large gains to religious nones category.

Complexity: Multiple Religious Changes

It is easy to imagine religious change as occurring once during a person's life. But some people change their religious affiliation multiple times, often at key turning points in the life course (e.g., completing high school or beginning college, getting married, having a child). Most research assumes that religious change is a one-time occurrence, partly because longitudinal data on religious affiliation are rare. However, the PSID data contain information on religious affiliation for the same respondents at multiple points in the life course, allowing me to explore the prevalence of multiple religious affiliation changes over time.

Table 5.3 shows religious change for the same individuals studied at multiple points between 1997 and 2021. In this table, *religious change* refers to a respondent reporting one religious affiliation in any PSID data year and another religious affiliation in a subsequent year. For example, a religious change of 1 indicates that the respondent changed affiliation once (e.g., from conservative Protestant to Catholic) and remained with the second affiliation for the remaining survey years. Changing religious affiliation two or more times includes various combinations or types of changes. For example, a respondent might change among distinct religious traditions (e.g., from conservative

Table 5.3 MULTIPLE RELIGIOUS CHANGES

Religious change (# of changes)	Frequency
1	3,205
2	183
3	8
Total	3,396

Notes: Data are from the 1997–2021 Panel Study of Income Dynamics (PSID), a dataset that interviews the same respondents regularly over time. Religious change refers to a respondent reporting one religious affiliation in any PSID wave and another religious affiliation in a subsequent wave (e.g., 233 respondents changed their religious affiliation twice between 1997 and 2019).

Protestant to Catholic to religious none) or from one faith back to the original (e.g., from conservative Protestant to Catholic and back to conservative Protestant). In the table, *frequency* refers to the number of respondents who made the associated number of changes. For example, 183 respondents changed their religious affiliation twice between 1997 and 2021.

As Table 5.3 shows, one religious change over a person's life is, by far, the most common, suggesting that research that assumes a single religious change is likely to be fairly accurate. However, 183 respondents changed their religious affiliation twice during the PSID study period, and another 8 respondents changed their religious affiliation more than twice. Analyses that are not included in the table showed two broad, common patterns among PSID respondents who switched religions. First, most changes occurred following a major life event, most commonly at turning points in education (completing an educational milestone), marriage (i.e., marriage, divorce, the death of a spouse), or the birth of a child. As the life course model of social behavior (see Chapter 1) suggests, educational, marriage, and fertility milestones are markers that define life trajectories and can prompt other important changes, such as religious change. Second, for those who changed religions multiple times, it was particularly common to change from one religion to a second religion and then back to the original religion.

Retrospective Editing: Evidence for More Exits from Protestant Churches

A unique data pattern suggests potentially more exits from Protestant Churches—but not from the Catholic Church—than previous research has found. The pattern is evident in GSS respondents' reports of childhood religion.

Researchers often use retrospective survey questions (i.e., about past events or conditions) to study changes during the life course. For example, the GSS uses retrospective questions to ask adult survey respondents to identify their childhood religious affiliations. Responses to these questions are crucial for studying religious mobility because they allow researchers to study change without interviewing the same respondents multiple times. However, retrospective questions may be inaccurate if respondents do not remember details from the past (recall bias), which is particularly common for issues that are not important to respondents. Respondents may also report inaccurate information, with at least some sense that the information is inaccurate; I will call this pattern *retrospective editing*. Retrospective editing could occur for a large number of reasons, reflecting the large number of life trajectories that individuals follow. Retrospective editing may also reflect social pressure that encourages answers that are more consistent with a respondent's current—rather than past—situation and contemporary social norms.

Figure 5.2 exploits patterns in retrospective GSS responses to better understand how much religious change has occurred in recent decades. GSS question RELIG16—used in some of the results shown in this chapter—asks, "In what religion were you raised?" Figure 5.2 compares responses to this question between two types of respondents: (1) a group of respondents from any GSS survey year, assigning their childhood religion (using RELIG16) to the year in which they would have been age 16; and (2) a group of respondents from that survey year, assigning their adult religion (RELIG) as the current reported religion. If all respondents reported childhood religion accurately, the responses of these two types of respondents would be nearly identical (see the Appendix for details). By contrast, if respondents alter their childhood religion, the responses of these two types of respondents will differ. Figure 5.2 shows that although most respondents responded accurately to this question, some appear to have responded inaccurately and in a way suggesting more religious change than previous research shows.

The figure shows intriguing differences across faith groups in the recall of childhood religion. Catholics appear to over-remember being Catholic. That is, for Catholics, the retrospective (darker, left) bars are significantly larger than the other bars for each decade. That means that there is a higher percentage of respondents who claimed they were Catholic when asked "What was your religion in childhood?" in each decade than there were adults who said they were Catholic in those decades. Notably, Catholics are the only religious group shown in the figure that have this pattern.

Mainline Protestants edited their religion more than the other groups shown in the figure and were more likely to remember not being a mainline Protestant than was probably true. In addition, their tendency to edit has declined over time. For example, in the 1970s, 33% of respondents said they were mainline Protestants, but when respondents in future decades were asked

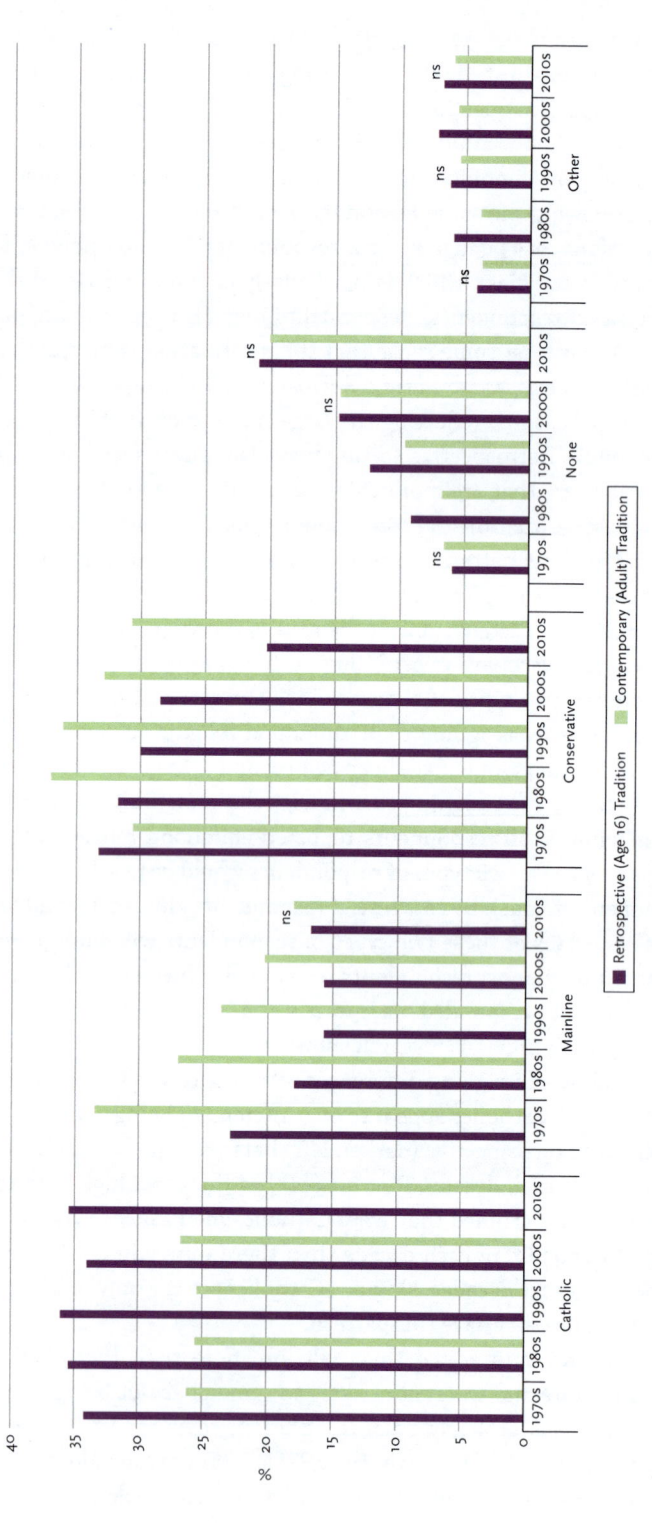

Figure 5.2 Retrospective editing: Do people alter their religion when looking backward?

what their religion was in the 1970s, only 23% of them said they were mainline Protestants in the 1970s. This general pattern (editing) was evident for mainline Protestants in the 1980s, 1990s, and 2000s as well. However, in the 2010s, the difference between current and retrospective reports had disappeared.

The pattern was different still for conservative Protestants: these respondents edited less than Catholics or mainline Protestants, but, like mainline Protestants, they were likely to remember not being a conservative Protestant. However, their tendency to edit has increased over time. For example, in the 1970s, current and retrospective percentages were not significantly different from each other. However, by the 2010s, 31% of respondents said they were conservative Protestants in the 2010s, but, in 2021, only 20% of respondents said they had been conservative Protestant in the 2010s.

Religious nones and members of other faith groups (i.e., Muslim, Hindu, Jewish, etc.) seem to edit the least. There were slight reporting differences for religious nones in the 1980s and 1990s, but these were minimal. For members of other faith groups, reporting differences were even smaller. For example, only about 6% of respondents reported being a member of one of the "other" faith groups both currently and retrospectively. Recall that sample sizes for the faith groups force me to include these very different groups in a single category labeled "other."

There are at least three reasons for the differences shown in Figure 5.2. First, there may be recall bias. This is possible, and certainly some people do not remember their childhood religion or would, for some other reason, mistakenly give an incorrect response to a survey question about childhood religion. However, it is unlikely that recall bias accounts for the differences shown in Figure 5.2 because most people know their childhood religion. Second, some respondents—particularly Protestants—might either not recall the specific denomination with which they were affiliated or may have changed to a slightly different Protestant denomination in adulthood. However, the figure shows patterns for broad Protestant groups (i.e., mainline and conservative Protestants) rather than particular Protestant denominations, making this explanation unlikely.

The third, and most likely, explanation for the patterns in Figure 5.2 is retrospective editing: some respondents edited—that is, changed—their childhood religion. Moreover, the figure shows that retrospective editing varies by childhood religious affiliation, suggesting that there might be something meaningful in these patterns. One potential explanation for the inconsistency of Catholic reports is ethnic Catholicism, or the tendency for people to consider Catholicism both an ethnicity and a religion. Whereas current adults might not call themselves Catholic—thinking of Catholicism as a religion—respondents looking back at their childhood might recall being Catholic—thinking of it as part of their ethnicity.

Protestants also edited, but they edited differently than Catholics. Some respondents who were probably mainline and conservative Protestants in childhood reported not being a Protestant as a child. One explanation for this pattern is that some respondents' families were loosely affiliated with a religion, and the respondent either does not recall that affiliation or no longer identifies with the group as an adult. A stronger explanation for this pattern is that current social norms favor being a religious none rather than a Protestant, and these norms encouraged some respondents to retrospectively disavow their childhood religions. Of course, there is no way to determine with any certainty the reason for retrospective editing, but future research might usefully explore the reasons that people mistakenly report or deliberately edit their childhood religious affiliation.

Importantly, these data inconsistencies do not undermine the rest of the findings reported in this chapter. Rather, the reports vary systematically by respondents' childhood religious affiliations and suggest that trends in religious change in the United States may be even more extreme than previous evidence suggests.

A LOOK AT LEAVERS

A close look at who leaves their childhood religion shows that many of the characteristics that distinguish Catholics from each other and from members of other religions are associated with patterns of leaving religious groups. Tables 5.4 through 5.7 show how religious mobility between childhood and adulthood varies by several critical individual and family characteristics, focusing on the characteristics discussed in previous chapters: personal characteristics (Chapter 2), family characteristics (Chapter 3), and socioeconomic characteristics (Chapter 4). I include leavers, joiners, and stayers in each table for comparison, and these results are largely consistent with estimates from other data sources (Heft and Stets 2021; MacGregor and Haycook 2021). I focus my discussion on leavers because disaffiliation has been such a pronounced trend in the U.S. religious landscape. Moreover, leavers are—by definition—reflected in other columns as well: that is, a respondent who left one faith group necessarily entered another. Focusing on leavers allows me to avoid being redundant. The penultimate column in each table includes all people who changed religion—leavers and joiners—to enable comparison to people who are inclined to change religion, regardless of the direction they move (into a faith or out of a faith).

Personal Characteristics

Several personal characteristics distinguish those who left the Catholic Church. First, *they are young, though not younger than the U.S. national average.*

Table 5.4 SOCIAL ORIGINS AND RELIGIOUS CHANGE

	Catholic			MP			CP			None			All	
	Left	Joined	Stayed	Left	Joined	Stayed	Left	Joined	Stayed	Left	Joined	Stayed	Changed	Stayed
Gen Z	8.25	1.76	10.56	9.32	11.24	6.15	11.27	6.12	3.6	10.05	10.99	19.63	9.54	9.29
Mill	33.07	25.67	25.37	24.47	19.25	17.44	32.22	22.4	23	32.28	38.53	35.67	31.53	25.54
Gen X	25.96	29.99	25.34	23.67	29.79	24.71	27.6	29.18	28.25	32.89	23.74	26.92	26.33	26.2
Y BB	16.62	13.65	17.38	18.32	20.18	23.61	14.08	23.38	23.13	16.64	12.58	12.17	16.26	19.15
O BB	11.37	17.77	14.04	16.63	10.59	17.13	8.33	13.1	14.49	5.3	9.58	4.72	10.81	13.01
Silent	4.73	11.15	7.31	7.58	8.94	10.96	6.49	5.81	7.53	2.85	4.57	0.89	5.53	6.82
Male	52.81	32.61	51.51	51.95	40.51	47.48	45.37	41.97	41.49	42.03	56.52	49.3	49.75	48.28
Female	47.19	67.39	48.49	48.05	59.49	52.52	54.63	58.03	58.51	57.97	43.48	50.7	50.25	51.72
White	67.48	78.62	57.14	84.42	70.58	79.63	67.62	66.03	60.9	67.4	72.1	67.49	70.55	63.5
Latino	24.32	9.07	35.51	2.94	15.18	2.29	9.76	13.5	7.72	12.38	14.24	11.43	13.61	16.23

Notes: Data are from the 2021 General Social Survey (GSS). Left, joined, and stayed refer to change between childhood and adult religion. "All" refers to all GSS 2021 respondents who left or stayed with their childhood religion. Cells indicate the percent of respondents who left/joined/stayed who have that demographic trait. In the penultimate column, "changed" refers to all leavers and joiners.

The largest groups of those who left the Church are Millennials (33%) and Generation X (26%). A notable portion of those who exited are also members of Generation Z (8%), even though this generation is still relatively young. This age pattern is consistent with other research that shows an increase in disaffiliation over cohorts (Voas and Chaves 2016). Notably, however, this age pattern is also consistent with population averages. That is, the U.S. population is now heavily weighted toward Millennials, Generation Z, and younger people. Indeed, by 2020, more than half of the U.S. population was Millennial or younger (Frey 2020).

Catholic leavers are similar to conservative Protestant leavers (32% Millennial, 28% Generation X) but slightly younger than mainline Protestant leavers (25% Millennials, 24% Generation X).

Perhaps most important for understanding the future of the Catholic Church, those who left the Catholic Church are younger than those who joined the Church, suggesting that the Church's age structure will increasingly tilt toward older cohorts if this trend continues.

Second, *Catholic Church leavers are slightly more likely to be male than female*. It is well-documented that women are more religious than men, and, consistent with this, the GSS shows that those who left the Catholic Church are slightly more likely to be male (53%) than female (47%). However, of those who joined the Church, considerably fewer are men (33%) than women (67%), suggesting the potential for a pronounced gender skew in the future. Patterns are similar for mainline Protestant leavers and joiners: of those who left mainline denominations, 52% were male and 48% were female. By contrast, females (55%) were more likely than males (45%) to leave conservative Protestant denominations. Patterns not shown here suggest that the women who exited conservative Protestant churches were young; equal portions joined other Christian faith groups and disaffiliated.

Third, *Catholic leavers are more likely to be white than Latino*. About 68% of those who left the Catholic Church are white and about 24% are Latino. Importantly, the Catholic Church is 34% Latino, meaning that Latinos are underrepresented among those who exit the Church. Mainline (84%) and conservative Protestant (62%) leavers are also disproportionately white.

Family Characteristics

Marriage, divorce, and children are all associated with leaving religious groups as well (Wilson and Sherkat 1994). I show patterns for those who were ever married, ever divorced, and have any children in Table 5.5, but patterns are similar when I define marriage (e.g., currently married, recently got married), divorce (e.g., currently divorced, recently divorced), and children (e.g., number of children, childless) in other ways.

Table 5.5 FAMILY AND RELIGIOUS CHANGE

	Catholic			MP			CP			None			All	
	Left	Joined	Stayed	Left	Joined	Stayed	Left	Joined	Stayed	Left	Joined	Stayed	Changed	Stayed
Ever Married	69.05	84.91	73.99	69.24	77.95	77.41	63.05	82.03	79.95	82.66	60.3	53.68	68.84	72.68
Ever divorced	41.47	20.19	33.15	39.59	53.28	43.51	46.97	40.59	39.78	34.89	38.06	42.67	40.77	37.57
Has children	59.79	84.59	71.33	64.26	77.55	73.23	64.7	80.97	78.95	81.94	52.28	58.7	63.77	70.76

Notes: Data are from the 2021 General Social Survey (GSS). Left, joined, and stayed refer to change between childhood and adult religion. "All" refers to all GSS 2021 respondents who changed or stayed with their childhood religion. Cells indicate the percent of respondents who left/joined/stayed who have that demographic trait. In the penultimate column, "changed" refers to all leavers and joiners.

Catholic leavers are less likely than the average Catholic to have been married and less likely to have any kids; yet they are more likely to have been divorced. Table 5.5 shows that 55% of Catholic leavers were ever married, 41% were ever divorced, and 60% have children. It is useful to compare these numbers to the average Catholic (not shown). Of all Catholics, not considering ethnicity, 75% have ever been married, 32% have ever been divorced, and about 71% have at least one child. Patterns are similar for Protestants with two exceptions. Conservative Protestant leavers are somewhat less likely than both Catholic and mainline Protestant leavers to have been married; both mainline and conservative Protestant leavers are more likely than Catholic leavers to have kids.

Despite these differences, the pattern is clear: marriage and children keep people in Christian faith groups, and divorce is associated with exit. Patterns for religious nones reinforce this interpretation. For nones, leaving means joining another group, and 82% of those who "left" the religious nones were ever married, 35% were ever divorced, and 82% have kids.

Socioeconomic Characteristics

Education, work, income, and wealth are all strongly correlated with movement out of the Catholic Church. Wealth is a particularly revealing SES measure because it simultaneously reflects many behaviors and processes that interact over the life course, including birth cohort, gender, race/ethnicity, family background, adult family, and the other SES measures. Table 5.6 uses GSS data to illustrate trends in religious mobility by education, work, and income. Table 5.7 turns to the PSID to illustrate wealth trends; I rely on the PSID data to show wealth trends because the GSS does not include wealth measures (see Appendix for details). Table 5.7 includes ethnicity to document similarities between the GSS and PSID.

Those who left the Catholic Church are highly educated, have high incomes and high wealth. About 40% of Catholic leavers versus 27% of Catholic stayers have more than a bachelor's degree (Table 5.6). Compared to those who left the Catholic Church, those who left mainline Protestant churches are even more likely (47%) to be highly educated, whereas those who left conservative Protestant churches (33%) are less educated. Similarly, those who left the Catholic Church (50%) are more likely than those who joined (47%) and those who stayed (43%) to have income above the median. Income patterns for those who left, joined, and stayed with mainline Protestant churches are similar: 51% of MP leavers and only 39% of MP joiners have income above the median. By contrast, those who leave (39%) conservative Protestant churches are slightly less likely than joiners (44%) to have high incomes.

Recall that the average Catholic today has relatively high wealth (Chapter 4). It follows that both Catholic leavers (about 60%) and Catholic stayers (62%)

Table 5.6 SOCIOECONOMIC STATUS AND RELIGIOUS CHANGE

	Catholic			MP			CP			None			All		
	Left	Joined	Stayed	Left	Joined	Stayed	Left	Joined	Stayed	Left	Joined	Stayed	Changed	Stayed
BA or higher	40.01	34.83	27.22	46.66	28.31	36.99	32.88	31	28.54	24.61	42.54	28.9	37.7	31.96
Works full time	74.81	71.3	74.08	67.53	74.73	77.56	77.39	66	76.15	69.65	75.59	72.42	73.21	74.8
In poverty	17.87	27.87	21.78	20.36	23.98	17.98	26.52	23.28	22.21	34.11	19.29	26.07	26.07	21.31
>Media income	50.22	46.86	42.69	51.09	39.18	43.5	38.97	43.48	41.15	35.77	49.91	42.3	45.93	43.44

Notes: Data are from the 2021 General Social Survey (GSS). Left, joined, and stayed refer to change between childhood and adult religion. "All" refers to all GSS 2021 respondents who changed or stayed with their childhood religion. Cells indicate the percent of respondents who left/joined/stayed who have that demographic trait. In the penultimate column, "changed" refers to all leavers and joiners.

Table 5.7 WEALTH AND RELIGIOUS CHANGE

	Catholic			MP			CP			None			All	
	Left	Joined	Stayed	Left	Joined	Stayed	Left	Joined	Stayed	Left	Joined	Stayed	Changed	Stayed
Net Worth Poverty	32.8	31.8	30.5	22.9	23.6	21.5	32.5	32.4	41.1	36.0	32.8	41.0	31.1	33.8
NW>Medias	59.7	61.6	59.9	67.4	66.5	69.3	55.1	58.7	47.5	56.0	56.8	48.1	59.5	55.8
Ever Inherited	4.9	2.9	4.3	5.5	4.6	4.8	4.1	5.1	5.1	6.6	4.6	5.2	4.7	4.2
	74.1	52.1	63.2	95.3	87.6	87.6	88.3	87.0	87.0	88.5	88.7	67.3	81.7	65.3
Latino	23.6	44.3	30.7	2.7	8.3	1.5	8.7	9.8	9.8	9.5	8.5	8.5	14.9	10.9

Notes: Data are from the 1997–2021 Panel Study of Income Dynamics (PSID) and include multiple interviews the same respondents over time. Leaving, joining, and staying refer to any change from one wave to another in religious affiliation. Cells indicate the percent of respondents who left/joined/stayed who have that demographic trait. In the penultimate column, "changed" refers to all leavers and joiners.

have net worth higher than the median. Similarly, 62% of Catholic joiners have above-average net worth (see Table 5.7). Those who join the Church, however, are less likely than those who leave or stay to have inherited, suggesting that joiners are upwardly mobile households. Although the average Catholic leaver and the average Catholic stayer are white, Latinos are overrepresented in each group, and Latino Catholics are less likely than white Catholics to inherit. Across all categories shown in Table 5.7, mainline Protestants are among the highest wealth respondents in the PSID.

Table 5.7 also shows notable similarities between those who move in and out of conservative Protestant denominations and those who become religious nones. A portion of this similarity is simply about large numbers: because much of the religious change in the United States has been into the religious none category and, to a lesser extent, into conservative Protestant congregations, the demographic characteristics of these movers drive some of the averages shown in Table 5.4. However, it is still worth noting that those who have become religious nones and conservative Protestants are relatively low-wealth respondents. This pattern partly reflects age: younger people are more likely to become religious nones and conservative Protestants, and they are also less likely to have accumulated much wealth. Future research will want to explore whether these wealth trends continue as they age, particularly for religious nones.

Religious Changers and the Future of Catholicism

An important potential consequence of the religious mobility shown in this chapter is long-term reorganization of the religious character of the United States. Using estimates similar to those in this section, the Pew Research Center generated detailed demographic predictions of the religious affiliation in the U.S. in coming decades (Kramer, Hackett, and Stonawski 2022). The Pew research team showed that, by 2070, the U.S. Christian population is likely to decline dramatically from about 64% to less than half (54%) or just more than one-third (35%) of the total population. Over these same future decades, religious nones are estimated to increase from 30% of the population to somewhere between about one-third (34%) and about one-half (52%) of the population. The range in these projections reflects various scenarios with assumptions about whether religious switching continues at recent rates, increases, or stops. Of course, these projections are hypothetical, and, as Pew points out, they are not a suggestion about what *will* happen, only what *could* happen under various scenarios reflecting a range of demographic and religious affiliation patterns. Yet the various assumptions underlying these estimates incorporate realistic patterns of religious switching, age and sex composition of the country, fertility, mortality, migration, and the transmission of religious identity from parents to children.

These estimates offer intriguing insights into the potential future of Christianity in the United States. However, they do not distinguish Catholics from Protestants or account for critical demographic differences among Catholics. Combining insights from the Pew estimates with findings from this book suggests some details about the future of the Catholic Church.

In particular, at least partly because of fertility differences among Catholics—particularly differences between white and Latino Catholics—and between Catholics and Protestants (see Chapter 3), the decline in the population of Christians is likely to vary across the three large Christian groups (Catholic, mainline Protestant, conservative Protestant). In addition, differences between white and Latino Catholics in marriage and fertility (Chapter 3), SES (Chapter 4), and religious change (current chapter) suggest that changes in the Catholic population might differ by ethnic subgroup: white Catholics are likely to decline as a portion of the total population, whereas Latino Catholics are more likely to increase as a portion of the total. Indeed, similar demographic projections that include ethnicity suggest that Latino Catholics may increase to 18% of the population as soon as 2043 (Skirbekk, Kaufmann, and Goujon 2010).

In addition, education, income, and wealth differences in movement in and out of the Church (shown in this chapter) are also likely to create a very different demographic profile of Catholics in the future. Because those who are exiting the Catholic Church are, on average, highly educated, high-income, and high-wealth, it follows that the SES profile of Catholics may be quite different in coming decades than it is today. In particular, it is likely that high-SES white Catholics are likely to become a smaller portion of the Church in the future. Particularly high-SES Catholics—including highly visible individuals such as President Biden and Supreme Court justices—may be drawing attention to the Church today, and they stand as reminders that the overall SES of Catholics is much higher today than it once was. However, movement of high-SES congregants out of the Church—without high-SES converts to replace them—suggests that Catholic SES may be in flux, and the Church may experience an overall decline in SES.

WHY CATHOLICS LEAVE: THEIR OWN WORDS

The reasons people leave Catholicism vary widely, and the demographic correlates I showed above only begin to capture the diversity of explanations people have for leaving the Church. Since the 1990s—when disaffiliation sped up rapidly—scholars have studied and debated the origins of America's dramatic religious transformation and have puzzled over how long this trend will continue. They have also, on occasion, conducted surveys aimed to identify reasons for disaffiliation.

A lack of belief or a dislike for organized religion are common reasons given in surveys of those who left Christianity (Lipka 2016). Other correlates include rising education levels, smaller families, more religious intermarriage, and parents who are not involved or not active in their religious groups (Sherkat 2014; Smith et al. 2014). These demographic patterns are reflected in the patterns I showed above. More existential reasons include a greater reliance on science to explain phenomena and a sense of security as scientific progress allows people to live longer with fewer worries (Norris and Inglehart 2011). For liberals, the association between Christianity and conservative politics is a turnoff (Djupe, Neiheisel, and Conger 2018; Hout and Fischer 2002), and for Catholics, the clergy sexual abuse scandal has pushed many people away (Gecewicz 2019).

The AVP builds on this important literature by offering a rich source of information about how and why people disaffiliate, using their own words. The AVP is unique among surveys that contain reasons for religious disaffiliation because it (1) includes a representative sample of Americans; and (2) asks open-ended questions that, for many respondents, include insight into the motives and processes that prompted their decision to change religious groups or disaffiliate. Having qualitative survey information on a representative sample of the U.S. population is rare in itself, and having detailed responses to a large number of open-ended questions makes the AVP extremely useful for understanding how and why people make the decisions that affect their life trajectories. Moreover, AVP respondents voluntarily raise issues related to religion and their affiliation with particular religious groups when they have the opportunity. Thus, many respondent comments about religion reflect their thoughts and feelings, independent of topics suggested by interviewers. Two other excellent studies provide information on reasons for disaffiliation (Bullivant 2019; MacGregor and Haycook 2021) using different data sources. The patterns I describe below from the AVP are largely consistent with the patterns shown in these other works.

The AVP data are not perfect, of course. For example, the survey includes a question about religious affiliation, and many respondents address religious change in their response. However, respondents rarely talk about religious stability—staying with a religion—presumably because stability is less eventful and likely involves less active decision-making than does change. In addition, the AVP is not designed to gather information specifically about religion, and religious change may not be salient for some respondents. Despite these downsides, the AVP data contain rich detail about religious change that is unique among contemporary data sources.

The way former Catholics in the AVP data discussed the processes that led them to leave the Church can be grouped into five broad themes: (1) drifting away, (2) moral relativism, (3) beliefs and practices, (4) pushed away, and (5) pulled away. These themes echo some well-documented explanations of disaffiliation that emerged in previous literature. However, AVP respondents' accounts also add new insight into the disaffiliation process and clarify how and why individuals make this important life decision.

Drifting Away. Drifting away from the faith was a common reason former Catholics provided for leaving the Church. Drifting away took a variety of forms and started at many points in the life course. In each case, though, drifting away involved replacing active participation in the Church with other activities. Usually, drifting away was not a conscious decision or an active response with an underlying complaint about the Church or a draw toward some alternative. For most respondents who drifted away from the faith, leaving the Church was the culmination of years of neglect of religious practice that ultimately amounted to disaffiliation.

For many respondents, drifting away from Catholicism started in childhood and suggested that parents—particularly fathers—are important anchors to the faith, a finding that echoes that shown in previous research (Smith et al. 2014; Smith, Ritz, and Rotolo 2020). One AVP respondent summed up this process when he recalled that his parents just "didn't make (Catholicism) a priority." Other respondents described similar childhood experiences in which their parents had them baptized, or had their first communions (and possibly were confirmed) but then had no other interactions with the Church. As another respondent noted, despite participating in these sacraments, "we didn't go to Church or anything." For him, drifting away from the Church was natural, and having to recommit to Catholicism as an adult would have required a conscious decision akin to joining a faith.

Other respondents were raised in families that were actively involved in the Church, but they began to drift away in adulthood. Some found themselves less involved with the Church in college or when they started working their first job. In these cases, leaving the Church did not reflect an intellectual or moral statement that might reflect disagreement with Church doctrine or practices. Others remained practicing Catholics until later in life and then slowly left the Church: one respondent considered himself Catholic until he was married. He then converted to his wife's Lutheran church, and, shortly after his conversion, both he and his wife drifted away from Christianity. For all the respondents who drifted away from the Church, leaving seemed passive and appeared to involve little emotion or conscious reasoning. These respondents simply replaced participation in the Church with other activities and, in some cases, seemed unaware of this process until years later.

Moral Relativism. No AVP respondents used the term "moral relativism," but many former Catholics in the AVP data described their reasons for leaving the Church in a way that aligned closely with this important concept. Moral relativism—the idea that there are no absolute truths about right and wrong—was a particularly common theme for younger former Catholics who commented that they did not need the Church to tell them how to behave in a morally just way. Reflecting common relativist thought, some AVP respondents—young and old—suggested that there are no absolute moral truths and that all societies should accept each other's values (which, of course, is a general moral principle).

Beliefs and Practices. Some former Catholics in the AVP data pointed to the Church's beliefs and practices—either specific beliefs or what they saw as a more general ideology—as motivating their disaffiliation. Complaints about beliefs and practices fell into three categories. First, some respondents made statements that evoked the idea that "these beliefs are hard" (John 6:60). In this Bible passage, Jesus tells a crowd that they must believe in him to have eternal life and that his flesh is real food and his blood is real drink; in the Bible, these statements made many people turn away from Jesus. No AVP respondent referred specifically to this Bible passage, but they described the teachings of Christianity, including Catholicism, as requiring more faith than they had on a range of issues (e.g., the real presence of Jesus in the Eucharist, sexual ethics), very much akin to the people who walked away in this Bible passage.

Second, some AVP respondents described Catholicism as unintelligent. This second group of respondents fell into two camps. On the one hand, some respondents described a dumbed-down version of Catholicism; that is, they described beliefs that are not Catholic and are not taught by the Church. This dumbing down of the faith reflected an approach to simplifying Church teachings that has been described by others as common after Vatican II (not because of Vatican II) and inconsistent with the philosophical and theological roots of the faith (Barron 2020). A related group of respondents first described beliefs that are not what the Church teaches or are caricatures of teachings and then pointed to them as the reasons for their disaffiliation. Two female Millennial respondents exemplified these complaints. One said that she struggles to understand how educated, intelligent people—including her parents—can believe Church teachings, including describing heaven as in the clouds and referred to this idea as "comforting but silly." The other Millennial described Christians as the ones who crucified Christ and said, "Why did they put Jesus on a cross? Why is that a good thing? Why would I wanna follow a faith that treats people so poorly, but then tells you to be good to everyone and forgive everyone?"

A third group of former Catholics described the Church as not sufficiently spiritual. These respondents largely disaffiliated from religion entirely or now identify as spiritual but not religious. Some respondents referred directly to a lack of spiritualism in the Mass, and many of these turned to what they described as "New Age" practices to fill their need for a spiritual connection to a higher power.

Pushed Away. Anger at the Church, writ large, and its clergy, in particular, motivated some Catholics to disaffiliate. However, respondents who left because they were angry were not the majority among former Catholics in the AVP, and these angry disaffiliates were surprisingly varied in the reasons for their irritation. These AVP respondents were perhaps most similar to the former Catholics described by MacGregor and Haycook (2021), who noted that significant numbers of former Catholics describe the Church as overly involved in politics, too focused on rules and judgment, and too concerned about money and power.

Not surprisingly, some former Catholic AVP respondents referred to the clergy sexual abuse scandal and were clearly angry about the scandal, the efforts by Church leaders to cover up the scandal, and the lack of consequences for the abusers. However, respondents were angry for other reasons as well, including the Church's political stances and basic elements of its structure. For example, some respondents were angry about the political stances taken by recent Popes. One Cuban immigrant expressed deep anger that Pope Francis went to Cuba and shook hands with Fidel Castro. Another respondent was angry about the Church hierarchy, saying that "the Church power structure is not Christian."

Pulled Away. A final reason that AVP respondents mentioned for leaving Catholicism is being pulled toward another faith tradition, a process that was similar to what others have described as being "loved away" from the Church. This description of the disaffiliation process was only relevant for those who left Catholicism to join other faith groups, mostly Protestant churches. This explanation included both those who were intrigued and enticed by the joy and love they felt when interacting with evangelical Protestants; it also included those who wished their Catholic Churches had been more oriented toward community. A 61-year-old man (a young Baby Boomer) noted that, for his wife (who was Methodist), church is a community; for him, it was a building. Being pulled away from the Church echoes the description given by Jeff Cavins—a popular Catholic writer and speaker—who described why he left the Catholic Church and became a conservative Protestant pastor (before returning to Catholicism). Cavins notes that "I was intrigued by their sense of community. They did everything together and I desired to have the kind of friendships I saw" (Cavins 2022; Cavins June 2, 2023).

Despite these complaints and sometimes strong emotions, many former Catholics in the AVP described the Church fondly and made claims that suggested they still consider themselves Catholic. A common theme among the former Catholics in the AVP was a sense that they could always and easily return to the Church because Catholicism is, in the words of one 50-something male respondent, my "spiritual hometown."

Unlike respondents raised in other faith traditions, practicing and former Catholics referred to themselves as being "born Catholic" rather than being raised Catholic, as if Catholicism is more similar to an ethnicity than a religion. Consistent with this thinking, some Catholic and former Catholic AVP respondents insisted that they are a particular ethnic variant of Catholic (e.g., Irish Catholic, Italian Catholic, Mexican Catholic).

Many former Catholic respondents were clear that they still believe in God and in some basic tenets of Christianity; others recalled elements of Catholicism fondly or even described still following some Catholic practices and traditions. One man who was raised Catholic and now says he is no religion said "but every once in a while ... I do find myself missing the sign of the cross, and I find myself talking to, well, a higher power, and I say, well, you're not listening to me, but here's the deal."

Another man from Generation X whose parents were devout Catholics identified as a religious none. However, he was quick to say that "I do believe there's a God" and that "Jesus died on a cross for our sins," but "I don't need to go to church to worship him." Particularly interesting is that, in an unrelated portion of the interview, this respondent noted that his family's food expenses had been a bit high recently because they "are Catholic" and were eating fish on Friday during Lent.

Other former Catholics reminisced about elements of the Church and faith that they missed. For example, some respondents pointed to the beauty of the Mass and the church buildings. One respondent recalled being in Navy boot camp decades earlier and having been away from the Church for years already at that point; he needed a break from basic training and found his way to a Catholic Church, where the organ "gave him chill bumps." Another woman talked about missing the Mass, its rituals, and its beauty; she said she still occasionally goes to "some random (Catholic) church, and it isn't about anything but my relationship with God."

Other respondents missed elements of the morality of the Church and the weekly messages about living well contained in the sermon at Mass. One man realized—and appeared to appreciate—that Christian morality underlies much Western thinking (Holland 2019). Although this respondent appeared to be unaware of the scale of the statements he was making about the role of Christianity in Western thought and morality, he was grateful to have been raised in the faith that generated important moral precepts.

CONCLUSION

Religious mobility has been extreme in the United States since at least the 1970s. The growth in the religious nones has been dramatic and well-documented, consistent with evidence that the United States is no longer an exception to the movement of modern societies toward secularization (Voas and Chaves 2016). Yet other religious change has occurred recently as well: people have moved among faith groups, and religious nones have joined churches.

In this chapter, I studied religious change and how it affects and includes Catholics. First, I documented patterns of American religious mobility using GSS and PSID data. I showed how much movement there has been, with special attention to movement into and out of the Catholic Church. I revisited aggregate estimates—the percentage of Americans affiliated with major religious groups—from Chapter 1 that showed extraordinary disaffiliation from major religious groups. I also looked at individual-level religious change from GSS respondents who reported their childhood and adult religious affiliations. These estimates reaffirmed that disaffiliation has been dramatic but also underscored an important pattern that attracts little attention: large numbers of Americans continue to remain affiliated with Catholicism and Protestant churches over their lives. The individual-level analyses also showed that there are significant numbers of Americans who become Catholic and who affiliate with other religious groups. Finally, I exploited a pattern in the GSS data to show that there may be even more religious change in the United States than previous research has found: potential retrospective editing of childhood religion suggests that more GSS respondents may have been affiliated with Protestant churches in childhood than contemporary reports suggest. If this is true, it may be the case that the number of disaffiliates is larger than we recognize using current data.

Second, I explored who leaves the Catholic Church, showing important demographic correlates with exits from Catholicism and other faith groups. Those who left the Catholic Church are young, but not younger than most Americans, and slightly more likely to be male than female. It is well-documented that young people change faith more than do older people and that women are more religious than men. My findings confirm these patterns. My findings also showed that gender differences in leaving the Church are minimal, but men are, indeed, less likely to join the Church, suggesting that a future gender imbalance is likely. Ethnicity is also strongly correlated with exiting the Church: those who leave the Church are more likely to be non-Latino. I also showed that those who leave the Church are more likely to have been married, more likely to have been divorced, and less likely to have children than the average Catholic.

SES differences in movement in and out of the Church are also likely to create a different demographic profile of Catholics in the future. In particular, those who left the Catholic Church are, on average, highly educated and have high income and high wealth. Combined with findings from previous chapters, this suggests that the highly visible Catholics—President Biden, members of Congress, Supreme Court justices—are one type of high-SES white Catholics today (Chapter 4). However, it is also these high-SES people who are more inclined to exit the Church. If these trends continue, the social and economic character of the Catholic Church will also be much different in the future.

Finally, I used interview data to explore the reasons people leave the Church, and I found that their explanations fall into five broad groups. First, many people simple drift away from the faith over time. This path was not a conscious decision for the former Catholics, but rather, drifting away happened after many years of neglect of the faith. Second, other former Catholics were motivated by moral relativism, the idea that there are no absolute truths. These leavers typically expressed dissatisfaction with any organization, including religious organizations, that would offer guidance for how to live a moral life. A third theme that emerged involved disagreement with a host of Catholic beliefs and practices. Former Catholics who fell into this camp expressed disagreement with Church doctrine regarding either specific beliefs or more general ideology. This group included those who found Church teachings generally hard to accept, those who called Catholicism unintelligent, and those who wanted a more spiritual experience with religion. The fourth group of leavers include those who were pushed away. These disaffiliates included those who expressed anger—sometimes intense anger—regarding scandals—including the clergy sexual abuse scandal—and other political stances taken by the Church. The final group of former Catholics include those who were pulled away, leaving the Church for other religious groups. The more critical of these disaffiliates included those who found more joy and love in other faith traditions and expressed remorse that they could not find those in Catholicism.

PART II
Beliefs and Attitudes

CHAPTER 6
Religious Beliefs and Practices

White and Latino Catholics have similar religious beliefs and practices, including levels of religious strength, participation in Mass and other religious practices, and views of issues with religious significance. They differ in their reports of having a born-again experience and views of divorce. However, both white and Latino Catholics diverge notably from Church teaching on key beliefs and practices.

Religious beliefs and practices are fundamental to who people are, and they are critical to the well-being of individuals, families, and societies. Religion gives purpose to individuals' lives, can motivate hard work and moral behavior, and can have enormous positive physical and psychological benefits (Galek et al. 2015; Koenig, King, and Carson 2012; Krok 2015; Silton et al. 2014). Religious beliefs can affect political behaviors and opinions, including voting (e.g., voter turnout, candidate choice) and attitudes about taxes, government spending, and penalties for crime (Gorski and Perry 2022; Hout and Fischer 2002; Norris and Inglehart 2011; Perry 2022). Religious beliefs can also affect attitudes about social issues, such as abortion, assisted suicide, inequality and redistribution, and gender roles (Bartkowski and Grettenberger 2018; Hoffmann, Ellison, and Bartkowski 2017; Keister 2023; Schwadel and Ellison 2017). Beyond the individual, religious beliefs have the potential to create and maintain social unity and stability (Durkheim 1912/1954), and, as a result, religion may have played a central role in the development of modern human societies, economies, and political systems (Bellah 2011).

A well-developed academic literature has explored the role of religious affiliation, beliefs, and practices in social, economic, and political life. However, an updated portrait of Catholic religious beliefs—and a comparison of Catholics' beliefs to those of American faith groups—is timely for at least two reasons. First, it is no surprise that religious beliefs and practices vary across faith groups, but beliefs and practices can also vary among adherents to particular faith groups (Pew Research Center 2008, 2015). Changing Catholic demographics and stark differences among Catholics in social origins, family states, and socioeconomic status (SES) (shown in previous chapters) have the potential to create Catholic subgroups based on religious beliefs and practices. There are certainly differences among Catholics in their religious, political, and social beliefs and practices (D'Antonio, Dillon, and Gautier 2013; Ellison, Wolfinger, and Ramos-Wada 2013; Keister 2023). Yet membership in a shared faith with clear doctrinal teachings on religious and other issues could create unity that supersedes demographic differences or leads to differences only under particular circumstances (Davis and Robinson 1996). Exploring similarities among Catholics will show whether there are different types of Catholics practicing the faith today.

Second, there have likely been significant changes in recent years in religious beliefs for individuals from each of the major American faith groups, including Catholicism. The rapid and extreme changes in religious affiliation shown in Chapter 5 suggest that commitment to these faith groups has declined, particularly for younger people. Consistent with this, most Americans claimed that religion was very important to them until recently; however, remarkable declines in the strength of religious beliefs and dramatic changes in the content of both religious beliefs and practices have occurred recently (Pew Research Center 2008; Voas and Chaves 2016).

Up to this point, I have paid minimal attention to the religious beliefs, values, and practices that characterize Catholics. In this chapter, I tackle religion directly by examining Catholics' religious beliefs and practices and comparing them with those of other Americans. I accomplish this in two parts. First, I array differences in beliefs and practices that are explicitly religious, including (1) strength of religious beliefs; (2) religious service attendance, prayer, and meditation; (3) religious experiences and evangelization; (4) beliefs about God, the afterlife, and the Pope; and (5) feelings about the Bible. Although only one of these beliefs and practices is explicitly Catholic (i.e., beliefs about the Pope), each topic provides insight into how Catholics approach their faith and how their religious values compare to others' values.

Second, I examine views about the role of religion in select issues with broader political and social implications, including views of the role of religion in public schools and attitudes about sex, divorce, pornography, and abortion. I include these political and social topics in this chapter because they address how religion intersects with these other attitudes. I reserve Chapter 7 (political attitudes) and Chapter 8 (social attitudes) for discussions of additional political and social issues. There is no clear way to classify topics as religious, political, or social, and my decision to include particular issues in this chapter rather than in subsequent ones is ultimately arbitrary. For example, I could have discussed topics such as abortion, assisted suicide, and capital punishment in any of these chapters given that they reflect the interdependence of religion, politics, and social issues.

Throughout the chapter, I make three comparisons. First, I compare white and Latino Catholics to explore whether these groups differ in their religious beliefs and practices. Second, I make brief, contextual comparisons of Catholics' religious beliefs and practices to official Church teaching. My objective is sociological, and I use these references entirely to provide some context for interpreting Catholics' stated beliefs and practices. None of the theoretical approaches that guide this book—status attainment, life course, the cultural approach—suggests a direct association between the stated beliefs of a group—religious or other—and the beliefs and practices of the group members. However, membership in a faith group should create synergies between members' beliefs and practices and official Church doctrine. Indeed, dissimilarities between official doctrine and members' beliefs are potentially more interesting, as Dillon showed in her work on why people stay in a faith tradition with which they disagree (Dillon 1999).

Third, I compare Catholics and members of other faith traditions in the content and practice of their religious beliefs to situate Church members in the contemporary American religious landscape. Historically, there were pronounced differences between U.S. Catholics and Protestants in their religious beliefs, but declining social differences between these groups suggests that religious differences are likely to be much smaller today than they were in the past. Indeed, given similarities between white Catholics and white mainline Protestants on the various family and SES measures I studied in Chapters 3 and 4, it is likely that these groups are similar in their religious beliefs and practices as well. By contrast, I found some evidence of convergence between white Catholics and white conservative Protestants on family and SES measures, but these groups are clearly distinct on many other demographic measures. Given that white Catholics and white conservative Protestants also attend churches with significantly different stances on religious, political, and social issues, it is likely that there are notable differences between these groups in religious beliefs and practices as well.

What about those who left the Church? The religious beliefs and practices of former Catholics could provide additional insight into who exits the faith and how current Catholics fit into the U.S. religious landscape. Differences between the religious beliefs of leavers and current Catholics might also shed light on the future of the Church, assuming at least some exits continue in the future. Although a complete comparison of leavers and current Catholics is beyond the space limits of a single book, I offer snapshots of how leavers differ from current Catholics in sidebars in this and subsequent chapters.

The beliefs and attitudes that I study in the remainder of this book reflect—and follow from—the demographic behaviors and processes I studied in the previous chapters of this book. Following an extensive and well-developed literature in sociological research, I acknowledge that beliefs and attitudes are subjective and more challenging to measure with survey data than are demographic and behavioral outcomes such as birth cohort, place of birth, marital status, fertility, education, work, income, and wealth. Of course, respondents might inaccurately report objective measures, but these measures could be verified against other records (Alwin 2007).[1] By contrast, beliefs are notoriously difficult to verify. Nonetheless, responses to survey questions about beliefs are not only useful but are also critical to understanding who people are. Indeed, an enormous academic literature—spanning the social science disciplines and subdisciplines—with an extensive history documents important information from survey responses to questions about beliefs (Alwin 2007; Baldassarri and Goldberg 2014; Boutyline and Vaisey 2017; McCall 2013; Wilson et al. 2022).

BELIEFS AND PRACTICES
Strength of Religious Beliefs

The strength of an individual's religious beliefs is essential for understanding their commitment to a faith and how likely that faith is to affect other behaviors and attitudes. The strength of religious beliefs can be measured in many ways, including through respondent self-reports to survey questions. Figure 6.1 uses such self-reports from the General Social Survey (GSS) data to compare responses to several measures of the strength of religious beliefs across the six religious-ethnic groups. The figure shows whether respondents consider themselves a strong (vs. not very strong) member of their faith group,

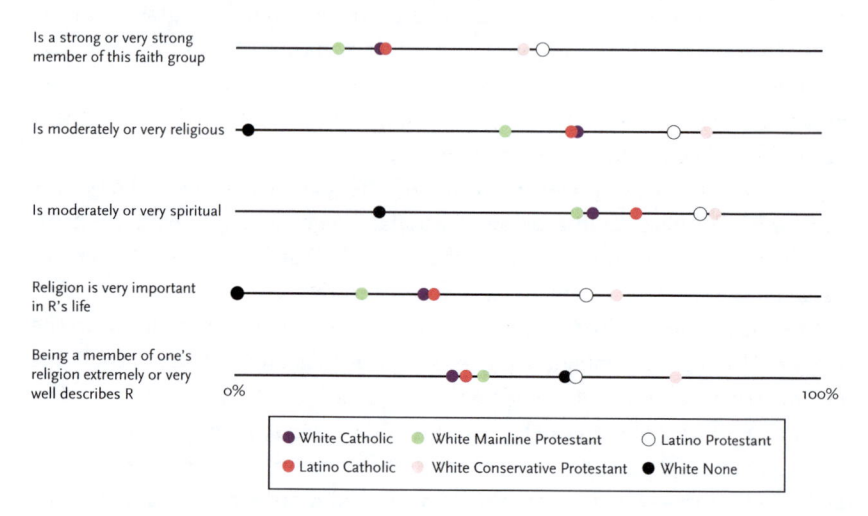

Figure 6.1 Strength of religious belief

moderately or very religious (vs. slightly or not at all religious), or moderately or very spiritual (vs. slightly or not at all spiritual). It also shows whether respondents consider religion very important (vs. somewhat, not too, or not at all important) and whether being a member of one's religion describes them extremely or very well (vs. somewhat, not very, or not at all well).

The figure provides a first glimpse into religious similarities between white and Latino Catholics, showing that these groups are remarkably comparable on all these measures of religious strength. Relatively few members of each ethnic group say that they are strong or very strong Catholics, that religion is important in their lives, or that being a Catholic describes them extremely or very well, consistent with evidence that attachment to Catholicism has declined over time (Hout 2016; Schwadel 2013). However, more members of both groups say that they are moderately or very religious or that they are moderately or very spiritual. In results not included here, white and Latino Catholics responded nearly identically to other questions about the strength of their faith. For example, about half of both groups say "we" versus "they" when talking about Catholicism, and most or all of them would feel greatly personally insulted if someone criticized Catholicism.

White and Latino Catholics are also similar to white mainline Protestants on religious strength measures, although white mainline Protestants report slightly lower levels of religious strength than Catholics on most measures included in Figure 6.1. One exception is that nearly identical percentages of white mainline Protestants and Catholics report that being a member of their religion describes them extremely or very well. Differences between white conservative Protestants and Catholics are more extreme: significantly larger percentages of white conservative Protestants report high levels of religious identification and strength on all measures included in Figure 6.1. Notably, white conservative Protestants are more similar to Latino Protestants in religious strength than they are to Catholics or white mainline Protestants; and Latino Protestants are more religious than Latino Catholics, consistent with previous research (Ellison, Acevedo, and Ramos-Wada 2011; Ellison et al. 2013). Not surprisingly, few religious nones are religious; however, it is more surprising that very few religious nones report being spiritual, a label that nones have used to describe themselves (Pew Research Center 2008).

Religious Service Attendance, Prayer, and Meditation

Religious practices provide additional information about the strength of belief; they are also useful for understanding whether and how often an individual is exposed to religious messages that can reinforce religious beliefs and create new ones. Three practices are particularly instructive: attending religious services, prayer, and meditation. Figure 6.2 shows how these practices

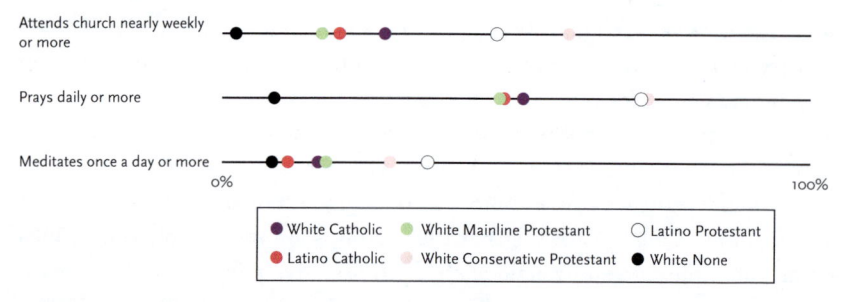

Figure 6.2 Religious practices

vary by religious affiliation and ethnicity. Attendance refers to attending religious services nearly weekly or more often (vs. attending less often). For prayer and meditation, I show the percentage of each group that prays or meditates daily or more (vs. praying or meditating less often).

Mass attendance and prayer are also fundamental to Catholicism. Catholic doctrine requires Mass attendance on Sundays and holy days of obligation (CCC 2000), and the Church considers prayer foundational to the faith (CCC 2000, paragraphs 2559–2565). White and Latino Catholics report similar levels of Mass attendance, prayer, and meditation; however, relatively low percentages of each group report engaging in these religious practices. Figure 6.2 shows that only about one-third of each group attend Mass weekly or more, although about one-half pray at least daily. Very few Catholics meditate, perhaps because meditation—which is a part of many Catholic spiritual practices—is not widely seen by Catholics as part of the faith.

Not only do few Catholics attend Mass regularly, but Mass attendance is at historic lows, continuing a well-documented trend (Hout 2016; Hout and Greeley 1987). Of all Catholics—including both white and Latino Catholics—about 30% reported attending Mass less than once a year, and about half those (16%) never attended (author's additional estimates from the GSS, not shown) in 2021. Only about 15% reported attending Mass weekly, and only a small percentage of Catholics (about 2%) attended Mass more than once a week. The decline in Mass attendance largely reflects disagreement with the Church's teachings on sexual morality, including birth control (Hout 2016; Hout and Greeley 1987). For comparison, about 26% of all Protestants attended services every week or more often in 2021. In 1972, these numbers were quite different: nearly 55% of Catholics attended Mass at least once a week, with more than 5% of those attending more often (author's estimates, not shown). By contrast, only about 8% of all Catholics reported attending Mass less than once a year, and only 3.6% of those never attended.

Catholics are similar to white mainline Protestants in the reported religious practices shown in Figure 6.2 but are notably different from white conservative Protestants. Similar percentages of Catholics and white mainline

Protestants report attending religious services, praying daily, and meditating daily. By contrast, higher percentages of white conservative Protestants and Latino Protestants attend religious services at least weekly and pray at least daily. Higher percentages of white conservative Protestants and Latino Protestants meditate daily as well, although daily meditation is relatively rare for each of the groups included in the figure.

Spiritual connection is another useful measure of religious strength that does not imply affiliation with any particular religious tradition, making it useful for comparing Catholics to religious nones. Considering a general measure of spiritual connection is also worthwhile given that increasing numbers of Americans refer to their religious beliefs and experiences as spiritual rather than as consistent with traditional religious organizations. In analyses not shown in Figure 6.2, I explored variation across religious groups in three measures of spiritual connection drawn from three related GSS questions: "Some people say they have experiences of being personally moved, touched, or inspired, while others say they do not have these experiences at all. How often, if at all, do you experience each of the following: felt particularly connected to the world around you, felt like you were part of something much larger than yourself, or felt a sense of a larger meaning or purpose in life?" I coded each of these measures as "yes" for respondents answering "at least once a day" or "almost every day." Other responses included "once or twice a week," "once or twice a month," "a few times a year," "once a year or less," or "never."

On each measure of spiritual connection, patterns are similar to those of the religiosity measures shown in Figure 6.2: white and Latino Catholics are very similar to each other and to mainline Protestants; and relatively low percentages of all three of these groups (around 30%) reported high levels of spiritual connectedness. Also similar to the patterns shown in Figure 6.2, white conservative Protestants and Latino Protestants were more similar to each other than to Catholics and mainline Protestants; and higher percentages of white conservative Protestants and Latino Protestants (approximately 50%) reported high levels of spiritual connection.

Religious Experiences and Evangelization

For Christians, *evangelization* refers to sharing information about their faith with another person, usually with at least an implicit desire to convert that person to the faith. Evangelization is often associated with conservative Protestants, and the terms "evangelical Protestant" and "conservative Protestant" are commonly used interchangeably. More properly, evangelical Protestantism is an interdenominational movement within Protestant Christianity that emphasizes having a personal conversion experience involving the acceptance of salvation (i.e., being "born again"). Evangelical Protestants also usually accept the authority of the Bible as the inerrant word of God and place high value on evangelization. Throughout this book, I use the term "conservative Protestant" rather than "evangelical Protestant" to be consistent with prior research. My conservative Protestant religious category refers to the group of Protestant churches that have more traditional religious beliefs than those I refer to as mainline Protestant. Importantly, not all the individuals I refer to as conservative Protestants are evangelicals, and some mainline Protestants are also evangelical (Green et al. 1996).

Yet evangelization is central to—or at least is supposed to be central to—Catholicism. A comprehensive discussion of evangelization is beyond the scope of this book, but it is useful to note that the Catechism of the Catholic Church requires evangelization of all the Baptized, referring to evangelization as a missionary mandate and calling it "a requirement of the Church's catholicity." The Catechism also cites the Gospel of Matthew to add Biblical backing to this mandate: "go therefore and make disciples of all nations, baptizing them in the name of the Father and of the Son and of the Holy Spirit, teaching them to observe all that I have commanded you; and Lo, I am with you always, until the close of the age" (CCC 849; Matthew 28:19–20). Pope Paul VI notably reiterated and emphasized this mandate in a well-cited apostolic exhortation (i.e., a magisterial document) (Pope Paul VI 1975).

Despite the Church's stated commitment to evangelization, Figure 6.3 shows that relatively few Catholics—white (27%) or Latino (35%)—in the GSS reported that they have "ever tried to encourage someone to believe in Jesus Christ or to accept Jesus Christ as his or her savior." Some readers might attribute these low percentages to evangelization being more of a Protestant activity than a Catholic one. Indeed, a slightly higher percentage (about 41%) of white mainline Protestants reported having done so. Nearly 77% of white conservative Protestants and about 83% of Latino Protestants (who, as I have noted, tend to be conservative Protestants) have tried to convert someone to Christianity. Additional data would be useful for exploring how

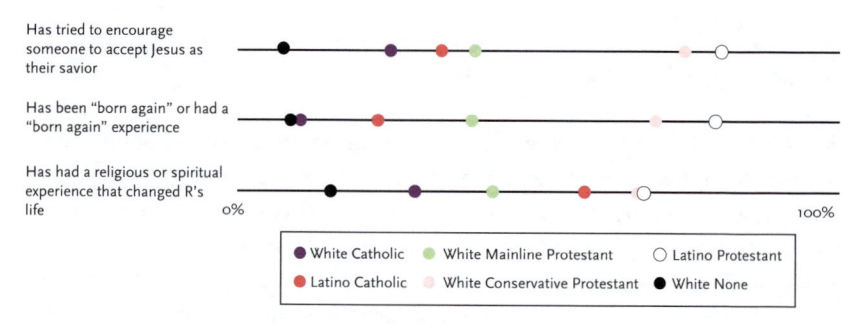

Figure 6.3 Religious experiences and evangelization

Catholics interpret this question. That is, many Catholics think of evangelization as living a life that reflects their commitment to Christ and his teachings, including regular worship and engaging in corporal and spiritual works of mercy. Yet the growing popularity of movements such as Bishop Robert Barron's Word on Fire ministry suggests that active evangelization may become more common for Catholics.

Having a born-again or other life-changing religious experience are two points on which white and Latino Catholics differ considerably. The GSS asked respondents two related questions about these sorts of experiences: (1) "Would you say that you have been born again or have had a born again experience?" and (2) "Did you ever have a religious or spiritual experience that changed your life?" Only about 11% of white Catholics said they had a born-again experience, and about 31% said they had some other life-changing religious experience. This low percentage of white Catholics is not overly surprising given that having a born-again experience does happen for Catholics, but this is more of a Protestant belief (and reflects the Protestant bias of the GSS).

However, having a born-again or other life-changing religious experience also highlights an important difference between white and Latino Catholics: nearly 25% of Latino Catholics reported having a born-again experience, and nearly 60% reported having some other life-changing religious experience. On these measures, Latino Catholics are more similar to white conservative Protestants and Latino Protestants. The majority of both white conservative Protestants (72% and 69%) and Latino Protestants (82% and 70%) reported having born-again or other life-changing religious experiences, respectively. Notably, these patterns are consistent with evidence of ethnic diversity in the way religion and ethnicity interact to shape vocation and the lived experience of vocation (Day 2018).

Beliefs About God, the Afterlife, and the Pope

Specific thoughts and ideas about God, the afterlife, and—for Catholics—the Pope provide insight into the details of individuals' religious beliefs. Figure 6.4 shows results for three measures related to these particular beliefs. The first measure asks respondents about their confidence in the existence of God with the following question: "Which of these statements comes closest to expressing what you believe about God?" I focus on those who responded, "I know God really exists, and I have no doubts about it (i.e., no doubts)" because this is the most common response for Catholic respondents and because the patterns that emerge across the various alternative answers are all similar to the patterns that emerge regarding having "no doubts." Other possible responses include "while I have doubts, I feel that I do believe in God"; "I find myself believing in God some of the time, but not at others"; "I don't believe

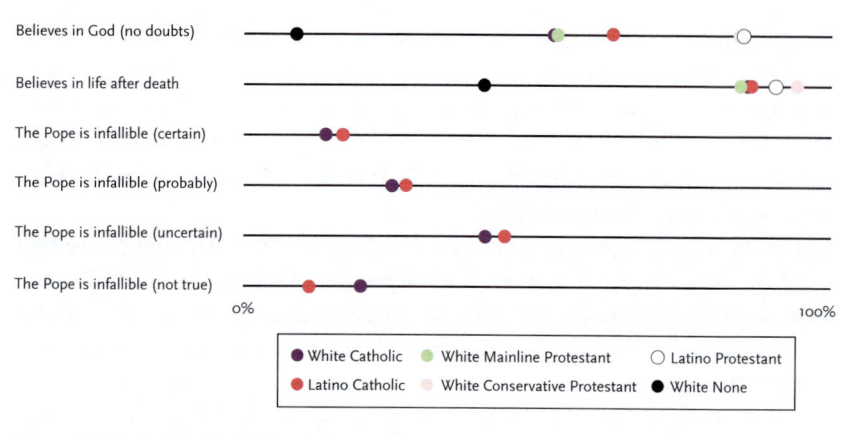

Figure 6.4 God, the afterlife, and the Pope

in a personal God, but I do believe in a Higher Power of some kind"; "I don't know whether there is a God and I don't believe there is any way to find out"; and "I don't believe in God."

Most white and Latino Catholics reported that they have no doubts about the existence of God; however, the percentage of those who are doubt-free is significantly higher for Latino (62%) than white (52%) Catholics. On this measure, white Catholics are nearly identical to white mainline Protestants (about 53% say they have no doubts in God's existence).

Although belief in God among Catholics seems high, changes over time suggest that their faith may be weaker than this pattern suggests. Among Catholic respondents to the 2021 GSS, most (52%) indicated no doubts about God's existence (analyses not shown). However, in 2006 (the first year the GSS asked the question about God's existence), 62% of Catholics had no doubts about God's existence, suggesting a dramatic short-term change between 2006 and 2021. Notably, these findings are consistent with Gallup research that shows belief in God—and in other spiritual entities such as heaven, angels, hell, the devil—have declined over short, recent time periods (Brenan 2023).

Belief in God is also weak for Catholics relative to white conservative Protestants and Latino Protestants. Similar to other measures of faith that I showed above, white conservative Protestants and Latino Protestants are nearly identical to each other in their faith in God, with much higher percentages of each of these groups (84% of each) saying that they have no doubt in God's existence.

A notably high percentage of religious nones (nearly 10%) have no doubt in God's existence, despite their lack of affiliation with a faith group. This percentage is, perhaps, not overly surprising given evidence that many religious nones have faith in God and are otherwise spiritual but lack faith in organized religion (Burge 2021; Levin et al. 2022; Lipka 2016).

Belief in some form of afterlife is an issue on which Americans appear to agree more than on most other religious issues. White and Latino Catholics are nearly identical to each other in their belief in an afterlife, and the differences among Christians of all forms are minimal. Even large percentages of religious nones agree that there is some form of afterlife. Figure 6.4 illustrates this by showing the percentage of each group that responds positively to the GSS question: "Do you believe there is a life after death?" Nearly identical percentages of white and Latino Catholics (about 85% and about 86%, respectively) hold this belief, as do about 84% of mainline Protestants. Slightly more white conservative Protestants (about 94%) and Latino Protestants (about 90%) also hold this belief. The percentage of those answering this question affirmatively is certainly lower for religious nones (about 41%), but this percentage is arguably high given that these respondents are not affiliated with a religious organization and—as previous figures in this chapter showed—largely do not consider themselves religious or hold other religious beliefs in common with Christians.

The GSS says little about beliefs that are specifically Catholic. However, it includes a question about papal infallibility, a central tenet of Catholic doctrine and a teaching that makes Roman Catholicism unique. According to the Catechism of the Catholic Church (paragraph 891), "The Roman Pontiff, head of the college of bishops, enjoys this infallibility in virtue of his office, when, as supreme pastor and teacher of all the faithful—who confirms his brethren in the faith he proclaims by a definitive act a doctrine pertaining to faith or morals." Consistent with this doctrine, the GSS asked Catholics (but not members of other religious groups) to react to this statement: "We are interested in what American Catholics think about religious matters. Please select the answer that comes closest to your own personal opinion about the following statement: Under certain conditions, the Pope is infallible when he speaks on matters of faith and morals." I compare white and Latino Catholic responses using all possible responses: "this is certainly true," "this is probably true," "I am uncertain whether this is true or false," "this is probably false," or "this is certainly false."

Responses to this GSS question show that white and Latino Catholics have similar views of papal infallibility, but large percentages of both groups have serious doubts about this teaching. Figure 6.4 shows that about 14% of white Catholics and about 17% of Latino Catholics are certain of the Pope's infallibility, and an additional 25% of white Catholics and about 27% of Latino Catholics say that the Pope is probably infallible. Together, this means that about 39% of white Catholics and about 44% of Latino Catholics are certain or fairly certain about this important Church doctrine. These are relatively high portions of each group; but, as the figure shows, large percentages of Catholics have doubts about this issue. Indeed, 25% of white Catholics and nearly 28% of Latino Catholics say they are uncertain about whether the Pope is infallible;

and nearly 20% of white Catholics and about 11% of Latino Catholics think that infallibility is probably or certainly false.

Feelings About the Bible

Given the Bible's centrality to Catholicism and other forms of Christianity, beliefs about the Bible—and how to best interpret and use it—are critical to understanding Americans. Figure 6.5 compares Catholics to other Americans using three responses to the GSS question: "Which of these statements comes closest to describing your feelings about the Bible?" I compare Catholics to each other and to other Americans on these possible answers: (1) "The Bible is the actual word of God and is to be taken literally, word for word"; (2) "The Bible is the inspired word of God but not everything in it should be taken literally, word for word"; and (3) "The Bible is an ancient book of fables, legends, history, and moral precepts recorded by men."

Relatively few white and Latino Catholics consider the Bible simply an ancient book, but they differ somewhat in whether they lean toward interpreting the Bible as the literal or inspired word of God. Arguably, the question and response options are poorly constructed: after all, the Bible is intended to be read in various ways. It is part ancient stories with moral precepts, part history, part poetry, and so on. Asking a respondent to decide among the options offered by the GSS forces them to omit options they might think are also true. I include this question because it offers insight into how respondents answer when they are forced to decide among these well-known options.

As Figure 6.5 shows, nearly equal percentages of white (about 19%) and Latino (about 17%) Catholics say that the Bible is an ancient book of fables, legends, history, and moral precepts. Both white (64% and 17%) and Latino (56% and 28%) Catholics are more likely to say the Bible should be interpreted as the inspired rather than the literal word of God. However, as those percentages suggest, Latino Catholics are more split on this issue than are white Catholics (Box 6.1).

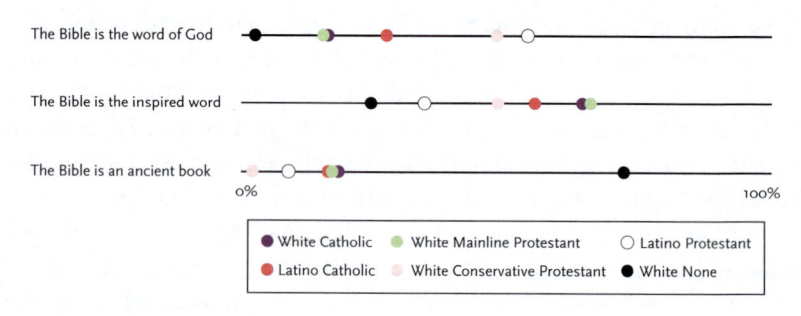

Figure 6.5 The Bible

Box 6.1 FORMER CATHOLICS: WHITE LEAVERS ARE MORE LIBERAL THAN LATINO LEAVERS

Compared to Latino former Catholics, white former Catholics are more liberal in their religious and related political and social beliefs. White GSS respondents who left the Catholic Church and joined other faith groups tended to join mainline Protestant churches; Latino respondents who left the Church tended to join conservative Protestant churches (Chapter 5). These differences are also reflected in the religious beliefs and related attitudes of the leavers. Beliefs about the Bible are a good example of this difference: white former Catholics who are now members of other faith groups tend to interpret the Bible as the inspired—rather than literal—word of God. By contrast, Latino former Catholics who are now members of other faith groups tend to interpret the Bible as the literal word of God. Not surprisingly, those who left the Church and became religious nones report similar views to other religious nones, including limited identification with religion, almost no attendance at religious services, and otherwise low levels of engagement with religion.

The figure also shows that nearly identical percentages of white Catholics and mainline Protestants view the Bible as the literal or inspired word of God. More Latino Protestants (54%) than any other group interpret the Bible literally, with white conservative Protestants (about 48%) following close behind. I included religious nones in this figure as a robustness check, and indeed, almost none (about 3%) of them view the Bible as the literal word of God and most (72%) consider it simply an ancient book. The fairly sizable group of religious nones (25%) who view the Bible as the inspired word of God overlap significantly (results not shown) with those who consider themselves religious despite not affiliating with a particular church.

RELIGION, POLITICS, AND SCIENCE

Religion has clear and significant implications for attitudes regarding politics, social issues, and science (Perry 2022; Sherkat 2017, 2021; Tope et al. 2017). Questions about the politics of Catholics have intrigued scholars and the popular media for decades, at least in part because it is challenging to categorize this large group that includes the U.S. President, prominent members of the Supreme Court and Congress, and some of the poorest Americans (D'Antonio et al. 2007; Greeley 1977; Orcés 2022; Smith 2020; Stark 2008). Catholic doctrine has also become part of public conversation and affected discussions of

R agrees or strongly agrees:

The government should not require reading Bible in public schools

Philosophy and science are best sources of truth, wisdom, and ethics

To understand the world, we must free our minds from old traditions and beliefs

R relies on reason and evidence to make decisions

All of the greatest advances for humanity come from science and technology

The success of the U.S. is part of God's plan

The federal government should advocate Christian values

The U.S. would be a better country if religion had less influence

0% 100%

● White Catholic   ● White Mainline Protestant   ○ Latino Protestant
● Latino Catholic   ○ White Conservative Protestant ● White None

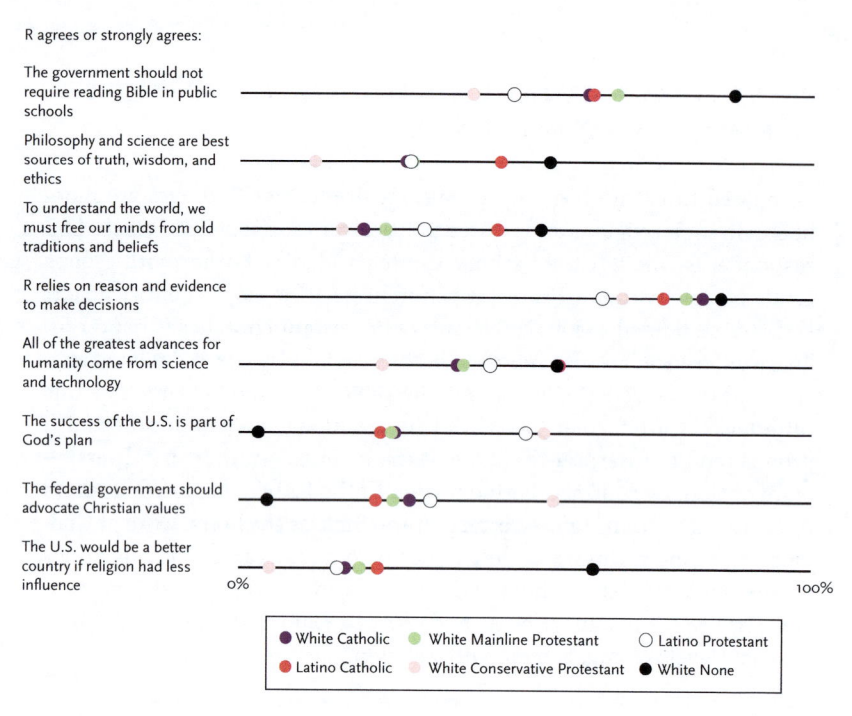

Figure 6.6 Religion, politics, and science

the role of religion in political life from time to time when Church teaching and doctrine intersect with critical political issues (Kaplan 2022; McCammon 2021; National Catholic Reporter 2021).

I explore attitudes about other issues that are political in Chapter 7, but I include a brief preliminary discussion here focusing on political, social, and scientific issues that have direct connections to religious beliefs. Figure 6.6 compares Catholics' and other Americans' responses to eight GSS questions. The first question asked respondents whether they approved of a Supreme Court ruling: "The United States Supreme Court has ruled that no state or local government may require the reading of the Lord's Prayer or Bible verses in public schools. What are your views on this—do you approve or disapprove of the court ruling?"

The figure shows the percentage of each group that approves (vs. not approving).

Subsequent questions ask respondents whether they agree with statements about the sources of wisdom, truth, ethics, and understanding and the role of religion in government and politics. The statements include:

"The great works of philosophy and science are the best source of truth, wisdom, and ethics."

[140] *Catholics in America*

"To understand the world, we must free our minds from old traditions and beliefs."

"When I make important decisions in my life, I rely mostly on reason and evidence."

"All of the greatest advances for humanity have come from science and technology."

"The success of the United States is part of God's plan."

"The federal government should advocate Christian values."

"The U.S. would be a better country if religion had less influence."

The figure shows the percentage of each group that agrees or strongly agrees (vs. neither agrees nor disagrees, disagrees, or strongly disagrees).

The broad pattern that emerges in this figure is that the attitudes of white and Latino Catholics and white mainline Protestants are largely similar and fairly moderate on these issues. However, the attitudes of religious nones, white conservative Protestants, and (to a lesser extent) Latino Protestants stand out from the other groups and are located closer to the poles on most of these topics. This pattern is largely consistent with evidence that polarization of attitudes regarding key political and social issues is not ubiquitous, and public discussion about polarization have been exaggerated to some extent (Gorski and Perry 2022). Indeed, Americans are becoming more liberal as a whole and, more importantly, are converging on many important moral and social issues (Baldassarri and Park 2020)

More specifically, the figure shows that on the first issue—reading the Bible in schools—similar percentages of white Catholics, Latino Catholics, and mainline Protestants (roughly 61%, 61%, and 65%, respectively) say that the government should not require reading the Bible in public schools. By contrast, nearly 86% of religious nones agree with this statement, and relatively few white conservative Protestants and Latino Protestants agree (roughly 40% and 48%, respectively).

There are similar patterns for the second two issues, although Latino Catholics change their positions: similar percentages of white Catholics, white mainline Protestants, and Latino Protestants indicate the importance of philosophy and science and the need to free our minds from old beliefs. Furthermore, Latino Catholics and religious nones have similarly high levels of agreement on these issues. By contrast, few white conservative Protestants agree with these statements.

The statement about using reason and evidence—designed to target the role of logic in an individual's thinking—is unique among the questions shown in this figure because, first, it asks respondents to reflect on their behavior rather than attitudes. Second, it asks respondents to evaluate the desirability of using scientific forms of reasoning to guide their actions. Third, nearly all respondents agree with the statement, perhaps because it is clear that logical thinking is a desirable trait. Of course, responses to this question say little about whether respondents use only logic in their decision-making; their decision-making might draw on other strategies, such as prayer, perhaps in conjunction with scientific logic.

The final four issues—regarding the role of science and technology in great advances and the role of God and religion in U.S. politics—highlight the broad patterns I mentioned above. On each of these issues, relatively small but similar percentages of white Catholics, Latino Catholics, and white mainline Protestants agree with each statement. Religious nones and white conservative Protestants are closer to the poles on these issues. Religious nones are more likely than the other groups to respond favorably to the question about the importance of science and technology and less likely to respond favorably about the role of God and religion in the United States. By contrast, relatively few white conservative Protestants agree with the question about the importance of science and technology. Particularly large percentages of white conservative Protestant respondents favor a more central role for God and religion in the United States, consistent with a large and growing academic literature on Christian nationalism, the idea that the United States should be a Christian nation (Gorski and Perry 2022; Perry et al. 2022; Perry, Davis, and Grubbs 2023; Perry, Schnabel, and Grubbs 2022).

Sex, Divorce, and Pornography

The Catholic Church and most other Christian churches have clear teachings about sexual morality, and the attitudes of adherents to each of the major U.S. faith groups also vary regarding these issues, as Figure 6.7 documents. The figure compares attitudes regarding nine issues related to sex and sexual morality from the following GSS questions: (1) Would you be for or against sex education in the public schools? (2) Should divorce in this country be easier or more difficult to obtain than it is now? (3) Is it wrong for a man and woman to have sexual relations before marriage? (4) What if they (i.e., the man and woman from question 3) are in their early teens, say 14 to 16 years old? (5) What is your opinion about a married person having sexual relations with someone other than the marriage partner? (6) Are sexual relations between two adults of the same sex wrong? (7) Should same-sex couples have the right to marry one another? (8) Should methods of birth control be available to teenagers between the ages of 14 and 16 if their parents do not approve? (9) What are your feelings about pornography laws?

On three of the sexual morality topics, there is considerable agreement across faith groups, including Catholics. More than 90% of white and Latino Catholics, white mainline Protestants, and Latino Protestants indicate that sex education in public schools is okay. Consistent with other attitudes, and

R is in favor of sex education in public schools		
Divorce should be easier to obtain		
Sex before marriage is not wrong		
Teenagers having sex is not wrong		
Extramarital sex is not wrong		
Same-sex sex is not wrong		
Homosexual couples should have the right to marry		
Birth control should be available to teenagers		
There should be laws against the distribution of pornography		

Legend: ● White Catholic ● White Mainline Protestant ○ Latino Protestant ● Latino Catholic ● White Conservative Protestant ● White None

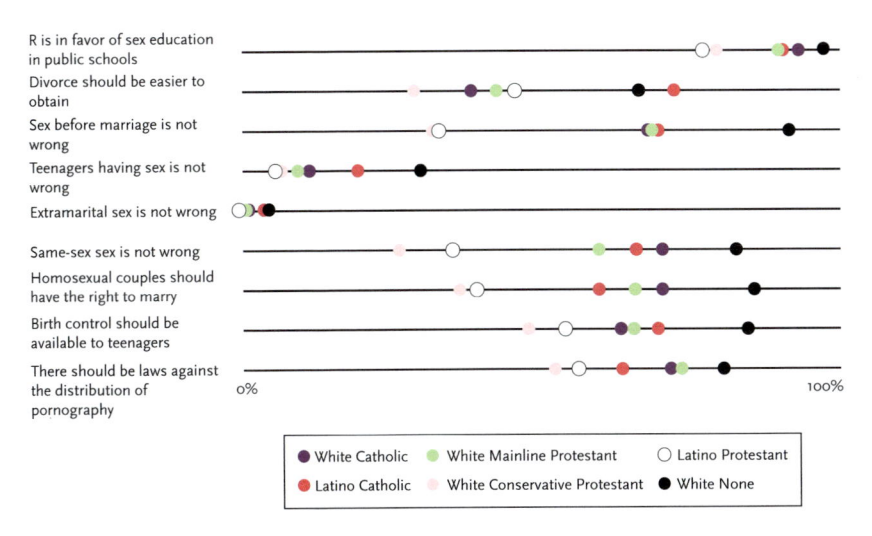

Figure 6.7 Sex, divorce, and pornography

conservative Protestants have the lowest at 80%. Very few respondents (fewer than 20%) think it is okay for young teenagers to have sex; again, religious nones (31%) are most likely to agree that teen sex is okay, and white conservative Protestants (8%) are most likely to disagree. On the issue of teen sex, Latino Protestants (7%) are more similar to white conservative Protestants than to the other religious groups. On the issue of extramarital sex, nearly all respondents (fewer than 5%) disapprove, with religious nones (about 6%) being most likely to approve.

On five sexual morality topics, the pattern was similar to that seen regarding many political attitudes (Figure 6.6): the attitudes of white Catholics, Latino Catholics, and white mainline Protestant are similar to each other and fairly moderate politically; white conservative Protestants tend to have relatively conservative attitudes; and religious nones have relatively progressive attitudes. The issues are sex before marriage for adults, sex between same-sex adults, same-sex marriage, birth control availability for teenagers, and legal regulation of pornography. Sex and marriage among same-sex couples generate the most polarization: 27% of white conservative Protestants but 83% of religious nones think sex among same-sex couples is wrong; 38% of white conservative Protestants but 86% of religious nones think same-sex marriage should be allowed. Attitudes about the legal regulation of pornography are also polarized, but this is the least divisive of the five highly polarized sexual morality topics.

Divorce laws generated a different ranking of the faith groups than did the other sexual morality issues. Arguably, divorce is not an issue of sexual morality, but it is certainly related, and the Catholic Church's teachings about divorce and sex are intertwined. For example, the Catholic Church "maintains that a new union cannot be recognized as valid [after a divorce] if the first marriage was [valid]" (Catechism of the Catholic Church, 1650). The Church also prohibits all sex outside of legal marriage, including for divorced Catholics (Catechism of the Catholic Church, 2335 and 2353). Similarly, Catholics who divorced and remarried civilly but have not been granted a declaration of nullity of their previous sacramental marriage are welcome to receive Holy Communion only if they abstain from sex. The Church encourages divorced Catholics who have civilly remarried to seek an annulment so that they can be free to obtain a sacramental marriage.

The issues of divorce and sex are divisive for Catholics, as popular writing (Hahn 2001; Rowland 2017), academic research (Ellison et al. 2013; Konieczny 2013), and the patterns in Figure 6.7 illustrate. Roughly 40% of white Catholics and more than 73% of Latino Catholics think divorce should be easier to obtain. Of course, that means that 60% of white Catholics and nearly 30% of Latino Catholics favor divorce laws that are at least as restrictive—or more restrictive—than they are currently. The difference between white and Latino Catholics on divorce is notable given the high levels of agreement between these groups on other issues, including other sexual morality issues. Additional analyses (not shown) indicate that young Catholics, particularly young Latino Catholics, are more likely than older Catholics to favor easier divorce rates. Differences in attitudes regarding divorce are consistent with patterns shown in Figure 3.4 (Chapter 3): Latino Catholics are less likely than white Catholics to divorce, but the differences are largely generational, with divorce rates being higher for younger rather than older Catholics. Another related pattern that further demonstrates the complexity of this issue for Catholics is who leaves the Church. As Chapter 5 showed, young people are more likely than older people to exit the Church, and Latino Catholics are less likely than white Catholics to exit. As a result, more older, never-divorced Latinos remain in the Church and may push attitudes about divorce toward the conservative end of the continuum.

Other differences among the religious-ethnic groups in attitudes regarding divorce laws are more consistent with patterns that have emerged in this book. For example, white Catholic attitudes regarding divorce laws are similar to those of white mainline Protestants, consistent with convergence in divorce rates (Chapter 3) and SES (Chapter 4) for these groups. Consistent with their tendency to hold more traditional views on social issues (Ellison et al. 2011, 2013), Latino Protestants are less likely than Latino Catholics to favor easier divorce. Perhaps least surprising, white conservative Protestants are more likely than any other group to oppose easier divorce rates (despite their own relatively high divorce rates shown in Chapter 3), and religious nones are highly likely to favor easier divorce rates. Although I do not show the details here, these groups also differ in religious strength, consistent with prior research showing that belief that the Bible is the word of God and religious

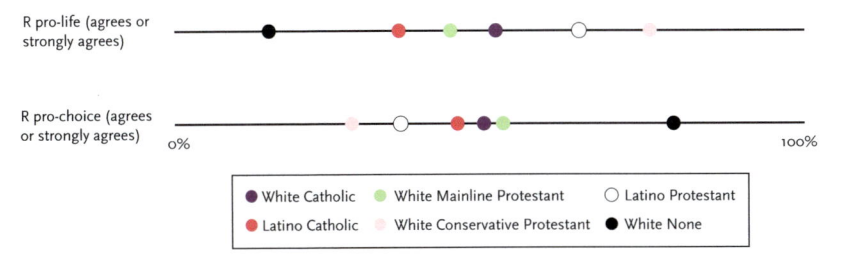

Figure 6.8 Abortion

attendance are associated with favoring more restrictive divorce laws (Stokes and Ellison 2010).

ABORTION

Attitudes regarding abortion—and the role of churches and other religious groups in advocating for various viewpoints—have attracted so much attention in the popular press, academic writing, and policy circles that the topic needs little introduction. It is also no secret that the Catholic Church stands in strong opposition to abortion. Yet the views of Catholics—like those of other Americans—are complex. Even Pope Francis has cautioned against American Catholics who have "a very strong, organized, reactionary attitude" and focus exclusively on issues such as abortion and neglect other issues such as care for the poor (Horowitz and Graham August 30, 2023).

The fairly simple and commonly accepted *pro-life* and *pro-choice* labels that individuals use to identify their beliefs regarding abortion are clearly an important first step in understanding views on this important issue. Yet views regarding abortion are more nuanced than these simple labels suggest. An individual's personal traits (i.e., age, ethnicity, religion, marital status, SES) affect their views and the labels they use to describe those views. In addition, contextual issues about abortion matter: the factors that led to the pregnancy, including whether it was a rape and the woman's financial situation, are important. Similarly, the mother's health, the baby's health, and the relationship between the parents can affect attitudes (Bruce 2020; Jozkowski, Crawford, and Hunt 2018) (Box 6.2).

Many Catholics—particularly white Catholics—consider themselves pro-life, but the percentages are not overwhelming, particularly given the Church's strong pro-life stance. Indeed, surprisingly high percentages of Catholics consider themselves pro-choice. Figure 6.8 shows the percentage of GSS respondents who respond "strongly agree" or "agree" with the statements "I consider myself pro-life" or "I consider myself pro-choice." Other options were "neither agree nor disagree," "disagree," or "strongly disagree."

> **Box 6.2 FORMER CATHOLICS: PRO-CHOICE CATHOLICS LEAVE THE CHURCH**
>
> Both white and Latino Catholics who left the Church are more strongly pro-choice (and less strongly pro-life) than current Catholics, but the differences are starker for white Catholics.
>
> For white Catholics, leavers clearly lean pro-choice: 51% of current white Catholics (Figure 6.8) are pro-life and 49% are pro-choice (agree or strongly agree that they are pro-life). By contrast, only 31% of white Catholics who left the Church are pro-life, whereas 73% are pro-choice (not shown in a figure).
>
> The differences are less dramatic for Latino Catholics given that they are more pro-choice overall: 36% of current Latino Catholics are pro-life and 45% are pro-choice; yet 46% of Latinos who left the Church are pro-choice and 61% are pro-choice.

The patterns I discuss below are similar across the various outcomes; I display only one outcome in the figure for brevity. The percentages do not necessarily add to 100% because the pro-life and pro-choice questions were asked separately and were not mutually exclusive. Rather, each question included multiple response categories to allow for nuanced answers that reflect the complexity of this issue, and respondents were able to indicate that they were some degree of pro-life and some degree of pro-choice. I measure the degree to which respondents gave complex answers using a complexity score below.

White Catholics are split nearly evenly on abortion: about 51% of white Catholics agree or agree strongly that they are pro-life, and about 49% agree or agree strongly they are pro-choice. Fewer Latino Catholics than white Catholics identify as pro-life: about 36% of Latino Catholics agree or agree strongly that they are pro-life, and about 45% agree or agree strongly that they are pro-choice. Young Catholics—both white and Latino—are more likely than older Catholics to be pro-choice (analyses not shown), suggesting that the attitudes of Church members may be changing and moving farther from official teaching in the future.

The ordering of religious groups by pro-life and pro-choice identification is similar to patterns on various issues shown in this chapter: white Catholics, Latino Catholics, and white mainline Protestants are somewhat similar to each other and fairly moderate in their attitudes; white conservative Protestants and Latino Protestants are comparatively conservative; and religious nones are comparatively liberal. This largely reflects the percentages of white conservative Protestants (28%) and Latino Protestants (36%) who agree or strongly agree that they are pro-choice.

Although the pro-life and pro-choice labels provide useful information about self-identification, they fail to capture the array of attitudes that individuals hold about an issue as complicated as abortion. A complexity score is designed to capture more detail about how individuals think about an issue and how they factor in various issues in arriving at their self-identification. In the case of abortion, a complexity score can efficiently summarize an individual's views about the contextual factors that surround and led to the pregnancy. Figure 6.9 illustrates variation in an abortion complexity score, following previous research (Jozkowski, Crawford, and Willis 2021) on Americans' complex views about abortion (details in Appendix).

To create this complexity score, I draw on responses to GSS questions about the conditions under which "It should be possible for a pregnant woman to obtain a legal abortion," with the following seven scenarios presented: a strong chance of serious defect in the baby, the woman is married and does not want more children, the woman's own health is seriously endangered by the pregnancy, the family has a very low income and cannot afford any more children, the woman became pregnant as the result of a rape, the woman wants an abortion for any reason.

The complexity score will equal 0 for an individual who is least complex or conflicted and who answered all questions as anti-abortion or pro-abortion. The score will equal 3 for an individual who was most complex or conflicted

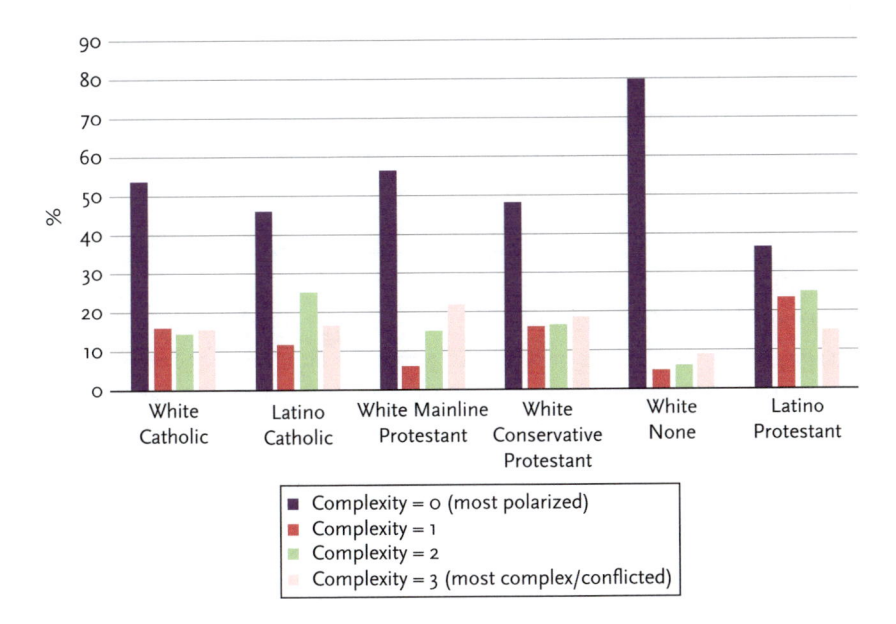

Figure 6.9 Abortion complexity

and who answered half of the questions as anti-abortion and half as pro-abortion. Scores of 1 or 2 indicate that an individual's complexity falls between these extremes. Figure 6.9 shows the percentage of each group with a complexity score of 0–3.

Consistent with American's strong views on abortion and differences in self-identification as pro-life or pro-choice, most GSS respondents had low complexity in their views on abortion. Indeed, about one-half of white Catholics (54%), Latino Catholics (46%), white mainline Protestants (56%), and white conservative Protestants (48%) had a complexity score of 0. Recall that 0 indicates that they gave either all pro-choice or all-pro-life responses to the questions about the conditions under which abortion should be legal. Of course, that means that the other half of each group responded in much more complex ways. Additional analyses (not shown) indicate that all four groups were likely to support abortion under most conditions, with lower percentages agreeing that abortion should be legal for a woman who wanted to end a pregnancy because she simply wants no more children or cannot afford to have another child. Across the conditions, few white conservative Protestants supported abortion rights, but the resulting complexity score was still 0 for nearly half (48%) of white conservative Protestants.

Religious nones had the least complex views: 80% of religious nones scored 0 on abortion complexity. Not surprisingly, large majorities of religious nones reported highly pro-choice views. For example, additional analyses (not shown) indicated that large percentages of religious nones said that abortion should be legal if the baby has a birth defect (95%), the mother's health is in danger (98%), and the pregnancy resulted from rape (98%). Compared to the other groups included in Figure 6.9, high percentages of religious nones (79% for each condition) also support abortion if the mother wants no more children or cannot afford another child.

Latino Protestants are the most difficult to summarize succinctly and are probably best described as moderate in their abortion views. Their abortion views are certainly complex, but their complexity scores vary more than the other groups. Compared to the other groups included in Figure 6.9, relatively few Latino Protestants (37%) scored 0 (i.e., entirely pro-life or pro-choice). Yet relatively few Latino Protestants (15%) scored 3, indicating that their answers were more or less evenly split across the conditions included in the survey. Latino Protestants are clearly unique in having fairly moderate abortion views.

CONCLUSION

In this chapter, I discussed how religious beliefs and practices vary among Catholics and how they compare to official Church doctrine. I also explored similarities and differences in the religious beliefs and practices of Catholics and members of other faith groups. I documented differences in strength of religious beliefs; religious service attendance, prayer, and meditation; religious experiences and evangelization; beliefs about God, the afterlife, and the Pope; and feelings about the Bible. I also showed how Catholics and others view the role of religion in broader political and social issues, such as prayer in public schools, the role of Christian values in U.S. politics, and abortion.

On most of the topics I studied, I found considerable similarity between white and Latino Catholics despite marked differences between these groups in social origins, family status, and SES (shown in previous chapters). This suggests that membership in the same faith with clear doctrinal teachings supersedes demographic differences. White and Latino Catholics report similar levels of religious strength. They also report similar patterns of Mass attendance, prayer, and meditation, although low percentages of each group report engaging in these religious practices. Despite the centrality of evangelization to Catholicism, few Catholics—white or Latino—report ever trying to convert someone to the faith. White and Latino Catholics are nearly identical to each other in their belief in an afterlife and papal infallibility, although large and comparable percentages of both groups report similar views on this teaching.

I also found similarity between white and Latino Catholics on topics related to religion, politics, and science. Indeed, Catholics' views on these issues were remarkably similar with just three exceptions: Latino Catholics were more likely than white Catholics to agree with statements about the centrality of philosophy and science to knowledge (i.e., philosophy and science are best sources of truth, wisdom, and ethics; we must free our minds from old traditions and beliefs; and all of the greatest advances for humanity come from science and technology).

Similarly, white and Latino Catholics had fairly similar views regarding abortion. In particular, I found that large percentages of Catholics—particularly white Catholics—consider themselves pro-life, but the percentages are not overwhelming given the Church's strong pro-life stance. Indeed, my findings showed that notably high percentages of Catholics consider themselves pro-choice.

Of course, the religious beliefs and practices of white and Latino Catholics differ in some notable ways. For example, relatively few Catholics reported having had a born-again or other life-changing religious experience, but Latino Catholics were significantly more likely than white Catholics to have had such an experience. By contrast, a majority of both white and Latino Catholics reported that they have no doubts about the existence of God; however, the percentage of those who are doubt-free is significantly higher for Latino than white Catholics. There were differences among Catholics in Bible interpretation as well: less than 20% of either group said that the Bible is an ancient book of fables, legends, history, and moral precepts; and both groups were more inclined to interpret the Bible as the inspired (rather than literal) word of God. However, Latino Catholics are more split on this issue than were white Catholics. Finally, there were important differences in the views of white and Latino Catholics regarding whether divorce should be easier in the United States. Latino Catholics were much more likely than white Catholics to prefer easier divorce, consistent with higher Latino divorce rates (shown in Chapter 3).

It is important to note that the GSS data do not include much information about issues that are particular to Catholics, and other research shows that white and Latino Catholics differ on some religious beliefs and practices that are unique to Catholicism. For example, Latino Catholics attribute greater importance to devotion to Mary the Mother of God, attending Mass once a week, participating in devotions such as Eucharistic adoration and praying the rosary, and going to private confession to a priest (D'Antonio et al. 2013; Day et al. Forthcoming).

Next, I compared Catholics to members of other faith traditions and found a fairly consistent rank order of the groups across the topics I explored. Most Americans—across religion and racial/ethnic categories—agree on the issues I explored in this chapter. Of course, I found exceptions, but a clear pattern emerged: white and Latino Catholic attitudes are largely similar to each other and to those of white mainline Protestants. By contrast, the attitudes of religious nones, white conservative Protestants, and (on most issues) Latino Protestants are located closer to the poles on most of these topics, with religious nones leaning to the liberal end and Latino Protestants leaning to the conservative end. This pattern was clear on most measures of religious strength; religious service attendance, prayer, and meditation; evangelization and religious experiences; belief in God and the afterlife; Bible interpretation; religion, politics, and science; many aspects of sexual morality; abortion; and assisted suicide.

Some aspects of sexual morality and divorce laws were issues on which the otherwise-consistent rank order changed. On three sexual morality topics, there was agreement across all faith groups: most agreed that teaching about sex in public schools is okay but that young teenagers having sex and extramarital sex are unacceptable.

Divorce laws generated different rankings of the faith groups than most of the other issues I studied. White Catholics are less likely than Latino Catholics to think that divorce should be easier to obtain, and Latino Catholics are more likely than all other groups, including the otherwise very progressive religious nones, to favor easier divorce laws despite their relatively low divorce rates. Other differences among the religious and racial/ethnic groups in attitudes regarding divorce laws are more consistent with other patterns that have emerged in this book. White Catholic attitudes regarding divorce laws are similar to those of white mainline Protestants, consistent with convergence in divorce rates for these groups. Consistent with their tendency to hold more traditional views on social issues (Ellison et al. 2011, 2013), Latino Protestants are less likely than Latino Catholics to favor easier divorce. Perhaps least surprising, from a conservative standpoint, white conservative Protestants are more likely than any other group to oppose easier divorce laws.

NOTE

1. Ethnicity and race are, perhaps, counterexamples given that individuals can change ethnic/racial identity over time.

CHAPTER 7
Politics

Catholics do not fit neatly into liberal or conservative boxes. White and Latino Catholics differ from each other in their views on many political issues, in contrast to their similarities in religious beliefs and practices (Chapter 6) and attitudes regarding social issues (Chapter 8). By contrast, there are clear similarities in the political views of white Catholics and white mainline Protestants.

The political gulf that exists between public figures such as liberal President Joe Biden and conservative Supreme Court Justice Amy Coney Barrett highlights the variety of political stances of Catholics today and illustrates why Catholic politics are not obviously categorized as left, right, or moderate. Classifying Catholics' politics is not just an issue with prominent Catholics. Although registered Catholic voters have been split somewhat evenly between the Democratic and Republican parties in recent years, their political leanings have changed even over short, recent time periods (Smith 2020). It is also difficult to identify the modal Catholic political attitude because Catholics have swung back and forth between political parties in presidential and other major elections for decades (Dionne Jr. 2000; Manza and Brooks 1997; Stine 2020).

Demographic changes among Catholics further complicate efforts to classify this large group. Some assume that there is a single Catholic political stance, in a way that they would not assume Protestants all agree on political issues. In reality, white and Latino Catholics may be particularly different politically and may have different attitudes toward many issues that follow from their demographic differences. Their political leanings may also be moving away from each other, particularly if white Catholics are becoming more conservative (Smith 2020). Yet even this movement cannot be taken for granted given rapid Latino population growth, changes in how young Catholics perceive and engage with politics (Gaunt 2022), the unique attitudes of Latino

Catholics of all ages and Latinos of all faiths (Ellison, Wolfinger, and Ramos-Wada 2013; Ramos, Woodberry, and Ellison 2017), and the clear movement of some Latinos toward the Republican Party, including in key swing states (Krogstad and Noe-Bustamante 2021; Sanchez October 15, 2022).

This chapter is divided into two parts. In the first part, I explore Catholics' political ideologies, that is the interrelated values and attitudes that individuals hold regarding how individuals and societies should function (Farmer, Kidwell, and Hardesty 2020). I document differences in self-assessed political party affiliation (i.e., Democrat, Republican, Independent) and political views (i.e., liberal, conservative, moderate) to address how individuals define themselves politically. However, self-assessed political identification does not necessarily reflect the broad set of politically related attitudes and ideas that individuals hold. Indeed, party affiliation and terms such as "liberal" and "conservative" are—at their heart—shorthand used to gauge views about how individuals and societies should behave. Thus, to get a better sense of how Catholics think individuals and society should function, I document their views on several specific issues that are part of public discussion in the contemporary United States, including taxes, government spending, gun laws, gun ownership, and the legalization of marijuana.

In the second part of the chapter, I study charitable giving to better understand the issues that are important to Catholics and the degree to which they invest their personal resources in charitable causes. Although charitable giving is not necessarily political or motivated by political interests, it says a great deal about what individuals value and the degree to which they are committed to certain causes because it requires making choices among many alternatives and identifying personal priorities. Charitable giving also speaks to whether individual values and priorities align with those of their faith groups. For example, the Catholic Church relies on members to support its churches and schools; it also prioritizes causes such as care for the poor. Thus, giving to religious causes and organizations that aim to alleviate poverty indicate whether Catholics' values are consistent with Church priorities.

As I did in the preceding chapter, I make three comparisons. First, I compare the political attitudes and chartable giving of white and Latino Catholics to clarify whether there are differences among Catholics in their political identities, attitudes about political issues, or giving behavior. Second, I make brief, contextual comparisons of Catholic attitudes to official Church teaching where possible. Given that the General Social Survey (GSS) does not include questions about political issues that target Catholics, I am unable to thoroughly assess issues that are uniquely Catholic. Moreover, although Church leaders frequently express opinions on the issues I study, official teaching on most of the topics I study is limited or does not exist. Thus, I make only a small number of references in this chapter to the alignment between the views of ordinary Catholics and Church doctrine. However, my data allow me to make comparisons between Catholics and other Americans on a host of political topics. For that, the third comparison I make in this chapter is between Catholics and members of other faith traditions in order to situate Church members in the contemporary American religious landscape.

I group the topics covered here under broad political labels, but I do so knowing that there are not always clear distinctions between the topics I study in this chapter and those I reserve for Chapter 8 (social issues). I also acknowledge that I am omitting issues and topics that are relevant to understanding Catholics, but that is unavoidable given the physical constraints of a single book.

POLITICAL IDEOLOGIES

Democrat, Republican, or Independent?

Catholics' political views are spread fairly evenly overall across the major political parties, but this masks differences between white and Latino Catholics. More specifically, white Catholic political identities are split between the Democratic and Republican Parties, with a slight lean to the right (Figure 7.1): about 36% of white Catholics considered themselves Democrats or

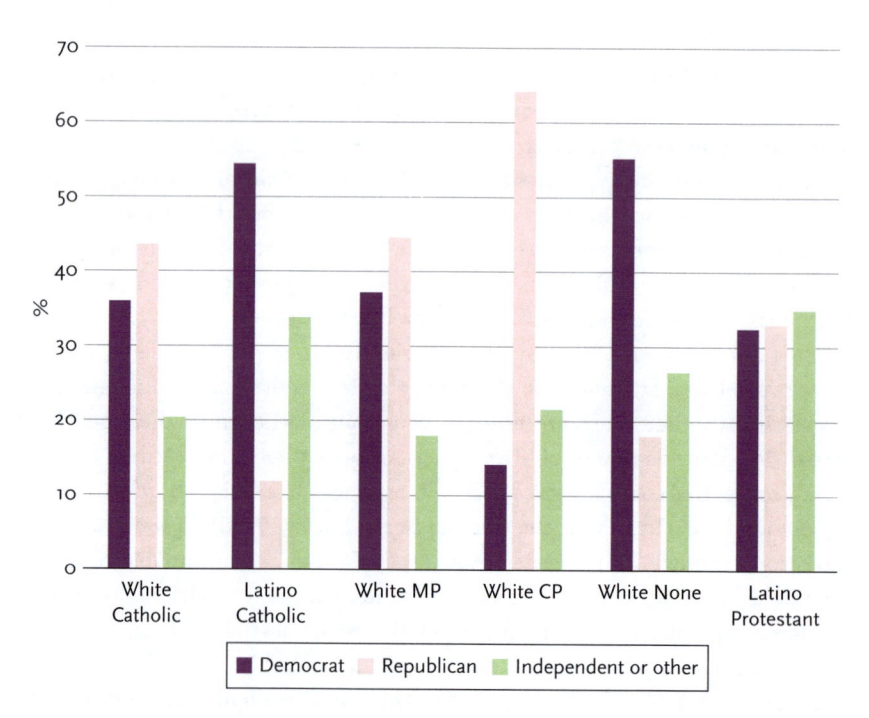

Figure 7.1 Political party identification

[154] *Catholics in America*

leaned toward the Democratic Party in 2021, and about 44% of them considered themselves Republicans or leaned toward the Republican Party.

The patterns shown in Figure 7.1 mark a change from the 1970s, when Greeley showed that 57–72% of Catholics were Democrats or leaned toward the Democratic Party (1977: 204). However, these percentages have changed slightly in the past 20 years: in 2002, 41% of white Catholics considered themselves Democrats or leaned toward the Democratic Party, and about 41% of them considered themselves Republicans or leaned toward the Republican Party (author's estimates from the GSS, not shown in a figure). Moreover, there was little change in these percentages in the intervening years in the political identities of white Catholics. These percentages are somewhat different from those found in other data (Smith 2020), possibly because other surveys ask about party registration whereas the GSS asks "Do you usually think of yourself as a Republican, Democrat, Independent, or what?" I sum responses across multiple categories: I combine "strong," "not very strong," and "independent close to Democrat" to create a single category called "Democrat." I do the same for Republican responses. However, coding the data in other ways does not affect the patterns I report, suggesting that question wording is largely responsible for differences across data sources.

In contrast to white Catholics, Latino Catholics lean heavily to the left. Political identification differences between white and Latino Catholics are among the more pronounced differences shown in Figure 7.1: compared to white Catholics (36%), Latino Catholics (54%) were much more likely to consider themselves Democrats or leaned toward the Democratic Party in 2021. By contrast, only about 12% of Latino Catholics (compared to 44% of white Catholics) considered themselves Republicans or leaned toward the Republican Party in that year. Moreover, unlike with white Catholics, there has been some change in the political party identification of Latino Catholics in the past 20 years. Indeed, since 2002, fewer Latino Catholics think of themselves as Republicans and more consider themselves Independents or members of some other political party: in 2002, 54% of Latino Catholics were Democrats or leaned Democrat, 21% were Republicans or leaned Republican, and 24% were independents or members of some other party. Most of this change has occurred since 2012, when 48% of Latino Catholics were Democrats or leaned Democrat, 22% were Republicans or leaned Republican, and 30% were Independents or members of some other party. If the growth of the Latino Catholic population continues, these patterns suggest that the Church will include increasingly large numbers of Democrats (Box 7.1).

The party identifications of white Catholics and white mainline Protestant are strikingly similar. That is, white mainline Protestants' political identities were also relatively evenly split between the two major parties, with a

> **Box 7.1 FORMER CATHOLICS: DEMOCRATS LEAVE, REPUBLICANS STAY**
>
> Former Catholics are more likely than current Catholics to be Democrats and politically liberal, but only if they are white. Whereas about 36% of current white Catholics are Democrats or lean toward the Democratic Party, about 53% of former Catholics are Democrats or lean toward the Democratic Party (analyses not shown in a figure). By contrast, about 44% of current white Catholics are Republicans or lean toward the Republican Party, and only about 13% of former Catholics are Republicans or lean Republican. Similar patterns are true for self-identified political views: liberal white Catholics leave, conservatives stay.
>
> By contrast, there is no difference in party affiliation or self-identified political views for Latino Catholics. I showed in Chapter 5 that those who left the Catholic Church are more likely to be white than Latino. Thus, sample sizes for Latino former Catholics are small. However, patterns are clear in these small samples: the political identities of Latino leavers are nearly identical to the political identities of current Latino Catholics.

slight slant to the right: about 37% of white mainline Protestants considered themselves Democrats or leaned toward the Democratic Party in 2021, and about 45% of them considered themselves Republicans or leaned toward the Republican Party. Figure 7.1 also shows that about 20% of both white Catholics and white mainline Protestants consider themselves Independents or members of some other political party. White mainline Protestant party identifications have also changed little over time: in 2002, about 38% of white mainline Protestants were Democrats or leaned toward the Democratic Party, and about 47% were Republicans or leaned Republican. However, this change in identity was fairly recent (occurring almost entirely since 2012) and largely a movement from the Republican Party to being an Independent rather than change between the two major political parties.

Political polarization is also clear in Figure 7.1. In 2021, white conservative Protestants leaned heavily toward the Republican Party, and religious nones leaned heavily toward the Democratic Party. Moreover, consistent with evidence of increasing political polarization, these differences have grown over time. More than 64% of white conservative Protestants were Republicans or leaned Republican in 2021 (Figure 7.1), an increase from 58% in 2002 and 53% in 2012 (author's estimates, not shown). By contrast, 55% of religious nones were Democrats or leaned Democratic in 2021, an increase from 21% in 2002 and 20% in 2012.

Liberal, Conservative, or Moderate?

Political views—self-identification as liberal, conservative, or moderate—are closely related to party affiliation and provide additional information about individuals' political ideologies. In addition to asking about political party identification, the GSS also asks respondents to place themselves on a seven-point political views scale ranging from extremely liberal to extremely conservative.

For white Catholics, white mainline Protestants, and white conservative Protestants, self-identified political views (author's estimates, not shown in a figure) follow patterns that are nearly identical to party identification patterns shown in Figure 7.1. Just as they were spread somewhat evenly across the three major political camps shown in Figure 7.1, white Catholics and white mainline Protestants are spread fairly evenly across the range of liberal-conservative political leanings (and are similar to each other). Both groups lean slightly more conservative than liberal, but the spread is otherwise fairly even.

For Latinos—both Catholic and Protestant—political views differ from their own political party identities (Figure 7.1). They also differ from party identifications of both white Catholics and religious nones. Both Latino Catholics and Latino Protestants are much more likely to call themselves moderates than either liberal or conservative. Indeed, about 50% of each group says they are "moderate or middle of the road." I note the difference between Latinos and nones because Figure 7.1 showed that Latino Catholics and nones have similar likelihoods of being aligned with the Democratic party, but Latino Catholics are less likely than nones to be Republicans and much more likely to be Independents.

Consistent with their political party identifications, white conservative Protestants lean strongly conservative: about 86% of this group called themselves slightly to extremely conservative in 2021. Religious nones lean the other direction: more than 50% call themselves slightly to extremely liberal.

The Catholic Vote

Of course, political attitudes are much more than self-assessed party identification and political leanings, and trying to identify where Catholics stand on key issues has been the subject of intense scrutiny by academics, journalists, and political pundits for decades. Naturally, much of this scrutiny focuses on voting in major elections (D'Antonio, Dillon, and Gautier 2013; Dionne Jr. 2000; Greeley 1977; Manza and Brooks 1997; Smith 2020). E. J. Dionne succinctly summarized the findings of this ongoing inquiry in the title of his op-ed called "There Is No 'Catholic Vote.' And Yet it Matters" (Dionne

Jr. 2000). Indeed, classifying a single "Catholic vote" seems elusive: the majority of Catholics voted for democratic presidential and congressional candidates from the 1950s through the 1970s, but they have shifted between major parties ever since. Patterns were no clearer by 2004, when Catholics voted for Republican George W. Bush rather than Democrat John Kerry, even though Kerry was Catholic. And the close margins have continued more recently: Catholics voted for Barack Obama (D) in 2008 and 2012 and Donald Trump (R) in 2016. They leaned left again in 2020 when both Donald Trump and Joe Biden made religion central to their presidential campaigns (Newport 2020). Trump tried to lure white conservative Protestants, while Biden made his Catholic faith a core component of his campaign. In that election, 52% of Catholics voted for Biden and 47% voted for Trump (Newport 2020).

Given that Catholic voting receives detailed analysis in other outlets, I do not delve into voting behavior more in this book; however, the elusive Catholic vote underscores the importance of studying political attitudes more broadly using a host of measures. Views about taxes, government spending, the nation's top problems, crime, guns and gun laws, and marijuana are all part of contemporary public discussions about how individuals and societies should behave and therefore provide useful insight into the range of issues that individuals care about and the political views that they hold.

POLITICAL ATTITUDES

Taxes and Government Spending

Taxes and government spending are fundamental to how societies function, and individuals' attitudes about these topics are a window into their political leanings and priorities. An individual's opinion about whether they pay too much in government taxes is particularly informative: prior estimates show that much higher percentages of conservatives (about 58%) compared to liberals (about 32%) think their taxes are too high (Newport 2021). Yet there is not a perfect correlation between political leanings and opinions on taxes, suggesting that views about certain national issues, such as taxes, are important but are only part of a complex set of factors reflecting underlying political leanings. For example, the percentage of Americans who think their taxes are too high tends to drop following well-publicized tax cuts such as those of the George W. Bush and Trump administrations (Newport 2021). Similarly, the more people pay in taxes, the more likely they are to think those taxes are too high; however, this relationship is difficult to measure (it is hard to know for certain how much tax households pay) and not perfectly clear.

Views about government spending are similar: conservatives tend to prefer less spending, liberals prefer more; however, Americans, overall, tend to be more liberal socially than economically (Brenan 2020). It is also well-known that opinions about government spending vary by the type of spending, with conservatives being more likely to support spending on issues such as the miliary and law enforcement and liberals being more likely to support spending on issues such as poverty alleviation and the environment. However, we know less about variation across religious groups in preferences for government spending.

Attitudes regarding taxes and government spending may also be relevant to understanding how Catholics internalize and apply their faith to realms that are not strictly religious. The Catholic Church's view of its role in society is clear in two key documents from Vatican II. *Lumen Gentium* (*Light of the Nations*), the Dogmatic Constitution on the Church, notes that "by its relationship to Christ, the church is a kind of sign or sacrament of intimate union with God and the unity of all humankind." To love God—the commandment of the synoptic Gospels—means to love one's neighbor (Himes 2019). In *Gaudium et Spes* (*Joy and Hope*), the Pastoral Constitution on the Church in the Modern World, the Council noted that the Church's religious mission implies certain action in the world, including "a function, a light, and an energy which can serve to structure and consolidate the human community according to divine law" (Vatican II 1965). That is, the common good is integral to Catholic social teaching and how Catholics live out that teaching in their social and political lives (Himes 2019).

A series of GSS questions allows comparison of religious groups' views of taxes and government spending. First, the GSS asks "Do you consider the amount of federal income tax which you have to pay as too high, about right, or too low?"

Responses to this measure are notable because they reveal a pattern that is not clear on other measures that I discuss in this chapter: white Catholics are highly conservative in regards to their federal income taxes. Indeed, they are very similar to white conservative Protestants in this regard: about 64% of each group says their taxes are too high (author's estimates, not shown in a figure). Each of the other groups—Latino Catholics, white mainline Protestants, Latino Protestants—is moderate to progressive on this measure, with about 55% of each group reporting that their taxes are too high. Religious nones (50%) are the most progressive and least likely to say they pay too much in taxes. Not too surprisingly, few respondents think their taxes are too low: about 4% of Latino Catholics, white mainline Protestants, religious nones, and Latino Protestants say their taxes are too low. Fewer white Catholics and white conservative Protestants (about 1% of each group) agree that their taxes are too low.

Second, the GSS includes a detailed list of problems on which governments spend money and asks respondents whether they think we are spending too much, too little, or about the right amount of money on each problem. Figure

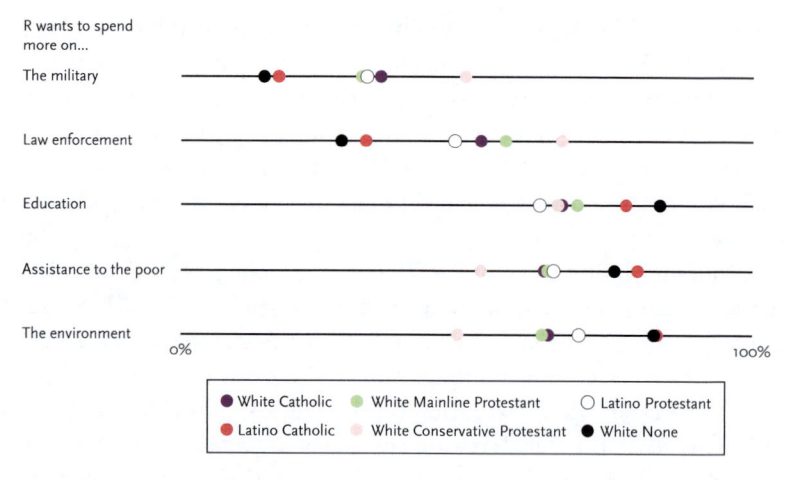

Figure 7.2 Government spending

7.2 illustrates differences in responses regarding four types of spending: the military and defense, law enforcement, education, assistance to the poor, and improving and protecting the environment. I focus on these spending categories because they highlight political differences that might not be evident in self-reports of political ideology.

Opinions about government spending follow a similar pattern across expenditure categories: Figure 7.2 shows that white Catholics, white mainline Protestants, and Latino Protestants have views that are similar to each other and are moderate to progressive. Latino Catholics and religious nones are similar to each other and are relatively progressive; and white conservative Protestants are the most conservative of the groups on each measure included in the figure. These patterns are reinforced in responses to other forms of government spending that I excluded from the figure for brevity.

Some specific estimates illustrate these broad patterns. For example, Figure 7.2 shows that about 30% of white Catholics, white mainline Protestants, and Latino Protestants feel that the United States should spend more on the military; about 50% of each of these groups think we should spend more on law enforcement; about 63% think we should spend more on education and assistance to the poor; and about 63–69% think we should spend more on the environment. Latino Catholics and nones are more progressive: only about 15% of these respondents think we should spend more on the military; about 30% think we should spend more on law enforcement; 75–79% think we should spend more on education and assistance to the poor, and more than 80% think we should spend more on the environment.

White conservative Protestants are, not surprisingly, more conservative than the other groups on each of these measures; however, Figure 7.2 suggests that a somewhat more complex pattern in white conservative Protestant preferences for spending on these categories underlies these estimates. The figure shows that about 50% of white conservative Protestants think that we should spend more on three categories: the military, assistance to the poor, and the environment. About 66% think we should spend more on law enforcement. Each of these estimates suggests that white Conservative Protestants are politically conservative. On preferences for education spending, white conservative Protestants express views similar to those of white Catholics, white mainline Protestants, and Latino Protestants. The figure does not show that white conservative Protestants are also more likely than members of the other faith traditions to say "we spend enough" on these categories, a pattern that suggests that a significant number of moderates—in terms of government spending—are in the white conservative Protestant category.

The unique preferences of white conservative Protestants suggest that not all members of these conservative faith groups are extreme political conservatives. Rather, there appears to be a significant component of the conservative churches that leans moderate or even progressive on these measures. Notably, this pattern is consistent with patterns shown in Chapter 5: on some measures such as self-identification regarding abortion, white conservative Protestants leaned conservative, but there were significant numbers of this group who were more moderate than the group mode. These patterns suggest that efforts to classify the political leanings of white conservative Protestants should be aware of both central tendencies (e.g., the modal patterns such as those I show in Figure 7.2) and unique patterns of deviation from that central tendency that reveal meaningful variation within this large group.

National Problems

Political ideology is ultimately about how individuals feel that a society should address its problems, and the GSS includes multiple questions designed to identify respondents' views of America's problems. For example, the survey allows respondents to select two problems that they see as the top and second most important problems facing the country. Respondents select these problems from a list that includes healthcare, education, crime, the environment, immigration, the economy, terrorism, and poverty.

Responses to this question (not shown in a figure) are insightful because they show high degrees of similarity among contemporary religious groups: the average white Catholic, Latino Catholic, white mainline Protestant, and Latino Protestant all listed healthcare as the top problem and the economy as the second most important problem. White conservative Protestants, on average, agreed that healthcare and the economy were the top problems but these problems garnered equal support from this group. Consistent with conservative disdain for environmental causes, white conservative Protestants were the only group to rank the environment lowest on their list of problems. At the other end of the political spectrum, religious nones were the only group that differed from the other groups included in the figure: nones agreed that healthcare was the top problem facing the country, but they felt that the environment was the second most pressing problem. The economy was the third problem listed by nones.

Although this relatively high level of agreement among religious groups is interesting, it needs to be evaluated with two caveats in mind. First, context matters, and any evaluation of political ideology derived from individual evaluations of how a society should define and deal with problems does—and should—change depending on national and international context. Indeed, gauging sentiment about which current affairs are most pressing is the point of a question of this nature. Respondents to the 2021 GSS were answering this question during the COVID-19 pandemic and associated economic crisis. It is perhaps no surprise that healthcare and the economy weighed heavily on their minds. Abortion was also attracting national attention at the time the 2021 GSS was in the field, and *Roe v. Wade* was overturned in 2022 shortly after the survey was completed. A second caveat that is useful in interpreting responses about the nation's top problems is that each general GSS question asks nothing about how respondents would address the problems that they identify as important. For example, although respondents agreed that healthcare was an important issue in 2021, there was likely considerable disagreement among them in what constitutes a healthcare problem and how the nation should address the issues.

Crime, Guns, Marijuana

Because the general question about national problems only allows respondents to identify top national problems (and does not give them an opportunity to express opinions about addressing the problems), the GSS also asks targeted questions about particular nationally prominent issues. Figure 7.3 summarizes responses to four of these questions, including one general question about preferences for dealing with crime and three additional questions about specific issues that can be criminal. I focus on these questions because they involve important issues that attract considerable national attention, are useful for deducing political leanings, and are not redundant with other topics I have explored elsewhere in this book (e.g., abortion, taxes, government spending).

The first question included in Figure 7.3 asks respondents whether they think the courts deal too harshly or not harshly enough with criminals. The second question asks whether respondents favor or oppose a law which would "require a person to obtain a police permit before he or she could buy a gun."

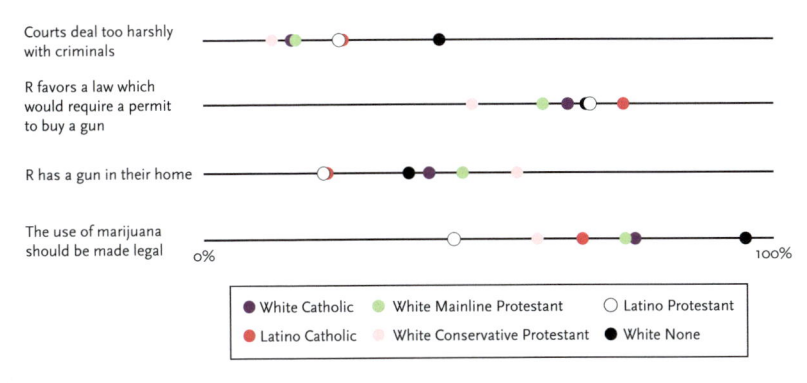

Figure 7.3 National problems: Crime, guns, and marijuana

Box 7.2 FORMER WHITE CATHOLICS: COURTS ARE TOO HARSH

White Catholics who left the Church are more inclined than current Catholics to think the courts deal too harshly with criminals. About 16% of current white Catholics agree that the courts are too harsh, but nearly 37% of former Catholics who identify as white agree with this statement (estimates not shown in a figure). This pattern is consistent with my findings that former Catholics—but only those who are white—are largely more liberal than current white Catholics. Indeed, I find no difference in views on crime between current and former Latino Catholics.

A third, related question asks whether the respondent has any guns in his or her home. Gun laws have played a central role in political discussions for years in the United States, in light of mass shootings. Because these laws are highly politicized, responses to this question will illustrate variation across religious groups in political ideology that might not be clear in other GSS questions. I include the question about personal ownership of a firearm to explore whether there are differences across the religious groups in the actualization of their views on gun ownership. The final question included in the figure asks whether respondents "think the use of marijuana should be made legal or not." The legalization of marijuana use is another controversial issue that will reveal respondents' political leanings (Box 7.2).

White and Latino Catholics have relatively similar views on each of these nationally prominent issues, despite slight differences in the degree to which members of each group support the issues. Both white and Latino Catholics, overall, are somewhat conservative on crime and liberal on gun laws, but

Latino Catholics lean slightly left of white Catholics on both issues: Latino Catholics are somewhat more likely than white Catholics to say that courts deal too harshly with criminals (25%, 16%) and to favor a law which would require a permit to buy a gun (73%, 64%). Both groups are fairly liberal on marijuana legalization, but, on this issue, white Catholics are more liberal than Latino Catholics: 75% of white Catholics and 66% of Latino Catholics favor legalization.

There is a notable divide among Catholics in gun ownership that is consistent with their preferences on gun laws: significantly fewer Latino Catholics (22%) than white Catholics (40%) have a gun in their homes. In fact, both Catholic and Protestant Latinos report nearly identical—and comparatively low—rates of gun ownership, consistent with prior reports that indicate low rates of firearm ownership among all Latinos (Parker et al. 2017). Additional analyses of the GSS (not shown in a figure) indicate that hunting accounts for a significant portion of the differences among Catholics. White Catholic respondents (about 20%) are much more likely than Latino Catholic (about 7%) or Latino Protestant (about 10%) to report that they, their spouse, or both hunt. Although hunting is only one of many reasons that individuals own firearms, hunting explains a significant amount of the difference between white and Latino Catholics on this issue. A full exploration of the other factors that contribute to these differences—including urban–rural, gender, and cohort differences in preferences for firearm ownership—are beyond the scope of this book.

White Catholics and white mainline Protestants are, once again, nearly identical in their views of the issues included in Figure 7.3. Both groups are more conservative in their attitudes regarding dealing with crime than they are on other issues I have highlighted. Indeed, on this issue, white Catholics, white mainline Protestants, and white conservative Protestants are similarly conservative: 15% of white Catholics, 17% of white mainline Protestants, and 15% white conservative Protestants feel that the courts deal too harshly with criminals. White Catholics and white mainline Protestants are more characteristically moderate to progressive on the other issues shown in the figure. About 60% of each group favors a law requiring a gun permit, and about 75% favor marijuana legalization. Similar percentages of white Catholics (40%) and white mainline Protestants (46%) also report that they own a firearm.

Once again, religious nones and white conservative Protestants report fairly predictable opinions on each of the issues included in Figure 7.3, with nones leaning left on each topic and white conservative Protestants leaning right. However, the views of these groups are not extreme and reflect notable percentages of each group with views that lean moderate. I find, for example that very few white conservative Protestants (13%) think that the courts deal too harshly with criminals, whereas more nones (42%) than any other group shown in Figure 7.3 think the courts are too harsh. The nones' views on this issue highlights the variation that characterizes the opinions of this group: the nones' response is, indeed, different from the responses of members of the faith groups shown in the figure, but their responses also reflect the reality that many nones have fairly moderate views on this issue.

Views of gun laws, gun ownership, and marijuana legalization also underscore differences between white conservative Protestants and religious nones. Indeed, white conservative Protestants (47%) are less likely than the other groups to favor a legal permit to buy a gun. By contrast, more nones (67%) favor such a law. Consistent with their preferences regarding gun laws, many more white conservative Protestants (55%) compared to nones (36%) own guns. Finally, the figure shows that 58% of white conservative Protestants and 95% of nones think that the use of marijuana should be made legal.

Latino Protestants are more challenging to classify on the issues included in Figure 7.3: they lean left and resemble Latino Catholics on dealing with crime, gun permit laws, and gun ownership. However, Latino Protestants are notably conservative in their views of marijuana legalization. About 25% of Latinos—both Catholic and Protestant—say the courts deal too harshly with criminals. Similarly, about 73% of Latino Catholics and about 68% of Latino Protestants favor a law requiring a gun permit, and only about 22% of each group reports owning a gun. Large percentages of both Latino Catholics (66%) and Latino Protestants (44%) support marijuana legalization, but the difference in support between the two groups is notable given their similar views on other issues shown in Figure 7.3.

CHARITABLE GIVING

Charitable giving is often studied because of its benefits: giving to important causes makes people healthier and happier, it sustains organizations that support the vulnerable, and it allows societies to grow and thrive in ways they might not without donors (Greater Good Science Center 2017). In addition to these benefits, however, charitable giving provides useful information about what individuals value and the degree to which they are committed to particular issues. Given that most individuals have finite financial resources, charitable giving forces them to make decisions about how to allocate the funds they are able to contribute. Thus, the extent to which individuals use their financial resources to promote particular causes through charitable giving is an excellent objective indicator of their beliefs, values, and priorities.

Giving can also provide a window into individuals' political ideologies. The relationship between political views and giving is complex; however, when researchers consider broad patterns of giving, there is evidence that political conservatives give more than liberals (Brooks 2003; Yongzheng and Peixu 2021). Brooks (2003) points out that conservative generosity reflects skepticism about government and the government's ability to redistribute resources effectively, traditional values about family that manifest in support of causes such as the pro-life movement, and views about the importance of individual effort and entrepreneurship. Yet when researchers study giving to particular causes, they find more variation by political ideology. For example, liberals—who are often seen as more easily won over by causes that support the vulnerable—appear to give more than conservatives to certain causes like support for the poor (Yongzheng and Peixu 2021).

For Catholics, giving is an important component of their faith. The Catholic Church and other Christian Churches depend on the service and donations of their members to sustain parishes, schools, and other causes. Giving—and supporting the vulnerable—are also critical components of Catholic social teaching. Care for others, particularly the poor and vulnerable, have clear biblical roots, with references to generosity and giving appearing throughout the Old and New Testaments. Giving is no less important today. Pope Francis has emphasized care for the poor in statements such as "(e)ach individual Christian and every community is called to be an instrument of God for the liberation and promotion of the poor, and for enabling them to be fully a part of society. This demands that we be docile and attentive to the cry of the poor and to come to their aid" (Pope Francis 2020). Similarly, Pope Francis has said "(t)rue justice comes about in people's lives when they themselves are just in their decisions; it is expressed in their pursuit of justice for the poor and the weak: (Pope Francis 2018).

Despite the importance of charitable giving to Catholicism, it is challenging to identify whether giving differs among the major U.S. faith groups (Greater Good Science Center 2017), and changing Catholic demographics suggest that an updated portrait of giving by Catholics and other Americans is in order. Religious people give more to charitable causes than do secular people, including to organizations that help the poor (Brooks 2003; Regnerus, Smith, and Sikkink 1998), but the association between religion and giving is not consistent across giving categories (Yongzheng and Peixu 2021). In addition, the giving behavior of members of the major American faith groups changes over time in reaction to broader social and cultural influences (Bekkers and Wiepking 2011; Eagle, Keister, and Read 2017; Havens, O'Herlihy, and Schervish 2006). Charitable giving also varies by ethnicity, age, education, family type, and socioeconomic status (SES) (Bekkers and Wiepking 2011; Eagle et al. 2017; Wiepking and Bekkers 2012).

Three components of giving are useful for identifying the issues that matter to individuals: giving to any cause, the amount given to charitable causes, and giving to particular categories of charities. My estimates come from the Panel Study of Income Dynamics (PSID), which contains sufficiently large samples of each of the major American religious groups to make sensible statistical comparisons.

Giving to Any Cause

Figure 7.4 shows that there are, indeed, considerable differences across faith groups in charitable giving. The figure sums all types of giving and shows the portion of respondents, by ethnicity and religion, who gave any donation greater than $25 to any type of cause or organization. The causes and organizations include religious and spiritual organizations (e.g., church, synagogue, mosque, radio ministry); organizations that help the poor, provide healthcare, do medical research, provide international aid, or some combination of these (e.g., the United Way); education, organizations for boys and girls, the arts, cultural diversity, or the environment; to help people affected by the COVID-19 pandemic; or any other cause. The figure includes those who did not donate to any cause, but the patterns do not change if I remove these individuals from the analyses.

White Catholics and mainline Protestants are the most likely of the groups shown in the figure to give to any organization or cause: about two-thirds of each group gave some amount of money in the previous year. White conservative Protestants were also highly likely to give: more than one-half of them made some sort of donation. Religious nones were less likely than white Catholics and white Protestants to give, consistent with research that shows that secular people give less to most causes (Brooks 2003; Greater Good Science Center 2017; Regnerus et al. 1998). Sizable percentages of Latinos gave some amount to a charitable organization; 42% of Latino Protestants gave, and more than 30% of Latino Catholics did as well.

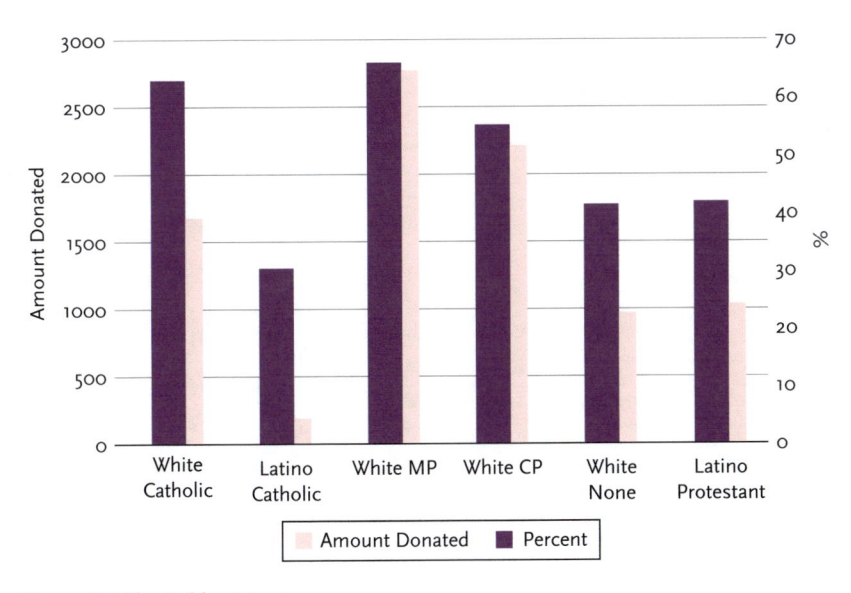

Figure 7.4 Charitable giving to any cause

Amount Given

The amount given to charitable causes underscores important cross-faith differences in giving and highlights how challenging it is to document an association between political ideology and giving. That is, PSID data illustrate that white Catholics give somewhat moderate amounts to all formal charitable causes compared to other Christian faith groups: white Catholics give about $1,668 per year, white mainline Protestants give about $2,773, and white conservative Protestants give about $2,200. Religious nones and Latino Protestants each give about $1,000, and Latino Catholics give about $200 (Figure 7.4). These differences are notable given similarities between white Catholics and white mainline Protestants in their self-assessed political party identifications and ideologies and their views on other issues described throughout this chapter.

Figure 7.5 uses predicted probabilities (see Chapter 3 for details about interpretation) and shows that these differences remain when total household income is held constant. Religious nones and Latinos—both Catholic and Protestant—give less overall than do white Catholics. These patterns do not vary substantively when I show basic percentages (i.e., when I do not control income). In other analyses (not shown), I find that the amount given to particular causes follows patterns that are very similar to those shown in Figure 7.6.

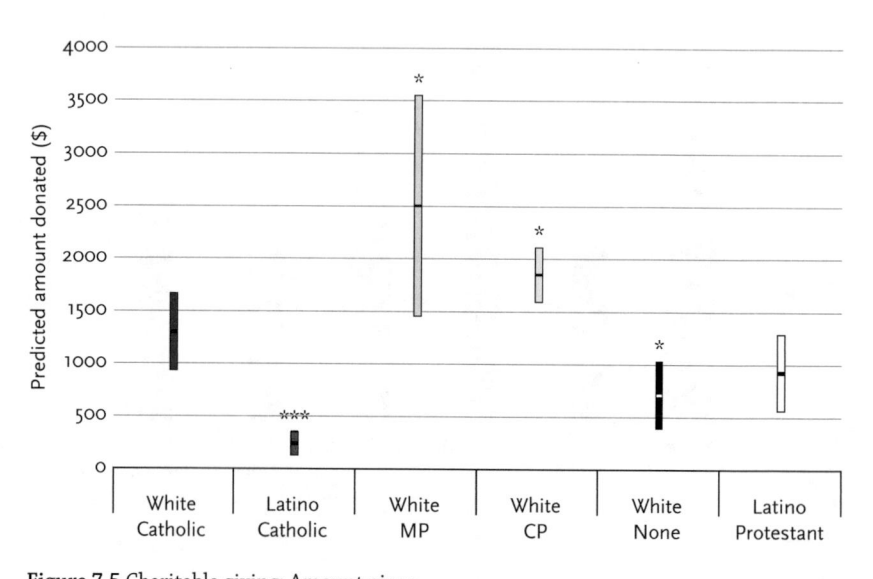

Figure 7.5 Charitable giving: Amount given

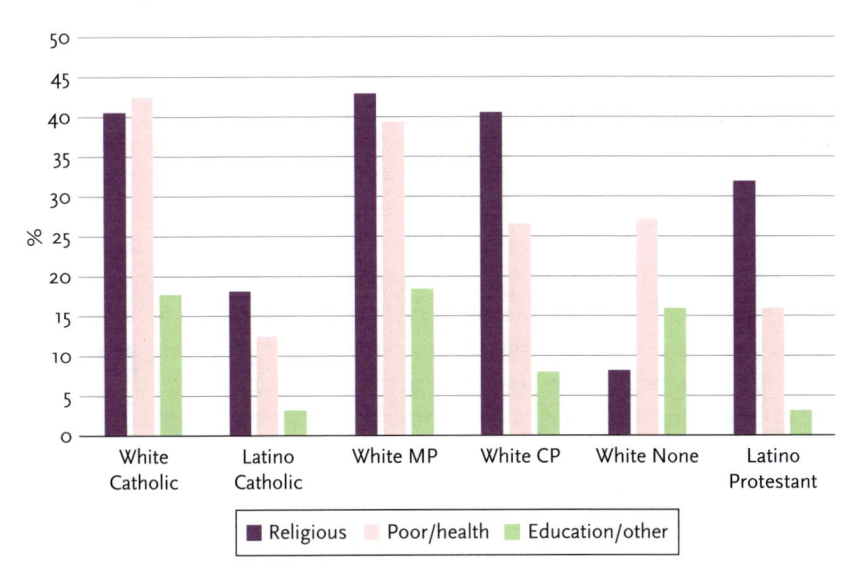

Figure 7.6 Charitable giving to religious, health, and educational causes

Giving to Particular Causes

Donations to particular types of organizations also vary by religious groups and are fairly consistent with the groups' views about how the government should spend money (Figure 7.2). Figure 7.6 highlights giving to three of the charity types included in Figure 7.4: religious organizations, organizations focused on poverty alleviation and healthcare, and organizations focused on education and related causes. I focus on these three organization types to highlight differences across the groups in priorities and values in giving. The figure shows that white Catholics and white mainline Protestants have similar giving priorities: about 40% of each group give to religious causes, about 40% give to organizations focused on poverty alleviation and healthcare, and about 18% give to organizations focused on education and related causes. White conservative Protestants are similar to white Catholics and white mainline Protestants in their propensity to give to religious causes (about 40% give to these organizations), but white conservative Protestants are less likely to support poverty alleviation and educational causes. These patterns are largely consistent with the views of these groups about government spending priorities—including for poor support and education—shown in Figure 7.2.

Religious nones were less likely to give to any of these organization; when they gave, they tended to support organizations targeting poverty alleviation and healthcare. Latinos—both Catholics and Protestants—also gave, with Latino Protestants giving more to each of the causes included in the figure.

Notably, both Latino groups favored religious organizations in their giving rather than the other two types of causes shown in the figure.

Do these results imply that Latinos are not generous? My findings show that Latino Catholics and Protestants were the least likely to give to any organizations or causes (Figure 7.4) or to particular causes (Figure 7.6). The amount they give (Figure 7.5) was particularly low and, indeed, striking. However, it is critical to keep in mind that I am only able to study giving to formal organizations. These figures do not include giving to family and friends; they also exclude giving to informal organizations, giving circles, and small groups. Other research shows that Latinos tend to give directly to people they know, particularly to friends and family who are in crisis or experiencing emergencies, and to other, often informal organizations that are not included in the PSID measures that I use (Indiana University Lilly Family School of Philanthropy 2021). Future research could usefully explore the degree to which informal giving varies by religion and ethnicity; unfortunately, I am unable to study this question in additional detail with my data.

CONCLUSION

In this chapter, I explored Catholics' political identifications, political attitudes, and charitable giving to profile their political leanings and views on several issues with national importance. In doing so, I built on a history of research that attempts to classify Catholics' political leanings but that often acknowledges important challenges to offering a definitive statement about whether Catholics lean left, right, or moderate. This chapter had two parts. In the first part, I documented Catholic political ideologies, including their self-assessed political party affiliations (i.e., Democrat, Republican, Independent) and political views (i.e., liberal, conservative, moderate). I also studied their views on several specific issues that are part of public discussion, including taxes, government spending, gun laws, gun ownership, and the legalization of marijuana. In the second part of the chapter, I explored patterns of charitable giving to better understand the issues that are important to Catholics. I noted that charitable giving is not political, per se, but it has the potential to identify how individuals divide their limited resources among important causes; as such, giving can identify issues that individuals consider important. As I have done in previous chapters, I compared white and Latino Catholics to show whether there are differences among Catholics in their political identities and attitudes. I also compared Catholic attitudes to official Church teaching where appropriate, and I compared Catholics and members of other faith traditions.

In contrast to the similarities in religious beliefs and practices I showed in Chapter 6, I found more notable differences between white and Latino

Catholics on many of the issues I explored in this chapter. Some of the differences were slight, but overall patterns provided evidence that Catholics do not fit neatly into liberal or conservative boxes. On most of the issues I studied, white Catholics identified as political moderates and expressed moderate views, with a slightly conservative lean. White Catholics' political identifications were split fairly evenly between the major political parties with slightly more white Catholics identifying as Republicans than Democrats. White Catholics also identified rather evenly across the liberal-moderate-conservative continuum with a slight conservative lean. By contrast, Latino Catholics were much more likely than white Catholics to identify as Democrats and to call themselves moderates. Latino Catholic views were also more liberal overall than white Catholic views on government spending and taxes; however, they had relatively similar views regarding crime, gun laws, gun ownership, and marijuana legalization. These findings are consistent with evidence that race and religion are deeply intertwined, including in the association between doctrinal and political conservatism: that is, doctrinal conservatism is closely linked to conservative political attitudes for white Catholics (and other majority white faith traditions), as Wuthnow's ideas about religious restructuring suggest (Wuthnow 1990). However, for Latino Catholics (and Muslims and black Protestants), there is no association between doctrinal conservatism and political conservatism (O'Brien and Abdelhadi 2020).

White Catholics and white mainline Protestants were similar on nearly all the issues I studied, with both groups expressing fairly moderate views. Indeed, white Catholics and white mainline Protestant self-identifications were both split nearly evenly between the major political parties, and both were slightly more likely to call themselves conservatives, but with high percentages identifying as moderates as well. On the political issues I studied, white Catholics and white mainline Protestants expressed nearly identical—and slightly left-leaning attitudes—with the exception of their views of crime. On this issue, both white Catholics and white mainline Protestants were uncharacteristically conservative, with relatively few of them indicating that courts deal too harshly with criminals.

Religious nones and white conservative Protestants were fairly predictable in both their self-identifications and views regarding political issues. Nones leaned left on most issues and white conservative Protestants leaned right. However, there was clearly variation within each group that underscores the complexity of political views and that is worth additional exploration. That is, some of my findings—for example, views of government spending, dealing with crime, gun laws, and marijuana legalization—all suggested significant variation within each of these groups that pulled the modal response for the group to a somewhat moderate position. A full exploration of this variation is beyond the scope of this book but worthy of additional research.

My findings regarding charitable giving underscored differences among Catholics and similarities between white Catholics and white mainline Protestants. I found that white Catholics and mainline Protestants are more likely than the other groups I study to give to any organization or cause, including when I controlled for household income. I also found that white conservative Protestants are also highly likely to give at all income levels. My findings showed that donations to particular types of organizations also vary by religious groups: white Catholics, white mainline Protestants, and white conservative Protestants have similar giving priorities—most of their donations go to religious causes and to organizations focused on poverty alleviation and healthcare. They also give to organizations focused on education and related causes but at lower levels, consistent with members of these groups wanting the government to spend more on support for the poor and education.

Sizable percentages of Latinos—both Catholic and Protestant—and religious nones gave some amount to a charitable organization, but they are less likely than the other groups to give to formal organizations or causes. Religious nones tend to support organizations targeting poverty alleviation and healthcare, whereas Latinos—both Catholics and Protestants—favored religious organizations in their giving. Lower levels of giving for these groups, particularly for Latinos, potentially reflect limitations in the data I used. I only study giving to formal organizations and cannot—with the PSID data—study informal giving (e.g., to family and friends, giving circles), which is more common among Latinos. Future research could usefully explore the degree to which informal giving varies by religion and ethnicity; unfortunately, I am unable to study this question in additional detail with my data.

CHAPTER 8
Social Issues

White and Latino Catholics agree on most social issues, including gender roles, economic inequality, suicide, and capital punishment. However, Catholics differ in their levels of generalized trust: white Catholics are more likely than Latino Catholics to express high levels of trust. White Catholics and white mainline Protestants have notably similar views of social issues.

Catholics have a long history of engaging with social issues and doing the work of social justice, and attitudes about social issues—those concerning how people interact with each other—are critical for understanding who Catholics are today. Social issues can be highly controversial because they often invite evaluations of how people *should* interact. Thus, attitudes about social issues can say a great deal about deeply held beliefs that define individuals and that affect decision-making. Indeed, many of the misperceptions about Catholics that I referenced in Chapter 1 stem from confusion about their attitudes regarding issues such as gender roles in and out of the home, inequalities (e.g., by gender, race, and class), how societies confront and address inequalities (e.g., with taxes or preferential treatment for some groups), and society's role in life and death decisions (e.g., assisted suicided, capital punishment). Generalized trust and confidence in institutions are related social issues that also offer windows into individuals' identities and decision-making. Generalized trust—"belief in the benevolence of human nature" (Yamagishi and Yamagishi 1994)—and confidence in major institutions—such as the federal government and military—are critical for societies to function. For everyday interactions to occur smoothly, it is necessary for individuals to trust each other and to have at least a basic level of confidence in the institutions on which social and economic life depend.

The Catholic Church has a long history of engaging with social issues and social justice, including in its teaching and activism (Day 2020). Teachings about the sacredness of human life and the importance of treating others with dignity are pervasive in Church doctrine, including in the Catechism. The introduction to the Catechisms' third pillar on morality summarizes several articles of the document about how individuals should interact with each other (CCC paragraphs 1699–1715). This introduction underscores the role of human dignity in social relations when it notes that "(t)he dignity of the human person is rooted in his creation in the image and likeness of God (*article 1*); it is fulfilled in his vocation to divine beatitude (*article 2*). It is essential to a human being freely to direct himself to this fulfillment (*article 3*). By his deliberate actions (*article 4*), the human person does, or does not, conform to the good promised by God and attested by moral conscience (*article 5*)" (paragraph 1700). Of course, Catholics are not unique in valuing human dignity, but their faith places strong emphasis on this virtue and may contribute to differences between Catholics and other Americans in their social attitudes.

It is well-documented that religion is a strong predictor of social attitudes, but, once again, an updated portrait of Catholics is in order given the significant changes that have occurred in the Church. Attitudes toward women's roles in the home and labor force vary by religious affiliation and ethnicity; religious and ethnic groups also differ in their perspectives of how societies should address these differences (Ellison and Bartkowski 2002; Ellison, Wolfinger, and Ramos-Wada 2013; Lehrer 2004; Sherkat 2000). Similarly, religious groups take different stances on inequality, suicide and assisted suicide, capital punishment, trust, and confidence (Keister and Sherkat 2013; Sherkat 2017; Welch et al. 2004). These attitudes and approaches reflect many of the behaviors and outcomes that I have studied in previous chapters: social origins, adult family, and socioeconomic status (SES) interact with each other to influence religious beliefs and political attitudes; these processes, in turn, contribute to creating and maintaining attitudes regarding social issues. Given the significant differences I have found both among Catholics and between Catholics and members of other religious groups, it is likely that I will also find meaningful differences in attitudes regarding social issues.

This chapter has two parts. In the first part, I explore differences among Catholics in their attitudes regarding four social issues that attract significant attention in both academic research and popular discourse: gender roles in and out of the home, economic inequality and poverty, suicide and assisted suicide, and capital punishment. In the second part, I study generalized trust and confidence in institutions, including the related issue of volunteering. As I have done in previous chapters, I compare white and Latino Catholics to clarify whether there are differences among Church members. I also provide brief, contextual comparisons of the views of Catholics to Church doctrine where possible, and I compare Catholics' attitudes to those of other Americans.

Each of the topics I study in this chapter has social interaction at its core. Thus, studying these topics together offers a reasonably comprehensive portrait of Catholic social attitudes. Yet I acknowledge that I could easily have discussed some of these topics in my discussion of political issues (Chapter 7) given their relevance to voting and other political behaviors. I also acknowledge that I have omitted some important issues, but I am forced to be selective given the constraints of a single chapter.

GENDER ROLES

Gender equity in the United States has certainly increased. However, gender inequality is extraordinarily persistent, and attitudes about gender roles contribute to this deeply entrenched inequity. As I showed in Chapter 4, more American women of all faith traditions work out of the home today. Yet women still lag behind men in countless ways, including in labor force participation, income, job benefits, occupational and career mobility, and representation in political positions. One reason that gender inequality persists is that attitudes regarding ideal gender roles and gender differences in capabilities are tenacious. Individuals' expectations and collective norms regarding how women and men should behave, whether they belong in certain positions, and their abilities to perform tasks work together to inform who is encouraged and enabled to enter and progress through various educational and work arenas.

The negotiation of gender roles in couples illustrates how attitudes become inequalities. As I noted in Chapter 4, couples negotiate how they allocate paid and unpaid work, and this gender division of labor affects a host of outcomes in and out of the family, including parents' involvement in their children's lives, career progression for the couple, income, job benefits, and wealth accumulation. The household division of labor also affects inequality more broadly, including how equity is maintained over the generations (Yavorsky et al. 2023). Three factors affect how couples divide their labor, and each of these factors reflects attitudes toward women's ideal roles and how societies should approach gender inequality. First, couples negotiate—not necessarily explicitly—their contributions to the household, and attitudes toward ideal gender roles affect these negotiations. Second, family structure—single, divorced, married, cohabiting, same-sex, opposite-sex—reflects attitudes regarding women's ideal roles and affects the division of labor in and out of the home (Lehrer 1995; Thébaud and Halcomb 2019). And third, social and cultural norms are critical contributors to the household division of labor, and these norms echo the attitudes of individuals. In the United States, gender norms continue to encourage women to stay home when a couple decides to sacrifice one income (England et al. 2016; Killewald and Gough 2010). Workplace norms regarding gender also reflect individuals' attitudes regarding the ideal role of women and exacerbate household norms regarding the division of labor by creating challenges to women's participation in the paid labor force, particularly when they have young children (Padavic, Ely, and Reid 2020; Thébaud and Halcomb 2019; Yavorsky et al. 2023).

Catholic teaching about gender roles is complex (see Chapter 4 for additional discussion) and can create challenges to the way Catholics live out their faith in their families—including how they divide their labor—and to the attitudes they have regarding women's roles in and out of the home. Despite these competing influences, white Catholics are quite similar to other Americans, including white mainline Protestants, in their propensity to have dual-earner marriages. By contrast, Latino Catholics are significantly less likely than white Catholics to have two incomes (Figure 4.4).

To explore whether attitudes regarding gender vary across religious and ethnic groups, I array attitudes toward women's and men's roles in and out of the home using five General Social Survey (GSS) questions (Figure 8.1). The first question asks respondents whether they agree with the following statement "(i)t is much better for everyone involved if the man is the achiever outside the home and the woman takes care of the home and family." The second and third questions deal with working mothers. Question two asks whether respondents agree that "(a) working mother can establish just as warm and secure a relationship with her children as a mother who does not work." Question three asks about agreement with the phrase "(a) preschool child is likely to suffer if his or her mother works."

The final question asks about attitudes regarding preferential treatment for women. It says: "(s)ome people say that because of past discrimination, women should be given preference in hiring and promotion. Others say that such preference in hiring and promotion of women is wrong because it

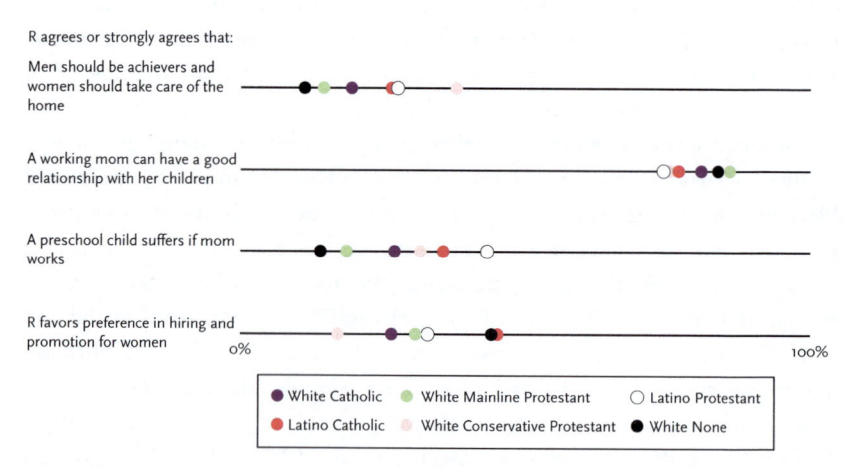

Figure 8.1 Gender roles

discriminates against men. What about your opinion—are you for or against preferential hiring and promotion of women?" Respondents are able to answer "strongly favor," "not strongly favor," "not strongly oppose," or "strongly oppose." I combine the two positive answers ("strongly favor" and "not strongly favor") and report them as "favor" in Figure 8.1. Reporting results from this question as "strongly favor" or "not strongly favor" did not change the substance of the results; similarly, reporting results for "not strongly oppose" or "strongly oppose" did not change the results.

Consistent with increasing gender equity in women's work and the household division of labor, there is considerable agreement across religious and ethnic groups in their attitudes toward gender roles (Figure 8.1). For example, fewer than 40% of respondents agree or strongly agree that it is better for everyone if the man is the achiever outside the home and the woman takes care of the home. Likewise, more than 74% of respondents agree or strongly agree that a working mother can have as good a relationship with her children as a nonworking mother, and fewer than 45% of respondents agree or strongly agree that a preschool child is likely to suffer if his or her mother works.

Americans also agree, overall, about preferential treatment for women: they by and large oppose it. As Figure 8.1 shows, fewer than 50% of respondents favor preferential hiring and promotion of women regardless of religion or ethnicity. This may seem to contradict the relatively progressive attitudes regarding gender roles shown in the same figure, but it might also suggest that Americans largely oppose preferential treatment for any group. I address this possibility in more detail in the next section of this chapter when I discuss preferential hiring and promotion for African Americans.

Despite this overall consistency among GSS respondents, there are notable differences in attitudes regarding gender roles both among Catholics and between Catholics and other Americans. In particular, Latino Catholics express somewhat more conservative views about gender than do white Catholics; however, Latino Catholics are significantly more likely than white Catholics to favor preferential treatment for women. As Figure 8.1 shows, Latino Catholics (27%) are more likely than white Catholics (20%) to think it is better for men to be the achievers outside the home and for women to take care of the home and family. Latino Catholics (36%) are also more likely than white Catholics (27%) to think that children suffer when their mothers work. Latino (76%) and white (80%) Catholics have more consistent views about whether working mothers can have good relationships with their children.

However, Latino Catholics (more than 45%) are much more likely than white Catholics (27%) to support preferential treatment for women. This finding is noteworthy because it suggests that—at least for Latino Catholics—ethnicity might be more salient than religion. That is, Latino's attitudes may reflect their membership in an ethnic group that has faced challenges to economic and social advancement, potentially including discrimination, in the labor force. However, there are also gender differences in support for preferential treatment that shape these findings: women express more progressive attitudes than men on each of these GSS questions, including being more supportive of preferential treatment (analyses not shown). Again, I return to the issue of preferential treatment for particular groups in the next section of this chapter and explore whether these differences among Catholics extend to preferential treatment for African Americans.

White Catholics' attitudes regarding gender roles are similar to—but slightly more conservative than—those of white mainline Protestants. Figure 8.1 shows, for instance, that white Catholics (20%) are more likely than white mainline Protestants (15%) to say that everyone is better off when men are the achievers; white Catholics (80%) are also slightly less likely than white mainline Protestants (86%) to agree that working mothers can have relationships with their children that rival those of nonworking mothers. More white Catholics (27%) are also much more likely than white mainline Protestants (19%) to think that children suffer when their mothers work. Finally, differences between white Catholic (27%) and white mainline Protestant (31%) attitudes regarding preferential treatment of women are modest.

Consistent with patterns I showed in their political leanings (Chapter 7), white conservative Protestants and religious nones have attitudes regarding gender roles that are consistently and significantly different from each other. White conservative Protestants are significantly more likely than any of the other groups included in Figure 8.1 to agree that everyone is better off when men are the achievers and women stay at home; similarly, they are the least likely to support preferential treatment for women. However, consistent with the comparatively high propensity for white conservative Protestants to work out of the home (Chapter 4), I find that their attitudes regarding the potentially detrimental effects of women's work are remarkably similar to those of the other groups shown in Figure 8.1. By contrast, religious nones are highly—and consistently—progressive in their views regarding each of the issues included in the figure.

Consistent with their political views (Chapter 7), Latino Protestants' attitudes regarding gender roles are difficult to summarize succinctly. Despite their own relatively high propensity to have dual-earner couples, Latino Protestants express fairly conservative views of the detriments of women's work, at least compared to the other groups included in Figure 8.1. Yet Latino Protestants are also fairly moderate in their views regarding the benefits of men being the achievers and women taking care of the home. In addition, their support of preferential treatment for some groups is low but fairly moderate compared to the other groups included in the figure. Latino Protestant views are notably similar to those of Latino Catholics, with the exception of their views of preferential treatment for women: 33% of Latino Protestants favor preferential treatment for women, whereas 45% of Latino Catholics support this strategy for addressing gender inequality.

ECONOMIC INEQUALITY AND POVERTY

Economic inequality is extreme and persistent in the United States. As I noted in Chapter 4, the top one percent of households receives about 20% of total household income, and the next nine percent receives an additional 28%. Inequality in wealth ownership is even more extreme: the top one percent of households owns about 37% of all wealth (assets less debts), and the next nine percent owns another 39%. Remarkably, this means that the top ten percent owns 76% of all household wealth. By contrast, the bottom eighty percent of households owns only about 13% of wealth. Moreover, this inequality has persisted for decades and makes the United States one of the most unequal countries in the developed world (Bhutta et al. 2020; Keister 2014; Keister and Southgate 2022; Killewald, Pfeffer, and Schachner 2017).

Poverty is closely related to economic inequality and is one of the visible manifestations of the problems of inequality: for example, children living in poverty are at increased risk of deficits in nutrition, physical and emotional health, cognitive development, and educational attainment (Gibson-Davis, Keister, and Gennettian 2020; Thomas, Miller, and Morrissey 2019; Yang et al. 2020). Underlying much of this inequality are vast racial differences—particularly between African American and white Americans—in educational attainment, income, wealth, and other measures of well-being (Cheng 2016; Gibson-Davis et al. 2020; Killewald et al. 2017).

A well-documented body of research shows that attitudes and beliefs about economic inequality and poverty are instrumental in identifying collective priorities and the policies that societies use to address problems associated with economic inequality and poverty. Attitudes and beliefs about inequality and poverty affect voting behavior, other forms of political engagement, charitable giving to organizations that focus on poverty reduction, and volunteer work intended to aid those in need (McCall 2013; McCall and Kenworthy 2009; Ritzman and Tomaskovic-Devey 1992; Wilson et al. 2022). Moreover, beliefs about addressing economic inequality and poverty—such as taxing high-income households, the utility of labor unions, and preferential treatment for some groups—may affect how governments and organizations allocate financial and other resources (e.g., time) and may feed back into individual- and household-level inequities.

Care for one's neighbors is a core Catholic teaching that follows from the centrality of the dignity of humans (Himes 2019; Vatican II 1965a, 1965b). Similarly, the Church has a long history of supporting working-class issues, including the need for organizations—such as labor unions—to protect workers (Pope Leo XIII 1891). Thus, Catholic support of programs designed to address the problems associated with inequality and poverty could be high. However, the relationship between doctrine and attitudes is by no means certain. For example, differences among Catholics in their experience of poverty may affect the degree to which Catholics support particular programs that target the problems associated with inequality and poverty. In particular, Latino Catholics are much more likely than white Catholics to have income and wealth below the poverty line (Chapter 4), and the experience of poverty might make Latinos comparably more aware of inequality and more inclined to support efforts to address inequality and poverty. Moreover, care for the poor is—ideally—a priority for all Christians, and the esteem of labor unions has changed dramatically in recent decades, suggesting that attitudes regarding economic inequality and poverty among the various American faith groups might converge.

I use four GSS questions to explore whether there are differences among Catholics—and between Catholics and other Americans—in their assessments of economic inequality and approaches to address inequality and poverty. The first question asks respondents to assess the general problem of income inequality by asking whether they agree or disagree that "(d)ifferences in income in America are too large." The other three questions ask about attitudes regarding particular efforts to address inequality and poverty. Question two asks: "Do you think that people with high incomes should pay a larger share of their income in taxes than those with low incomes, the same share, or a smaller share?" Question three addresses protection for the working class through support of labor unions. The questions asks whether respondents agree that "(w)orkers need strong trade unions to protect their interests."

The final question asks about preferential hiring and promotion for African Americans and is worded: "(s)ome people say that because of past discrimination, blacks [sic] should be given preference in hiring and promotion. Others say that such preference in hiring and promotion of blacks [sic] is wrong because it discriminates against whites [sic]. What about your opinion—are you for or against preferential hiring and promotion of blacks [sic]?" Respondents are able to answer "strongly favor," "not strongly favor," "not strongly oppose," or "strongly oppose." I combine the two positive answers ("strongly favor" and "not strongly favor") and report them as "favor" in Figure 8.2 (comparable to my reporting of attitudes regarding preferential treatment of women in Figure 8.1). Reporting results from this question as "strongly favor" or "not strongly favor" did not change the substance of the results; similarly, reporting results for "not strongly oppose" or "strongly oppose" did not change the results. I use a question that specifies preferential treatment for African Americans because poverty among African Americans is notably high but also because the GSS does not ask about programs that target other groups, such as Latinos.

R agrees or strongly agrees that

The income gap in America is too large

High-income people should pay more taxes

Workers need strong trade unions

R favors preferential hiring and promotion for African Americans

0%   100%

● White Catholic   ● White Mainline Protestant   ○ Latino Protestant
● Latino Catholic   ○ White Conservative Protestant ● White None

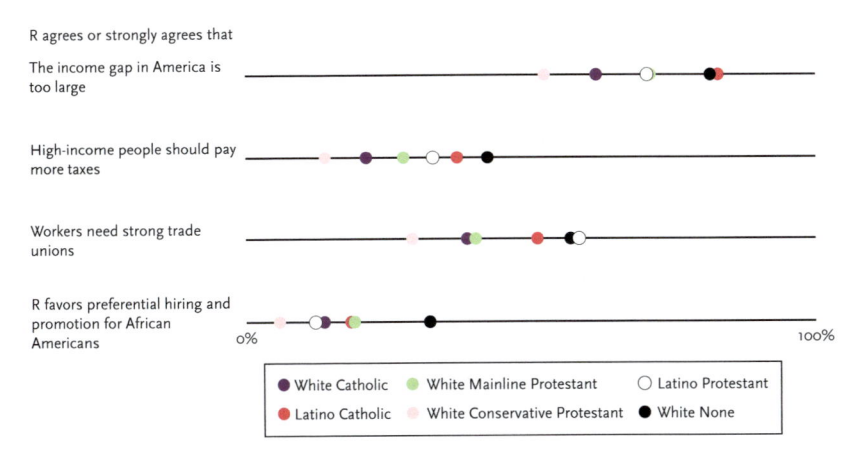

Figure 8.2 Economic inequality and poverty

Consistent with Church doctrine, white and Latino Catholics agree that income differences in America are too large, but significantly more Latino than white Catholics agree with this sentiment. Similarly, large percentages of both Latino and white Catholics support efforts to address the problems associated with inequality and poverty, but support is higher among Latino Catholics, with the exception of support for preferential treatment for African Americans. Figure 8.2 shows that more than 82% of Latino Catholics compared to about 61% of white Catholics think that the income gap in the United States is too large. More Latino Catholics than any other group included in the figure think the income gap is too large. Latino Catholics (37%, 51%) are also more likely than white Catholics (22%, 39%) to think that high-income people should pay a larger share of their income in taxes than those with low incomes and that workers need trade unions to protect their interests.

Differences between Latino (19% in favor) and white (14% in favor) Catholics are minimal, however, regarding preferential treatment for African Americans. Recall from Figure 8.1 that Latino Catholics—particularly female Latino Catholics—are much more likely than white Catholics to support preferential treatment for women. This suggests that if the GSS asked about preferential treatment for Latinos, Latino Catholics might have expressed additional support for such initiatives.

White Catholics have more conservative views of inequality than do white mainline Protestants, similar to the pattern I showed in Figure 8.1 regarding attitudes toward gender roles. Fewer white Catholics (61%, 21%) than white mainline Protestants (71%, 28%) think the income gap is too large or that high-income people should pay a larger share of their income in taxes than those with low incomes. Similarly, slightly fewer white Catholics (14%) than white mainline Protestants favor preferential treatment for African Americans. By contrast, white Catholics (39%) and white mainline Protestants (41%) express similar agreement for the need for labor unions.

Once again, white conservative Protestants and religious nones have attitudes that are at the poles of the continuum on each inequality issue shown in Figure 8.2. White conservative Protestants (52%, 15%) are the least likely of the groups to think that the income gap is too large or that high-income people should pay a larger share of their income in taxes than those with low incomes. Notably, white conservative Protestants offer these opinions despite having incomes and wealth that are relatively low (Chapter 4). White conservative Protestants (30%) also express lower levels of support for labor unions than the other groups. Their support for preferential treatment for African Americans (7%) is most glaring and extreme among the groups included in the figure. By contrast, religious nones offer more liberal views of these issues than the other groups. More than 80% of nones say the income gap is too large, and 43% of them prefer that high-income people pay more taxes. Nearly 57% of nones think workers need labor unions, and about one-third support preferential treatment for African Americans.

Anger about Inequality

Anger about economic inequality and poverty is a related issue that sheds additional light on individuals' attitudes. Concern and anger about inequality attract a considerable amount of research attention, and this research shows that—despite high levels of income and wealth inequality in the United States—general levels of dissatisfaction with the state of inequality are relatively low (Keister 2017; Winship 2013). To be clear, this literature does not propose that people *should not care* about inequality. On the contrary, it explores reasons for the empirical reality that—on average—they *do not care* much. The literature offers at least four reasons, including (1) *homophily*, the notion that we tend to spend most of our time with people like us and are, therefore, just not aware of inequality. Moreover, (2) as overall incomes and wealth increase, individuals tend to be less concerned about differences than they might otherwise; and (3) individuals' own experiences with change in their incomes and wealth over time (mobility) further diminish their concern. Finally, (4) most people are busy, distracted, and stressed, leaving them little time to be concerned about big-picture social issues.

To assess levels of dissatisfaction and anger about inequality, the GSS asks respondents "How do you feel when you think about differences in wealth between the rich and the poor in America?" Respondents are able to give a number ranging from 0 (not angry at all) to 10 (extremely angry).

In results not shown in a figure, I find that anger about inequality is fairly comparable between Latino and white Catholics. Fairly high—but comparable—percentages of each group are very angry: about 26% of Latino Catholics and about 22% of white Catholics express high levels (7–10) of anger. By contrast, nearly one-half of white Catholics and about one-third of Latino Catholics register low levels (0–4).

Catholics and white mainline Protestants have similar levels of anger about inequality; however, differences between white conservative Protestants and religious nones are stark on this metric. More than 61% of white conservative Protestants express low levels of anger (0–4) about inequality (see description of variable above), whereas only 30% of religious nones have low anger. By contrast, only 14% of white conservative Protestants compared to more than 45% of religious nones voice high levels (7–10) of anger regarding inequality.

Who Is Responsible for Addressing Inequality?

Latino and white Catholics differ in their assessments of who is responsible for addressing inequality and its consequences. Latino Catholics are more likely than white Catholics to hold the government—rather than other parties—responsible for addressing income inequality (results not shown in a figure). The GSS asked respondents who they think should have the greatest responsibility for "reducing differences in income between people with high incomes and people with low incomes?" Possible responses included "the income gap is fine" as well as various options such as private companies, the government, trade unions, and rich or poor people. Only 11% of Latino Catholics (results not shown in a figure) responded that they think the income gap is fine, and the majority of Latino Catholics (53%) think the government is primarily responsible for addressing this problem. Another 19% of Latinos think that private companies are responsible. Only small percentages of Latino Catholics (less than 3% each) hold rich or poor people themselves responsible. By contrast, more than 21% of white Catholics think there is no income inequality problem, and 34% of white Catholics think private companies should be responsible for fixing the problem. About 28% of white Catholics hold the government responsible. Similar to Latino Catholics, few white Catholics (less than 7% each) hold rich or poor individuals responsible.

SUICIDE AND ASSISTED SUICIDE

American attitudes regarding suicide—including physician-assisted suicide (hereafter, *assisted suicide*)—are complex but can provide important insight into individuals' identities. These attitudes can also affect behaviors such as voting, financial support for political candidates, giving to charitable organizations, and volunteering. Suicide stands in contrast to the broad Catholic principle that respects human life from conception to natural death. The Catholic Catechism (#2280) states: "everyone is responsible for his life before God who has given it to him. It is God who remains the sovereign Master of life. We are obliged to accept life gratefully and preserve it for his honor and the salvation of our souls. We are stewards, not owners, of the life God has entrusted to us. It is not ours to dispose of." The Catechism also draws attention to the social problems associated with suicide, stating that it "offends love of neighbor because it unjustly breaks the ties of solidarity with family, nation, and other human societies to which we continue to have obligations. Suicide is contrary to love for the living God" (#2281).

The U.S. Conference of Catholic Bishops summarized the Church's approach to assisted suicide as follows (United States Conference of Catholic Bishops [USCCB] 2011; Pope John Paul II 1984): "our society should embrace what Pope John Paul II called 'the way of love and true mercy'—a readiness to surround patients with love, support, and companionship, providing the assistance needed to ease their physical, emotional, and spiritual suffering. This approach must be anchored in unconditional respect for their human dignity, beginning with respect for the inherent value of their lives."

Views about an individual's right to take their own life by suicide are complex. Similar to views about abortion (Chapter 6), views about the right to commit suicide vary by the conditions under which the suicide would occur. To capture this variation, the GSS included a general question about assisted suicide, followed by questions about the conditions under which suicide might be considered acceptable. The general question was, "When a person has a disease that cannot be cured, do you think doctors should be allowed by law to end the patient's life by some painless means if the patient and his family request it?" The respondent then indicated their agreement or disagreement with statements about suicide more broadly and the conditions under which a person has the right to take their own life, including if the person (1) has an incurable disease, (2) has gone bankrupt, (3) has dishonored his or family, or (4) is tired of living and ready to die. Because the rank order of religious groups' attitudes regarding assisted suicide is similar to the rank order of their attitudes regarding other issues described above, I describe the patterns in text and do not include a figure in this section.

Despite Church teachings, high percentages of white (68%) and Latino (62%) Catholics agree that a doctor should be allowed to end a patient's life if the patient and family request it (i.e., they agree with the first, broad GSS question about assisted suicide, shown in Figure 8.3). Catholics are not unique in this support: large percentages of white mainline Protestants (79%) and religious nones (92%) also agree. Even the more conservative religious respondents indicate broad support for assisted suicide, although few white conservative Protestants (57%) and Latino Protestants (44%) agree that doctors should be legally allowed to end a patient's life.

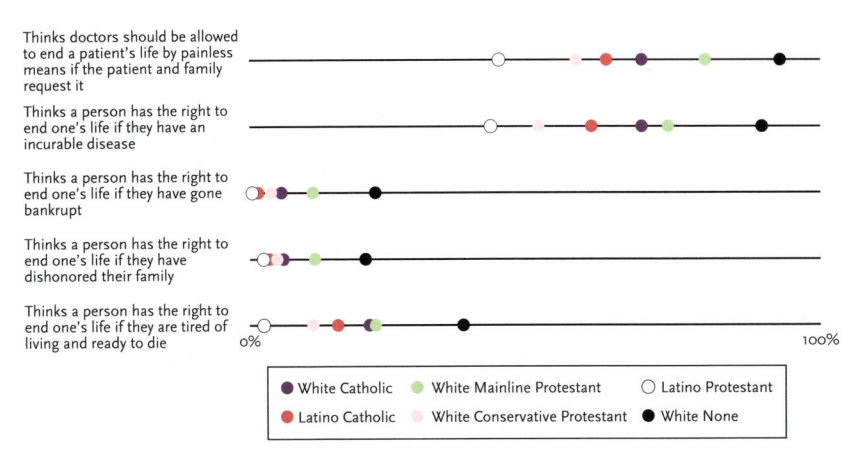

Figure 8.3 Suicide and assisted suicide

Importantly, however, support for an individual's right to commit suicide varies for both Catholics and other Americans depending on the context. In the first GSS scenario—the patient has an incurable disease—support is high among all respondents and is nearly identical to the patterns for assisted suicide: 68% of white Catholics, 59% of Latino Catholics, 73% of white mainline Protestants, 92% of religious nones, 89% of white conservative Protestants, and 42% of Latino Protestants agree.

However support for an individual's right to commit suicide is dramatically lower across the religious and racial/ethnic groups for the other scenarios. Very few Catholics think suicide is acceptable if it is motivated by bankruptcy or family honor (the second and third scenarios). Very few white (6% for each scenario) or Latino (2% and 4%) Catholics agree that bankruptcy or family honor justify suicide. Similarly low percentages of white conservative Protestants (4%, 5%) and Latino Protestants (1%, 3%) agree. By contrast, white mainline Protestants (12% for each scenario) and religious nones (22% and 20%, respectively) are more likely to agree that suicide is acceptable in this case.

Support for an individual's right to commit suicide is much higher among Catholics and most other groups if the person is simply tired of living and wants to die. More than 21% of white Catholics, 16% of Latino Catholics, 22% of white mainline Protestants, and 37% of religious nones support suicide in this case. Latino Protestants (3%) are unique in being very unlikely to support suicide in this instance.

CAPITAL PUNISHMENT

Capital punishment is another issue on which Americans have strong—and often divided—views and that can affect voting, other political behaviors, and other behaviors. The Catholic Church strongly opposes capital punishment because it takes a human life. The United States Conference of Catholic Bishops (USCCB) summarizes the Catholic approach to capital punishment when it says: "[A] principled Catholic response to crime and punishment is rooted in our convictions about good and evil, sin and redemption, justice and mercy. It is also shaped by our commitment to the life and dignity of every human person, and the common good.... No matter how heinous the crime, if society can protect itself without ending a human life, it should do so." In a similar plea, Pope John Paul II wrote that "the dignity of human life must never be taken away, even in the case of someone who has done great evil" (Pope John Paul II January 27, 1999).

The GSS captures Americans' views of capital punishment with a single question: "Do you favor or oppose the death penalty for persons convicted of murder?" Large percentages of white and Latino Catholics (roughly 58% and 53%, respectively) support capital punishment—much like they support abortion rights and assisted suicide—despite Church teachings to the contrary (Figure 8.4).

Yet capital punishment is unique among the topics I have explored in this book, perhaps because it is a highly politicized issue in the United States that taps into views about policing, the role of government in people's lives, and related issues that have become part of the complex relationship between religious groups and the state. The religious groups I study are arrayed differently on the issue of capital punishment than on other issues. Despite their relatively moderate stances on many issues, 68% of white mainline Protestants support capital punishment. High percentages of white conservative Protestants (77%) support capital punishment, consistent with the tendency of this faith group to ally with conservative political causes (Gorski and Perry 2022). Latino Protestant support (46%) is more similar to Latino Catholic (53%) support on the issue of capital punishment than it is on many of the other issues I have discussed.

Finally, 51% of religious nones support capital punishment, in contrast to their progressive attitudes on other issues, and the views of religious nones regarding capital punishment are somewhat similar to those of all but white conservative Protestants. This support provides further evidence that capital punishment is a unique issue on which there is considerable agreement among

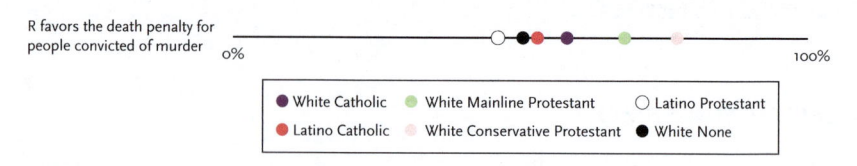

Figure 8.4 Capital punishment

Americans. As others have shown, nones hold a wide variety of attitudes and opinions (Burge 2021; Levin et al. 2022).

TRUST AND CONFIDENCE

Generalized Trust and Confidence in Institutions

Generalized trust and confidence in institutions can be important components of individuals' identities; these concepts are also critical to the functioning of societies, economies, and political systems. Generalized trust (hereafter, *trust*) binds social systems together (Paxton 2007), facilitates social order (Parsons 1937), makes economic transactions more efficient (Coleman 1988), contributes to cooperation (Arrow 1974), and has been linked to the creation and maintenance of democracy (Paxton 2002) and economic development (Tolbert, Lyson, and Irwin 1998). Confidence in institutions (hereafter *confidence*) is closely related to trust and also foundational for social functioning (Brady and Kent 2022). For everyday interactions to occur smoothly, it is necessary for individuals to trust educational institutions to teach children, the military and police to protect, the government to solve collective problems, and business, lawyers, doctors, and other professionals to supply the goods and services on which social and economic life depend (Brady and Kent 2022).

Despite being critical to the basic functions undertaken in all societies, trust and confidence vary across individuals, and both have changed over time (Brady and Kent 2022; Paxton 2007; Welch et al. 2004). There is evidence, for example, that American conservative Protestants have lower trust than mainline Protestants (Welch et al. 2004). Researchers also find differences in trust and confidence by political party affiliation: Republicans tend to have high confidence in business, the police, religion, and the military; by contrast, Democrats have historically had higher levels of confidence in labor, the press, higher education, and public schools (Brady and Kent 2022). Increasing political polarization and declining trust in governmental organizations has resulted in declines in confidence in most institutions—except for the military and science—over time.

Trust and confidence offer unique information about how Catholics—and members of other faith groups—view the social world. The GSS includes a series of variables that are useful for clarifying differences among these groups; Figure 8.5 includes six of these measures. First, trust is captured by responses to the question: "Generally speaking, would you say that most people can be trusted or that you can't be too careful in dealing with people?" The figure shows the percentage of respondents who answer "can trust" rather than "can't be too careful" or "it depends." Most respondents say either they "can trust" others or you "can't be too careful."

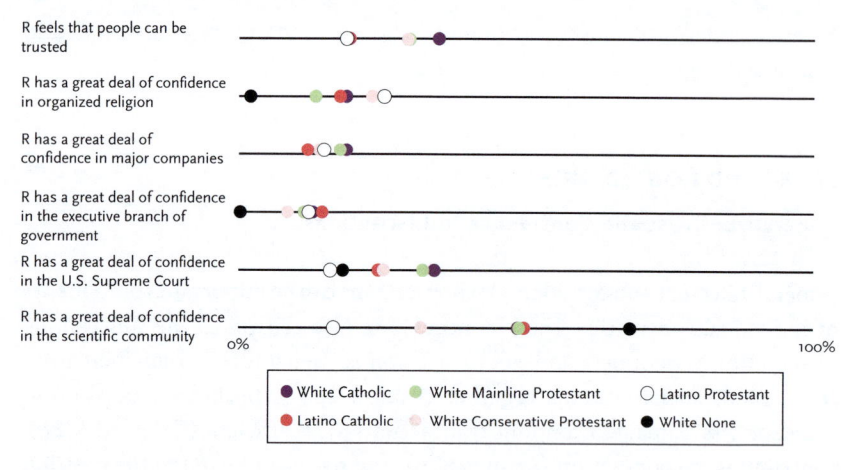

Figure 8.5 Generalized trust and confidence in institutions

The remaining measures included in Figure 8.5 are from the following GSS question: "As far as the people running these institutions are concerned, would you say you have a great deal of confidence, only some confidence, or hardly any confidence at all in them?" Respondents can answer "a great deal," "only some," or "hardly any" regarding a series of institutions. The figure shows the percentage of each group that responds "a great deal" of confidence in (1) organized religion, (2) major companies, (3) the executive branch of the federal government, (4) the United States Supreme Court, and (5) the scientific community. The GSS includes eight additional institutions that I do not include for brevity and because including them does not change the substance of my findings.

The results in Figure 8.5 show that Latino Catholics have lower levels of trust than white Catholics, but the two groups express similar confidence in most institutions. The trust gap among Catholics is, indeed, large: only 20% of Latino Catholics and more than 35% of white Catholics say that people can be trusted. This difference likely reflects the various social origin, family, and SES differences that I showed in the first part of this book and that others have documented. For example, underrepresented groups and those with lower SES (i.e., education, income, occupational prestige) tend to have lower trust perhaps because disadvantage makes them feel vulnerable (Taylor, Funk, and Clark 2007) (Box 8.1).

Yet there are few differences between white and Latino Catholics in their confidence in the institutions included in the figure: the Catholic groups have similar levels of confidence in organized religion (18% of Latino Catholics, 19% of white Catholics), the executive branch of the federal government (15%, 13%), and science (50%, 49%). They also express similar levels of confidence in institutions that are not included in the figure, including the press,

[188] *Catholics in America*

Box 8.1 FORMER CATHOLICS: LEAVERS HAVE LOW
CONFIDENCE IN RELIGION *BUT* HIGH TRUST

It is no surprise that former Catholics—both white and Latino—have low confidence in organized religion: only 3% of white and 11% of Latino Catholics who left the Church have a great deal of confidence in organized religion (results not shown in a figure). Naturally all those who have left major faith groups express low confidence in religion.

However, those who left Catholicism are more trusting than current Catholics. Indeed, white Catholics who left the Church are the most trusting group of any I study, including current and former members of all faith groups: about 43% of white Catholics who left the Church say you can trust people compared to 35% of current Catholics. Latinos who left the Church are also relatively trusting, though not as much as white Catholics: about 28% of Latino Catholic leavers say you can trust people compared to 20% of current Latino Catholics.

education, organized labor, medicine, and banks and financial institutions. Latino Catholics have lower confidence than white Catholics in only three institutions: major corporations (13%, 19%), the Supreme Court (24%, 34%), and the military (38%, 56%).

Another takeaway from Figure 8.5 is that both trust and confidence are low for all Americans, yet there are meaningful differences among the groups that offer insight into social attitudes. For example, white Catholics and white mainline Protestants also express highly similar levels of both trust and confidence, with one difference: higher percentages of white Catholics express a great deal of confidence in organized religion. Figure 8.5 shows that trust is similar for white Catholics (35%) and white mainline Protestants (30%). Likewise, similar percentages of white Catholics and white mainline Protestants respond that they have a great deal of confidence in major corporations (19%, 18%, respectively), the executive branch of the federal government (13%, 12%), the Supreme Court (34%, 32%), and science (49% for each group). By contrast, more white Catholics (19%) than white mainline Protestants (14%) express a great deal of confidence in organized religion.

White conservative Protestants express levels of trust (30% say you can trust people) similar to those of white Catholics (35%) and white mainline Protestants (30%). Their levels of confidence also line up with those of the other groups.

Religious nones are similar to the other groups in trust, but their levels of confidence make them unusual among the groups shown in Figure 8.5. About

36% of religious nones say that you can trust people. However, nones—not surprisingly—have very low confidence in organized religion: only 3% say they have a great deal of confidence in organized religion. By contrast, two-thirds (67%) of religious nones have hardly any confidence in organized religion (results not shown). Their levels of confidence in corporations (16%) and the executive branch of the federal government (13%) are similar to those of Catholics (both white and Latino) and white mainline Protestants. Nones also stand out in their confidence in the Supreme Court: 19% of them express a great deal of confidence in the Supreme Court (Figure 8.5), but more than 53% say they have "only some" confidence in the Court (not shown). Context might matter here: respondents were answering the GSS questions as the Supreme Court was preparing to overturn *Roe v. Wade*, and many religious nones describe themselves as pro-choice (Chapter 6). Dissatisfaction with the Court might reflect this event rather than a generalized lack of confidence in the court.

Volunteering

Catholic social justice includes a long history of engagement in issues through volunteering (Day 2020). "Volunteering" refers to freely chosen, uncompensated work typically done through formal organizations and usually with the intention of helping others or furthering a cause. *Stated evaluations* of trust and confidence—shown in Figure 8.5—are an individual's own assessments of their expectations and attitudes regarding others (trust) and institutions (confidence). The *hours spent* working as a volunteer can be a behavioral indicator of this same trust and confidence: allocating scarce hours to assist others through volunteer work signals trust and confidence in those organizations and their causes. Although the causal relationship between trust/confidence and volunteering is complex and difficult to untangle empirically, there appears to be a mutually reinforcing relationship between confidence in an organization and the number of volunteer hours individuals are willing to work (Bekkers and Bowman 2008; Bowman 2004). Volunteering has clear benefits for the organizations and individuals who are the recipients of the work; it also has potential benefits to the volunteer, including improved physical health, mental well-being, and social connection (Bryant et al. 2003; Fegan and Cook 2014).

Motivations for volunteering vary across individuals and groups and range from pure altruism to social influences and self-interested reasons (Bekkers and Bowman 2008; Bowman 2004). Figure 8.6 uses Panel Study of Income Dynamics (PSID) data to explore whether there are differences in volunteering by religion and ethnicity and to compare Catholics to members of other faith groups in their volunteering behavior. I turn to the PSID to illustrate

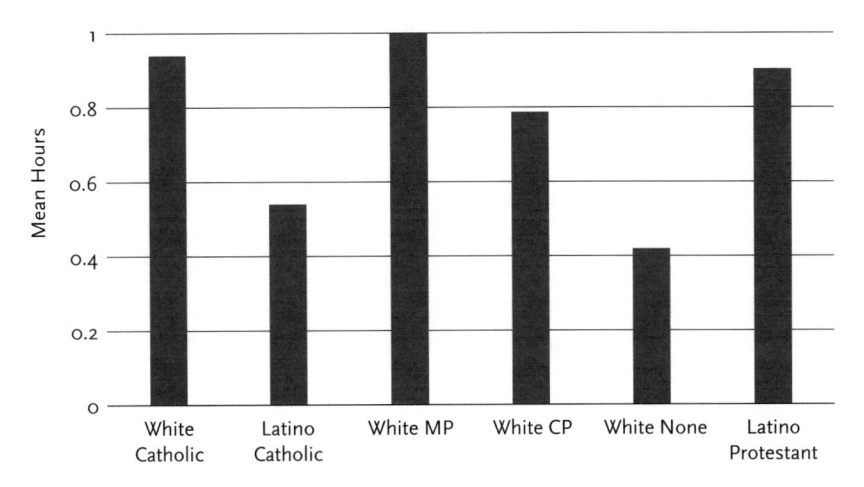

Figure 8.6 Volunteering: Average hours per week

these patterns because the GSS does not contain data on volunteering and the PSID is considered a reliable source of this information. Figure 8.6 shows the mean number of hours spent volunteering per week by individuals in 2020; additional analyses (not shown in a figure) indicate that controlling for age, income, gender, work, and other demographic traits does not change these patterns notably.

Three clear patterns emerge from Figure 8.6. First, the volunteer hours worked by any individual are low. On average, most respondents work one hour or less per week in a volunteer job, reflecting the other obligations that individuals have to work, family, and other activities. However, the low average volunteer hours might also signal at least some level of low trust and confidence—and a degree of apathy—consistent with other research findings of similar patterns. The second pattern that is clear in Figure 8.6 is that Latino Catholics, on average, volunteer less than white Catholics. The third pattern shown in the figure is that white Catholics and white mainline Protestants report similar levels of volunteering, and white conservative Protestants volunteer less than either of these groups. Again, these differences signal some difference in trust and confidence in organizations between the two groups.

Some additional caveats are in order in interpreting these patterns. Controlling for other demographic characteristics (including age, income, gender, and work) does not change these broad patterns; however, there are other potential influences on volunteering that I am unable to control. For example, socialization is a strong influence on volunteering that might vary by ethnicity and economic class (Ottani-Wilhelm, Estell, and Perdue 2014).

Latino Catholics, for example, may not be socialized to volunteer in formal settings in the same way as white Catholics. Similarly, white conservative Protestants—who tend to have education levels, income, and wealth that are lower than white Catholics and white mainline Protestants—may also have received fewer signals to volunteer as they grew up. Personality traits also affect volunteering (Carlo, Allen, and Buhman 1999), and the PSID does not allow me to control for these influences. Finally, the PSID only asks about formal volunteering (i.e., for an established organization), and many people devote unpaid work hours to helping friends and family. The PSID data would not include these hours. This omission might be particularly relevant for understanding Latinos and white conservative Protestants' volunteering. For example, much like other research that shows that Latinos tend to give financial resources directly to people they know (Indiana University Lilly Family School of Philanthropy 2021), they might also give time to those they know. Future research could usefully explore the degree to which informal volunteering affects the patterns shown in Figure 8.6.

CONCLUSION

In this chapter, I studied Catholic attitudes regarding social issues, generalized trust, and confidence in institutions. I started by noting that attitudes regarding human social interaction are essential for understanding who Catholics are and that many of the misperceptions about today's Catholics may result from confusion about their attitudes toward social issues. I explored differences among Catholics in their social attitudes, and I situated them among contemporary faith groups by comparing their attitudes on gender roles, inequality and poverty, suicide and assisted suicide, and capital punishment. I also compared Catholics' and other Americans' generalized trust and confidence in institutions to capture their orientations toward the people and organizations that comprise social life.

I found considerable similarity between white and Latino Catholics on most of the issues I studied. On gender roles, I found considerable agreement among Americans: it is rare for any respondents to say that everyone is better off if the man is the achiever outside the home and the woman takes care of the home. Similarly, most agree that a working mother can have as good a relationship with her children as a nonworking mother and disagree that children suffer when their mothers work. Consistent with this broad agreement, Latino Catholics expressed similar—but somewhat more conservative—views about gender than white Catholics. One notable difference among Catholics was Latino Catholics' high support of preferential treatment for women.

White Catholics' attitudes regarding gender roles were also similar to—although slightly more conservative than—those of white mainline

Protestants. White conservative Protestants and religious nones expressed views on gender that were different—albeit modestly—from those shared by members of other faith groups. For example, white conservative Protestants were significantly more likely than any of the other groups to agree that everyone is better off when men are the achievers and women stay at home; similarly, white conservative Protestants were the least likely to support preferential treatment for women. However, consistent with the comparatively high propensity for white conservative Protestants to work out of the home, their attitudes regarding the potentially detrimental effects of women's work on children were similar to those of the other groups.

White and Latino Catholics also had similar views of inequality, suicide, and capital punishment. They agreed, for instance, that differences in income in America are too large (although more Latino than white Catholics agreed with this sentiment). Similarly, large percentages of both Latino and white Catholics supported efforts to address the problems associated with inequality and poverty (e.g., high-income people should pay more taxes, a need for strong labor unions). However, Latino Catholics were much less likely than white Catholic to support preferential treatment for African Americans.

Despite Church teachings, high percentages of white (68%) and Latino (62%) Catholics agreed that a doctor should be allowed to end a patient's life if the patient and family request it. Notably, Catholics were not unique in this support: large percentages of white mainline Protestants (79%) and religious nones (92%) expressed support for assisted suicide. Even the more conservative religious respondents indicated broad support for assisted suicide, although few white conservative Protestants (57%) and Latino Protestants (44%) agreed that doctors should be legally allowed to end a patient's life. I also found, however, that support for an individual's right to commit suicide varies for both Catholics and other Americans depending on the context, with few members of any faith group supporting an individual's right to end his or her life in, for example, the case of bankruptcy or family honor. Large percentages of white and Latino Catholics (roughly 58% and 53%, respectively) support capital punishment—much like they support abortion rights and assisted suicide—despite Church teachings to the contrary.

Generalized trust was the one issue on which white and Latino Catholics expressed significantly different attitudes: significantly higher percentages of white Catholics than Latino Catholics expressed high levels of trust. However, Catholic confidence in institutions was more similar overall. Latino and white Catholics had similar levels of confidence in organized religion, the executive branch of the federal government, and science. However, Latino Catholics have lower confidence than white Catholics in major corporations and the Supreme Court. Latino Catholic confidence in corporations and the Supreme Court was more similar to those of white conservative Protestants than to those of Latino Catholics.

White Catholics and white mainline Protestants also expressed similar levels of both trust and confidence, with one difference: higher percentages of white Catholics express a great deal of confidence in organized religion.

White conservative Protestants were also highly trusting and were notably similar to white Catholics and white mainline Protestants on this general evaluation of the benevolence of people. By contrast, white conservative Protestants and religious nones have much different levels of confidence in institutions, consistent with the different worldviews that I consistently find between these two groups.

In the final section of the chapter, I compared Catholics to other Americans on volunteering—a behavioral indicator of trust and confidence—that built on my discussion of individuals' opinions of their trust and confidence. I found that the volunteer hours worked by any individual in any faith group were low. I also found that Latino Catholics, on average, volunteer fewer hours than white Catholics, in contrast to similarities in trust and confidence I found between these two groups. I also found that white Catholics and white mainline Protestants volunteer similar numbers of hours, whereas white conservative Protestants volunteer less than either of these groups. While I noted that these patterns are useful indicators of trust and confidence, they are yet simply suggestive and should be interpreted in light of data limitations. In particular, controlling for various demographic characteristics (including age, income, gender, and work) did not change the patterns I presented. However, I was unable to control for socialization and personality traits that might affect volunteering. In addition, I only measured volunteering for formal organization and did not include hours spent helping friends and family. Future research might usefully study these issues more closely than I was able.

CHAPTER 9
Conclusion

Catholics occupy a different place in American society today than they did historically. With this social portrait, I sought to document who contemporary Catholics are, including variations among Church members and how Catholics compare to other Americans. I started by observing that membership in the Catholic Church is large and has remained relatively stable since the 1970s. Some influential Catholics—including President Joe Biden and members of both the U.S. Congress and the Supreme Court—have helped fuel interest in the demographics, religious beliefs, and other attitudes of today's Catholics. However, the seemingly steadfast size of the Church potentially masks considerable underlying change in Church membership, including a dramatic growth in the Latino Catholic population. Previous research has shown that Catholic family behaviors and states have also changed dramatically, and white Catholics have experienced changes in social and economic status that have probably continued and that may be associated with significant changes in their beliefs, practices, and attitudes. These changes to Catholicism have occurred during a period of broader American religious transformation, including a substantial rise in religious disaffiliation (a rise in the religious nones). Given these changes and realities, I proposed that an updated social portrait of Catholics is in order and would improve understanding of Catholics and the broader U.S. religious landscape.

This social portrait had two parts. In Part I, I provided a portrait of Catholic demographics, including documenting differences among Catholics, changes in Catholic states and behaviors over time, and comparisons with other Americans. I explored Catholic social origins (e.g., birth cohort, gender, ethnicity, class background), family traits and behaviors (e.g., marriage, cohabitation, divorce, fertility), and socioeconomic status (SES) (e.g., education, work, income, wealth). I ended Part I by studying movement into and out of the

Catholic Church and situated that movement in the broader landscape of religious mobility. In Part II, I studied beliefs and attitudes, including religious beliefs and practices, politics and political attitudes, and attitudes regarding social issues. In each chapter in the second half of the book, I compared white and Latino beliefs and practices to document similarities and differences between these two largest Catholic ethnic groups. When I was able, I considered how Catholics' attitudes and beliefs compare to official Church teaching to consider whether there are gaps between Catholic teaching and the attitudes of Church members, and I compared Catholic beliefs and attitudes to those of other Americans.

This strategy revealed that Catholics are a complex collection of individuals and families. Although prominent Catholics have brought attention to the Church, these individuals are not necessarily representative of the multitude of demographic profiles represented among Catholics. Viewing Catholics solely through the most visible Church members would risk missing the important diversity in background traits, other demographics, and religious, political, and social beliefs that characterize Catholics today. My findings built on previous social science research that emphasizes the importance of ethnicity in contemporary society, but the analyses I offered also underscored the vital importance of religion in understanding Americans.

I found that today's Catholic Church is highly diverse and that ethnicity is a critical dimension on which Catholics differ. Chapter 2 underscored the reality that Latino Catholics comprise an increasingly large portion of the Church and that understanding Catholics requires understanding differences between non-Hispanic white (i.e., white) Catholics and Latino Catholics. Black Catholics, Asian Catholics, and other ethnic subgroups are certainly unique and important as well; however, these groups are not numerous enough in my data for me to provide detailed empirical estimates of their demographics, beliefs, and attitudes. Thus, I focused on differences between white and Latino Catholics in subsequent chapters. Chapter 2 also showed that today's Catholic Church is diverse in terms of birth cohort and gender, including large numbers of each living birth cohort: Generation Z, Millennials, Generation X, Baby Boomers, and the Silent Generation. However, Millennials and Generation X are the most numerous cohorts in the Church. This chapter also began to document differences between white and Latino Catholics, showing that white Catholics grew up in more affluent families than their Latino counterparts.

The remainder of Part I provided additional evidence that white and Latino Catholics are very different demographically; however, my analyses also showed that white Catholic parity with white mainline Protestants has continued. That is, Chapter 3 showed that high marriage rates, low divorce rates, and shrinking fertility are hallmarks of today's Catholic family. However, today's white and Latino Catholics have different adult families: compared to white Catholics, Latino Catholics are less likely to marry, more likely to cohabit, and less likely to divorce. By contrast, marriage and cohabitation rates are similar for white Catholics and white mainline Protestants, with one notable exception: white Catholics are less likely than white mainline Protestants to have ever divorced. Comparison of family patterns also showed that white conservative Protestants are different from white Catholics and white mainline Protestants, but the findings were suggestive of convergence as well. For example, Chapter 3 findings showed that white conservative Protestants are more likely than white Catholics to marry, equally likely to cohabit, and *slightly* more likely to have divorced. Long-term trends in divorce were particularly instructive and showed rising but converging rates for each of the groups I studied.

Chapter 4 focused on SES—education, work, income, and wealth—and showed that Latino Catholics lag behind white Catholics on nearly every measure I studied. Results showed lower education levels, overall income, homeownership, and wealth for Latino Catholics compared to white Catholics. Latino Catholics are also more likely than white Catholics to experience income and net worth poverty. Yet I found signs that the SES of Latino Catholics may be changing and could converge with that of white Catholics. For example, differences between white and Latino Catholics on working full time and having two earners are minimal; I also found that white and Latino Catholics have similar levels of self-employment, an important indicator of long-term upward SES mobility. Findings from Chapter 4 also underscored that SES parity between white Catholics and white mainline Protestants has continued: these groups had similar levels of each SES measure I studied. One intriguing finding was evidence that white Catholics may be moving ahead of white mainline Protestants on some SES measures. I found, for example, that white Catholics are more likely than white mainline Protestants to have high incomes and wealth. These findings are preliminary, but suggestive; future research might usefully explore these patterns in more detail.

Part I ended with an exploration of religious mobility, updating evidence regarding movement into and out of the Church and situating that movement within the broader U.S. landscape. Findings underscored well-documented evidence that movement out of the Catholic Church has been considerable. Indeed, I found suggestive patterns in the GSS that indicated there might be even more religious change than previous research has found because people revise (or edit) their childhood religion to be more congruent with their adult situations and current norms. My findings underscored the demographics of those who left the Catholic Church: that is, leavers are relatively young and more likely to be female, Latino, and divorced or previously divorced. I also explored the reasons that people leave the Church, using updated, nationally representative data that include interviews with a large number of Americans from all faith groups. These interviews highlighted five reasons that people leave Catholicism, including drifting away over time, a dissatisfaction with all religion motivated by a commitment to moral relativism, disagreement with Church doctrine, anger over Church scandals or politics, or being pulled away to other faiths.

Part II explored beliefs and attitudes, including religious beliefs and practices (Chapter 6), political attitudes (Chapter 7), and attitudes regarding social issues (Chapter 8). In each of these chapters, I compared white and Latino Catholics to better understand variation among Church members. I also studied how Catholic beliefs, practices, and attitudes compare to official Church teaching, where possible, to explore whether Catholics widely adhere to Church teaching. My ability to investigate this question thoroughly was limited by my data, but my findings revealed important patterns that would be usefully explored in future research. Finally, in each of these chapters, I situated Catholics' beliefs, practices, and attitudes in the broader U.S. religious landscape by comparing Catholics to members of other faith groups.

Chapter 6 showed that white and Latino Catholics are similar to each other on many measures of religious strength, Mass attendance and other religious practices, evangelization, and their beliefs about God, the afterlife, the Bible, and Papal infallibility. They differ, however, in their reports of having a born-again or significant religious experience and in their views of divorce. One of these findings is particular noteworthy: both white and Latino Catholics have serious doubts about the church's teachings about papal infallibility. Because my goal is to provide a contemporary portrait of Catholics, I do not study how attitudes regarding papal infallibility have changed over time. Moreover, data limitations prevent me from addressing some of the more important issues related to attitudes regarding papal infallibility. For example, it would be useful to know whether particular events in the Church or secular events contributed to declines in these attitudes. It is plausible that the erosion in belief in papal infallibility began in the late 1960s, when the Pope declared the immorality of artificial contraception or in reaction to other papal decisions or actions. Unfortunately, the GSS question that I use is only available back to 2004. Moreover, there are no related questions that would allow connecting attitudes about papal infallibility with other issues (e.g., there are no questions that probe reasons for these beliefs). Future research might usefully explore these issues.

In addition—as I pointed out in Chapter 6—it is important to keep in mind that the GSS data contain very little information about issues that are uniquely Catholic, and white and Latino Catholics appear to differ on some elements of the faith that I was unable to study. For instance, data with more Catholic-specific detail shows that Latino Catholics place greater emphasis than white Catholics on devotion to Mary, weekly Mass attendance,

Eucharistic adoration, praying the rosary, and going to private confession to a priest (D'Antonio, Dillon, and Gautier 2013; Day et al. forthcoming).

Nevertheless, white Catholics and Latino Catholics are remarkably similar on nearly all measures of religious belief and practice. For example, I found that Mass attendance is low for both white and Latino Catholics: about 30% of both white and Latino Catholics reported attending Mass less than once a year, and about half those (16%) never attend. Only about 15% attend Mass weekly, and only about 2% attend more than once a week. Despite Church teaching contrary to divorce, 40% of white Catholics and more than 73% of Latino Catholics think divorce should be easier to obtain; however, it is noteworthy that Latino support for easier divorce laws is significantly higher than white Catholic support for this issue. Catholics also have views regarding abortion that are contrary to Church teaching: only 51% of white Catholics and 36% of Latino Catholics call themselves pro-life. Relatively few Catholics—white or Latino—report that they have "ever tried to encourage someone to believe in Jesus Christ or to accept Jesus Christ as his or her savior."

In contrast to their religious similarities, white and Latino Catholics differ in their political attitudes and orientation (Chapter 7). White Catholics are similar to white mainline Protestants politically. I found, for example, that both white Catholics and white mainline Protestants are split across Democrat (20%), Republican (45%), and Independent Parties (20%). By contrast, the majority (more than 50%) of Latino Catholics and nones are Democrats and consider themselves liberals. Findings also indicated that Catholics have diverse views regarding issues such as federal income taxes and government spending. For example, white Catholics are highly conservative in regards to their federal income taxes. Latino Catholics, white mainline Protestants, and Latino Protestants are more similar to each other and lean moderate to progressive on taxes. By contrast, white Catholics, white mainline Protestants, and Latino Protestants all express moderate views on government spending I cut this to simplify the language. whereas Latino Catholics lean left on spending.

Finally, Chapter 8 showed that white and Latino Catholics agree on most social issues, including gender roles, economic inequality, suicide, and capital punishment. Despite Church teachings to the contrary, Catholics support physician-assisted suicide: both white (68%) and Latino (62%) Catholics agree that a doctor should be allowed to end a patient's life if the patient and family request it. Catholics also support capital punishment: more than one-half of both white and Latino Catholics support capital punishment. I found some relatively minor but notable differences among Catholics in their generalized trust. That is, my results showed that significantly higher percentages of white Catholics than Latino Catholics expressed high levels of trust. These differences are notable given the importance of trust for the functioning of social, economic, and political systems and because they are highly correlated with other behaviors such as voting.

BOUNDARIES AND NEXT STEPS

Although I was able to address a large number of demographic, religious, political, and social issues, my social portrait was necessarily bounded. For example, I was unable to provide details about the demographics, beliefs, and practices of groups other than white and Latino Catholics. Other ethnic groups—including Asian and African American Catholics—occupy unique positions in the Church. I was unable to study these groups in depth because there are too few of them in my data; however, their unique experiences, characteristics, beliefs, and practices are critical to understanding Catholics. Future research will hopefully explore the distinct contributions these groups make to Catholicism.

The constraints of a single book also forced me to provide only brief discussions of many issues that deserve to be unpacked further. Issues such as the Church's teaching on gender, divorce, and other family issues—and variations among Catholics on their approaches to these issues—could be the subject of entire books (and indeed, such books exist). Similarly, the continued fluctuations in income and wealth among Catholics and between Catholics and other Americans are worth unpacking, and my single chapter on the subject only began to explore the many issues that underlie the patterns I described. The same is true for many of the religious, political, and social beliefs that I described. However, to provide a broad social portrait, I am forced to leave this unpacking for future research.

I was also unable to discuss Catholic doctrine in depth or to say much about the beliefs and practices that are uniquely Catholic. As I noted in the Introduction, my goal was sociological, and my primary objective was to provide empirical estimates of the demographics, beliefs, and attitudes of Catholics. In addition, my data do not contain detail on topics that are uniquely Catholic—arguably the data I use (like many other survey datasets that include information about religion) have a Protestant bias (e.g., asking questions about Bible interpretation). Thus, I focused on issues that are relevant to all Americans. For example, I would ideally have studied Catholic beliefs about the Eucharist, how these beliefs vary among Catholics, and how they have changed—and may be changing—over time. Transubstantiation is the idea that bread and wine become the actual body and blood of Jesus during Mass. This core Catholic teaching has attracted attention in light of evidence that only 31% of Catholics believe in the Real Presence. Nearly 70% of Catholics say they believe that the bread and wine are merely "*symbols* of the body and blood of Jesus Christ" (Smith

2019). Related to this disconnect between the beliefs of ordinary Catholics and Church teaching, the Church is undergoing a "National Eucharistic Revival." This three-year effort that began in 2022 is intended to "renew the Church by enkindling a living relationship with the Lord Jesus Christ in the Holy Eucharist" (https://www.eucharisticrevival.org/). A study of Catholic beliefs following the Eucharistic Revival—including an exploration of whether their beliefs changed in light of this initiative—would be interesting and useful.

Tensions among Catholics—including tensions related to the political and social issues I studied—are also important for understanding the contemporary Church. Although I alluded to some of these tensions in my discussions of various attitudes, a full exploration of the origins, contemporary manifestations, and potential implications of these tensions is beyond the scope of this book. For example, tensions regarding abortion attitudes are strong enough that Pope Francis has issued sharp statements cautioning against "backward" attitudes held by some Catholics regarding abortion and sexual morality at the expense of other Church priorities such as care for the poor (Horowitz and Graham August 30, 2023). Related to these tensions are coalitions between some Catholics and members of other faith groups—typically conservative Protestants—that fuel frictions among Catholics. Although these issues are important for understanding Catholics and for situating them within the broader American religious landscape, I was unable to do them justice in this book.

Additional exploration of other empirical patterns would also be ideal. For example, differences between former and current Catholics would also be useful for understanding the current and future makeup of the Church. I included sidebars underscoring the ways former Catholics differ from current Catholics, and these showed that leavers have distinct beliefs and practices. However, a full exploration of who leaves the Church—and, related to this, who ultimately returns—is beyond the scope of this book. Similarly, my data prohibited me from offering a discussion of geographic—and corresponding cultural—differences among Catholics. There is little doubt that religious practices—and potentially religious beliefs and attitudes regarding political and social issues—vary across regions of the United States. However, my data do not include large enough samples to allow me to offer empirical evidence at the state or local levels.

Many of my findings—particularly from Chapters 7 and 8—showed that white conservative Protestants and the religious nones are on opposite sides of the spectrum on a variety of political and social issues. These patterns suggest that these two groups might contribute significantly to high levels of polarization in American society today. Although this is an intriguing hypothesis, studying it is beyond the scope of this book and not possible with my data. Future research might usefully explore this idea.

CONCLUSION

My findings allude to what the Catholic Church may look like in the future. For example, differences in the social origins, family behaviors and states, and SES of Catholics suggest that the demographic profile of the Church will continue to change. Differences between white and Latino Catholics in fertility (i.e., higher for Latino Catholics) and rates of disaffiliation (i.e., lower for Latino Catholics) suggest that the Latino Catholic population will continue to grow. As a result, other Latino Catholic demographic traits (e.g., marriage, cohabitation, divorce, income, wealth) are likely to become more common. Similarly, Latino Catholics' religious beliefs and practices, political orientations and attitudes, and attitudes toward social issues would also become more common. Of course, I found many areas of agreement among Latino and white Catholics on critical religious, political, and social issues (e.g., religious strength, views of papal infallibility, views regarding crime and gender roles); thus, the attitude of the modal Catholic might not change dramatically on these issues. However, on the issues on which Latino and white Catholics disagree (e.g., attitudes regarding whether divorce should be easier, abortion, government spending and taxes), the average Catholic will look different in the future.

Of course, responding to disaffiliation to retain and attract members would also affect the makeup of the Church in the future. Findings from Chapter 5—particularly those that indicate why Catholics leave the faith—are relevant here. For example, I found that many former Catholics simply drifted away from the Church over time and at turning points during the life course. This suggests that targeted efforts to engage—or re-engage—people of all ages in the faith or drawing back in young people at critical life stages might retain members. I also found that many former Catholics left the Church because they interpreted its message as unintellectual or even anti-intellectual. Moving away from simplified approaches to Catholicism and celebrating the Church's deep intellectual traditions might forestall disaffiliation by those who appreciate this tradition (see Barron 2020 on this issue). Other former Catholics pointed to the beauty of particular elements of Catholicism—such as the Mass and church buildings—and spoke about how they missed many aspects of the faith. These reminiscing thoughts suggest that drawing on the beauty of the faith in evangelization may be critical (Barron 2020).

The changing demographics of the Church also have implications for the United States, including in politics. I began this book by pointing to prominent Catholics such as President Biden and the Supreme Court justices. These influential individuals are clearly able to affect national politics and conversations about social issues. Yet ordinary Catholics can also affect change, for instance, through voting, other political behaviors, and charitable giving. If the growth in the U.S. Latino population continues and the proportion of Catholics who are Latino continues to increase as well, the Church may include more Democrats over time, and this would affect the Catholic vote. Regional differences in politics—for example, the potential that political ideologies vary across states and regions—would affect whether a change of this sort aggregates into an effect on elections.

My hope is that this social portrait showed that Catholics are much more complex than anecdotal evidence suggests. My findings underscored differences among Catholics that may be magnified if current trends in demographics and religious mobility continue. However, my findings also underscored continued similarities between white Catholics and white mainline Protestants—and evidence of convergence with white conservative Protestants on some issues as well—suggesting that it may well be that misunderstandings about Catholics are not based on facts but on misperceptions stemming from conclusions drawn from prominent Catholics.

Appendix

DATA

I use three datasets in this book. First, I use the 1972–2021 General Social Survey (GSS) to provide quantitative, cross-sectional estimates that are representative of the U.S. population. The GSS is a series of nationally representative cross-sectional interviews with the adult population of the United States that has occurred since 1972. I use all 50 years of GSS data, but I focus on the 2021 GSS panel to document contemporary patterns. I include relatively few over-time comparisons using the GSS because the GSS changed its survey strategy in 2021 from an in-person interview to an online interview to address concerns related to the COVID-19 pandemic. I weight all analyses using GSS-provided weights.

Second, I use the 1997–2021 waves of the Panel Study of Income Dynamics (PSID) to provide quantitative estimates of outcomes that are not included in the GSS. I also use the PSID to provide longitudinal estimates (i.e., estimates of outcomes over time for the same respondents). For example, I use PSID data to study wealth and inheritance (Chapter 4), religious change over individual lives (Chapter 5), charitable giving (Chapter 7), and volunteering (Chapter 8). The PSID is the longest-running longitudinal survey of individuals and families in the United States. Its sample includes individuals who were originally selected as part of a probability sample in 1968 and who have been reinterviewed regularly since that time. The PSID also includes individuals who were born to or adopted by these original sample members and those included in subsequent immigrant refreshers. I weight all analyses using PSID-provided weights.

Third, I use the American Voices Project (AVP) to provide case studies that illustrate the mechanisms underlying the empirical patterns that emerge from my GSS and PSID analyses. I also use the AVP to explore reasons people left the Catholic Church (Chapter 5). The AVP is a unique mixed-methods (quantitative and qualitative) data source that was collected in 2019 and 2020 from a representative sample of the U.S. population. The AVP sample was identified using a three-stage clustering methodology and included respondents in all 50 states plus Puerto Rico. The AVP's quantitative survey includes individual and household demographics (e.g., age, gender, ethnicity, education), religious affiliation, place of birth, current residence, and other information. It also contains a detailed interview with respondents that includes a detailed life history, information about important life events, and discussion of other issues such as religion, education, family, and work. The average AVP interview was 2.2 hours.

These datasets are ideal for my work, but they also have drawbacks. Each of the datasets includes enough Catholics and members of other faith traditions to allow me to study differences within the Catholic Church and to compare Catholics to other Americans. The datasets I use also have rich information on a range of demographic characteristics, beliefs, and practices that allows me to offer a detailed portrait of Catholics and members of other faith groups.

However, each of these datasets was collected during the COVID-19 pandemic and required special attention and changes to survey protocols to adjust for restrictions at the time. I conducted robustness checks to uncover data inconsistencies that might have resulted and did not discover any significant issues. However, I acknowledge that the time during which the surveys were collected might have influenced respondent answers.

In addition, these datasets are designed to make national comparisons rather than to study issues that are particularly Catholic in nature. As a result, I am unable to offer detailed analysis of issues that are important to Catholics. There is only one question in the GSS—regarding papal infallibility—that is about a Catholic belief; I use that question in Chapter 6. The PSID contains no Catholic-specific questions. Other research has used data that have more questions that are specifically Catholic (D'Antonio et al. 2007; D'Antonio, Dillon, and Gautier 2013; Smith et al. 2014), but these datasets tend to make national comparisons challenging.

VARIABLES

Many of the variables I use are self-explanatory. I provide additional detail here for variables that require clarification.

GSS Variables

Religious Affiliation. I use the GSS variables RELIG (religious affiliation) and DENOM (specific Protestant denomination) to code religious affiliation in adulthood. I compare Catholics to three other religious groups: mainline (or progressive) Protestants, conservative Protestants, and religious nones (those who claim no formal religious affiliation). I do not include people affiliated with other religious traditions because there are too few in the data to provide reliable statistical estimates on most of the topics I study.

I create the religious groups using the religious traditions classification scheme that has become the standard in the sociology of religion (Steensland et al. 2000). In Chapters 1 and 2, I modify the Steensland et al. approach by decomposing the black Protestant churches into mainline and conservative groups following other research (Perry and Schleifer 2019). Chapter 2 analyses clarify that white and Latino Catholics are the largest ethnic groups in the Catholic Church and are numerous enough in the GSS data to study in additional detail in subsequent chapters. However, Chapter 2 analyses also show that the GSS data contain too few black and Asian Catholics to analyze in subsequent chapters. Therefore, starting in Chapter 3, I begin to compare six religious ethnic groups: white Catholics, Latino Catholics, white mainline Protestants, white conservative Protestants, white religious nones, and Latino Protestants. This strategy allows me to compare the two main Catholic ethnic groups: non-Latino white Catholics and Latino Catholics to each other and to white mainline Protestants and white conservative Protestants, the two largest Protestant religious-ethnic groups in the United States. Using these groups also allows me to compare Catholics to the growing group of religious nones.

Age and Birth Cohort. I use respondents' self-reported age as a stand-alone variable and to create birth cohort. Because the GSS saw higher rates of non-response to its age question in 2021 (Davern et al. 2021), I used multiple imputation to estimate age for 333 respondents with missing data for age. I conducted extensive preliminary analyses and determined that the age variable was missing at random and not correlated with other variables that are central to my analyses. I used SAS's Proc MI (multiple imputation) procedure to impute the values (https://stats.oarc.ucla.edu/sas/seminars/multiple-imputation-in-sas/mi_new_1/). Specifically, I tested two auxiliary variables (age at which respondent's children were born or AGEKDBRN and work status or WRKSTAT) and found that they were, in fact, correlated with missing age, meaning that they should be included in the age imputation. These two variables are both highly age-dependent and reveal considerable information about respondent age. I followed the GSS dummy coding strategy for all imputation variables except age; for age, the GSS used 10-year categories, but I used generational cohort to create the categories I use in the book. Using all eight of the GSS imputation variables, plus my two auxiliary variables, I ran five imputations using the multivariate normal distribution (MVN) method. I then averaged the imputed values and recoded them into generational categories. Additional sensitivity testing showed that the imputed age information was highly consistent with what we would expect respondents to report.

Ancestry, Ethnicity, and Race. To create ancestry, I use two variables. First, I use the variable ETHNIC which asks, "From what countries or part of the world did your ancestors come? IF MORE THAN ONE COUNTRY NAMED: Which one of these countries do you feel closer to?" This variable has a single country answer. Second, I use the variable HISPANIC, which is asked of respondents who responded that they are Spanish, Hispanic, or Latino/Latina: "Which group are you from?" and presents two dozen different Hispanic countries. The Hispanic variable has only one value, so respondents are not able to select more than one country; however, they could choose a general category if they wanted, like "South American" or simply respond again with "Hispanic." I grouped these responses into broad global regions.

I use a four-category variable to indicate ethnicity and race throughout the book. The variable divides the GSS sample into four mutually exclusive categories (using GSS variables RACE and HISPANIC): non-Latino white, non-Latino black, Latino, or other ethnicity/race. I opted to use this strategy after extensive exploration and consideration of other variables that also contain information about ethnicity and race. For example, I explored using a series of variables that pose 16 races to the respondent, who could then choose as many races as he or she wanted. I also explored using a similar series of 16 other variables that asked about the respondent's ethnicity and race at age 16, and I explored using a different series of variables that ask about the respondent's ancestry.

I ultimately decided that the four-category strategy I use has several advantages. First, the four-category strategy is efficient, requiring only two variables (RACE and HISPANIC) for its construction; other strategies require using multiple variables, which can lead to additional missing values or inconsistencies across variables. Second, the four-category strategy is straightforward and easy to replicate. Third, the four-category strategy is most effective at identifying people who consider themselves Latino.

Fourth, few respondents take advantage of the option to identify as multiple races when given the opportunity, suggesting that there is little advantage to using a series of variables to code ethnicity and race. Fifth, the four-category strategy is consistent with most current research on ethnicity and race. One alternative is to divide respondents into those who identify as Latino versus non-Latino respondents and then letting race (e.g., black vs. white) vary separately. This strategy might become common in the future given that ethnicity and race are different concepts; however, this strategy is not common now. Moreover, most respondents still identify as black, white, Latino, or other, consistent with my coding. Finally, it is possible to create the four-category variable from 2000 forward in the GSS.

For 2021, GSS sample sizes are non-Latino white = 2,839; non-Latino black = 426; Latino (including those who identify as white or black and Latino) = 454; other race = 279; and missing = 34. The GSS has sufficient numbers of Latino Catholics to provide reliable comparisons of Latino and non-Latino white Catholics: of all GSS respondents in 2021, 454 identify as Latino, 824 are Catholic, and 204 are both Latino and Catholic. However, there are too few Latinos to study subgroups by nativity: of the 2021 GSS respondents who identify as Latino, 245 are Mexican, 51 are Puerto Rican, 46 are Spanish, 21 are Cuban, and 17 are Dominican. All other Latino groups have 10 or fewer respondents. Similarly, of Catholics in the 2021 GSS, 129 are Mexican, 19 are Puerto Rican, 4 are Cuban, 17 are Spanish, and 5 are Dominican. All others have 10 or fewer respondents.

Immigrant Generation. I use mother's, father's, and grandparents' place of birth to create measures of immigrant generation. Consistent with past research (Greeley and Hout 2006), I classify the respondent as first-generation if they have at least one parent born outside the United States. Similarly, if at least one of four grandparents was born outside the United States while both parents were born in the United States, I classify the respondent as second-generation. If all four grandparents and both parents were born in the United States, regardless of whether the respondent reported being US-born (or even if they did not report their place of birth), I classified them as non-immigrant.

Married/Cohabiting/Divorced. I model married as "ever married" and divorced as "ever divorced" using MARITAL and DIVORCE. I model cohabiting as currently cohabiting using MARCOHAB. The GSS historically included additional detail about cohabitation, but in 2021, they started providing information only about current cohabitation, which makes it impossible for me to model "ever cohabited."

Abortion and Assisted Suicide. The variables I used to create these measures are part of an experiment conducted in the 2021 GSS designed to reduce the length of some questions. In this experiment, the GSS chose two sets of items that shared question stems, response options, and conceptual topics—including abortion and assisted suicide—and presented them differently to two subsets of respondents (i.e., either in grid format or list format). The GSS codebook includes additional detail and examples of the two display options. I combine responses from both subsets of respondents in creating my abortion and assisted suicide measures. Robustness checks suggested that there were no significant differences by religious affiliation that would affect the substance of the results I present.

Federal Poverty Line (FPL). I used household income and household size to determine whether a household falls below the FPL. I calculated the FPL as closely as possible to the federally define threshold given the constraints of the GSS data.

First, I estimated household income using CONINC, which identifies household income categories. I coded CONINC into 26 ordinal categories, noting the income range of each. Second, I estimated household size. Because HOMPOP—the variable typically used for household size—was not collected by the GSS in 2021, I used an alternative strategy. I begin with 1 and add family members using the variables MARITAL (+1 if married), MARCOHAB (+1 if not married but living together), and CHILDS (+ number of children) with AGE as a control for respondents whose children may not live at home anymore.

Finally, I determined which ordinal bin to use as the FPL cutoff: if the official FPL cutoff fell above the middle of the ordinal category, I used that bin as "below the FPL." Otherwise, I determined that the bin was "above the FPL." If the official FPL limit falls below the middle of the ordinal category, I use that bin as "above the FPL" and the next lower bin as "below the FPL."

PSID Variables

Net Worth Poverty. I use the PSID's imputed household net worth variable to measure net worth poverty (NWP) and high wealth. Net worth is defined as assets less debts; assets include stocks, real estate, and checking and savings accounts net of a broad range of debt, including medical, legal, student, family loan, and credit card debt. Following previous work (Gibson-Davis, Keister, and Gennettian 2020), I exclude the value of retirement assets and the value of vehicles from net worth calculations. I define NWP relative to the 2019 poverty line (United States Census Bureau 2021). I consider households to be net worth poor if their net worth (total assets minus total debts) is less than 25% of the federal poverty line, adjusted for family composition.

AVP Variables

The AVP quantitative survey included a question about religious affiliation: "What religion do you identify with, if any?" The answer is open-ended, allowing respondents to identify with multiple faith traditions and to mention small or less well-known faith traditions. Despite the flexibility of this question, most respondents said they were affiliated with common religious groups (e.g., Catholic, various Protestant denominations) or no religion.

The qualitative interviews allowed respondents to offer information about religion in any part of the interview. In the life history portion of the interview, many respondents mentioned their religious backgrounds. The qualitative interview also included a question that addressed religion specifically: "Some people say that religion or spirituality is important in their lives, others not so much. How about you?" These qualitative details provide the bulk of the information I used to create the case studies included in the book.

ANALYSES

I used both descriptive statistics and multivariate models to present my findings. In Chapters 1 and 2, all estimates are descriptive statistics. Starting in Chapter 3, I also presented predicted probabilities from logistic and negative binomial regression models.

GSS Analyses

Predicted Probabilities. In my predicted probability figures, the point on each bar is the average probability for that group (e.g., white Catholics) based on a logistic regression model that includes only religion and ethnicity. For example, Figure 3.1 shows that a randomly selected white Catholic has a .83 chance of having ever been married. A predicted probability of 1 would mean that every white Catholic has been married at some point. The bar represents the 95% confidence interval (i.e., the probability that the true value for that group falls along the bar 95% of the time). An asterisks indicate that a given group differs statistically from white Catholics on that trait (i.e., the difference is not explained by chance alone). In all predicted probability figures, I showed results derived from base models (i.e., models that include only religion and ethnicity) to document simple, descriptive patterns across religious-ethnic groups. However, I ran a large number of other models with control variables to better understand the conditions under which the simple results are statistically significant. I comment on both the base models and the models with other control variables where appropriate. I include model details below.

Chapter 5: Retrospective Religion. In Chapter 5, I discussed whether GSS respondents accurately report their age 16 (childhood) religion. To estimate reporting accuracy, I compared how respondents to the 2021 GSS and respondents to other GSS survey years reported age 16 religion. To accomplish this, I started with the pooled 1972–2021 GSS. I then created a variable called SURVEY_YEAR: for each respondent, I used the YEAR variable (survey year) and the AGE variable (respondent's age) to calculate *in what year a respondent was age 16* (YEAR – AGE + 16). This result was a continuous variable (i.e., respondents were born in 1972, 1973, 1974, 1975, etc.). Because the GSS is not asked every year, I created a dummy SURVEY_YEAR variable and coded the 16-year-old respondents by GSS survey year. If a respondent was 16 in 2002, then their SURVEY_YEAR is 2002. For respondents who were age 16 in a non-GSS survey year, I assigned them to the prior year's GSS survey year given that the next survey year did not exist yet when they were 16. For example, a respondent who was 16 in 2003 would be coded as SURVEY_YEAR = 2002. This created two types of respondents: "original" respondents (those who actually took the GSS in a particular year) and the "hypothetical" respondents (those I calculated were 16 years old at the time the "original" respondents took the GSS). In Chapter 5, I compare the reports of age 16 religion for "original" and "hypothetical" respondents by decade. The "hypothetical" 16-year-olds could come from *any* future GSS survey. For this reason, the oldest decade (1970s) has the most observations because those retrospective observations (RELIG16) are coming in from *every* future GSS survey year (31 GSS years). Likewise, the 2010s have the fewest retrospective observations because its observations can necessarily only come for GSS years 2012, 2014, 2016, 2018, and 2021 (not 2010 because the youngest respondent is 18 years old). Preliminary explorations suggested that this imbalance did not affect the substance of the results.

Chapter 6: Abortion Complexity. Figure 6.9 compares abortion complexity scores for my religious-ethnic groups. I follow previous research (Jozkowski, Crawford, and Hunt 2018; Jozkowski, Crawford, and Willis 2021) in creating this score. I use responses to a series of GSS questions about the conditions under which "it should be possible for a pregnant woman to obtain a legal abortion," including a strong chance of serious defect in the baby, if she is married and does not want more children, the woman's own health is seriously endangered by the pregnancy, the family has a very low income and cannot afford any more children, the woman became pregnant as the result of a rape, and if the woman is not married and does not want to marry the man.

In each abortion scenario, I changed the value to 1 or –1 (where 1 was originally coded as 0). I then summed across measures and recoded the sum so that –6 and 6 = 0, –4 and 4 = 1, –2 and 2 = 2, and 0 = 3. The complexity score equals 0 for an individual who is least complex or conflicted, meaning they answered all questions as anti-abortion or pro-abortion. The score will equal 3 for an individual who was most complex or conflicted and who answered half of the questions as anti-abortion and half as pro-abortion. Scores or 1 or 2 indicate that an individual's complexity falls within these extremes. Figure 6.9 shows the percentage of each group that scores 1 through 3 on this complexity indicator.

PSID Analyses

Chapter 5: Religious Change. In Table 5.4, *leavers* are those who were affiliated with a religious group in any PSID wave and were not affiliated with that religious group in a subsequent wave. The religious group for leavers refers to the starting religious group. For example, a respondent who was Catholic in any PSID year and then not Catholic (i.e., affiliated with any other religious group or religious nones) in a subsequent year is considered a leaver and included in the "Catholic" column in the leaver segment of the table. By contrast, a respondent who was Catholic in any PSID year and not Catholic in the most recent report of religious affiliation is considered a *joiner* and included in the "Catholic" column in the joiner segment of the table. *Stayers* are those who were affiliated with the same faith tradition in the previous report of religious affiliation.

REFERENCES

CHAPTER 1

Agius Vallejo, Jody. 2012. *Barrios to Burbs: The Making of the Mexican-American Middle Class*. Palo Alto: Stanford University Press.

Bruce, Tricia Colleen. 2017. *Parish and Place: Making Room for Diversity in the American Catholic Church*. New York: Oxford University Press.

Bryk, Anthony S., Valerie E. Lee, and Peter B. Hollan. 1993. *Catholic Schools and the Common Good*. Cambridge: Harvard University Press.

Burge, Ryan P. 2021. *The Nones: Where They Came from, Who They Are, and Where They Are Going*. Minneapolis, MN: Fortress Press.

Center for Applied Research in the Apostolate (CARA). 2023. "Frequently Requested Church Statistics." https://cara.georgetown.edu/faqs

Chaves, Mark. 2017. *American Religion: Contemporary Trends*, 2nd ed. Princeton, NJ: Princeton University Press.

D'Antonio, William V., James D. Davidson, Dean R. Hoge, and Katherine Meyer. 2001. *American Catholics: Gender, Generation, and Commitment*. Walnut Creek, CA: Altamira Press.

D'Antonio, William V., James D. Davidson, Dean R. Hoge, and Mary L. Gautier. 2007. *American Catholics Today: New Realities of Their Faith and Their Church*. Lanham, MD: Rowman & Littlefield.

D'Antonio, William V., Michele Dillon, and Mary L. Gautier. 2013. *American Catholics in Transition*. Lanham, MD: Rowman & Littlefield.

Day, Maureen K., ed. 2018. *Young Adult American Catholics: Explaining Vocation in Their Own Words*. Mahwah, NJ: Paulist Press.

Day, Maureen K. 2020. *Catholic Activism Today: Individual Transformation and the Struggle for Social Justice*. New York: New York University Press.

Dillon, Michele. 2018. *Postsecular Catholicism: Relevance and Renewal*. New York: Oxford University Press.

Douthat, Ross. March 17, 2023. "What Liberal Catholicism Gets Right". *New York Times*. https://www.nytimes.com/2023/03/17/opinion/liberal-catholicism.html

Ellison, Christopher G., Nicholas H. Wolfinger, and Aida I. Ramos-Wada. 2013. "Attitudes toward Marriage, Divorce, Cohabitation, and Casual Sex among Working-Age Latinos: Does Religion Matter?" *Journal of Family Issues* 34:295–322.

Gaunt, Thomas. 2022. *Faith and Spiritual Life of Young Adult Catholics in a Rising Hispanic Church*. Collegeville, MN: Liturgical Press.

Gray, Mark, Mary Gautier, and Thomas Gaunt. 2014. "Cultural Diversity in the Catholic Church in the United States". https://www.usccb.org/issues-and-action/cultural-diversity/upload/cultural-diversity-cara-report-phase-1.pdf

Greeley, Andrew, and Michael Hout. 2006. *The Truth About Conservative Christians: What They Think and What They Believe*. Chicago, IL: University of Chicago Press.

Greeley, Andrew M. 1977a. *The American Catholic: A Social Portrait*. New York: Basic Books.

Greeley, Andrew M. 1977b. "How Conservative Are American Catholics?" *Political Science Quarterly* 92(2):199–218.

Hamilton, Laura T., and Elizabeth A. Armstrong. 2021. "Parents, Partners, and Professions: Reproduction and Mobility in a Cohort of College Women." *American Journal of Sociology* 127(1):102–51.

Horowitz, Jason. March 13, 2023. "10 Years on, Pope Francis Faces Challenges from the Left and the Right." *New York Times*. https://www.nytimes.com/2023/03/13/world/europe/pope-francis-catholic-church.html

Igielnik, Ruth, and Abby Budiman. 2020. "In Battleground States, Hispanics Grew More Than Other Racial or Ethnic Groups as a Share of Eligible Voters." https://www.pewresearch.org/2020/09/23/the-changing-racial-and-ethnic-composition-of-the-U-S-electorate/

Kaplan, Anna. 2022. "Pelosi Joins Biden, Kerry, Giuliani and Other Catholics Threatened with No Communion Because of Abortion Support." *The Economist*. https://www.forbes.com/sites/annakaplan/2022/05/24/pelosi-joins-biden-kerry-giuliani-and-other-catholics-threatened-with-no-communion-because-of-abortion-support/?sh=60eb35501d58

Keister, Lisa A. 2007. "Upward Wealth Mobility: Exploring the Roman Catholic Advantage." *Social Forces* 85(3):1195–225.

Keister, Lisa A., Jody Agius Vallejo, and E. Paige Borelli. 2014. "Mexican American Mobility: An Exploration of Wealth Accumulation Trajectories." *Social Forces* 89:763–74.

Keister, Lisa A., and E. Paige Borelli. 2013. "Religion and Wealth Mobility: The Case of American Latinos." In *Religion and Inequalities*, edited by L. A. Keister and D. E. Sherkat, 119–45. New York: Cambridge University Press.

Keister, Lisa A., Sarah Thebaud, and Jill Yavorsky. 2022. "Gender in the Elite." *Annual Review of Sociology* 48:149–69.

Konieczny, Mary Ellen. 2013. *The Spirit's Tether: Family, Work, and Religion among American Catholics*. New York: Oxford University Press.

Lopez, Mark Hugo, Ana Gonzalez-Barrera, and Jens Manuel Krogstad. 2018. "Hispanic Voters and the 2018 Midterm Elections." https://www.pewresearch.org/hispanic/2018/10/25/hispanic-voters-and-the-2018-midterm-elections/

McCammon, Sarah. 2021. "An Issue Dividing Catholics: Should Abortion Rights Supporters Be Denied Communion?" *National Public Radio*. https://www.npr.org/2021/11/15/1055749036/an-issue-dividing-catholics-should-abortion-rights-supporters-be-denied-communion

McConahay, Mary Jo. March 13, 2023. "Is the American Catholic Church Fueling the Far Right?" *New York Times*. https://www.nytimes.com/2023/03/13/books/review/playing-god-mary-jo-mcconahay.html.

Mulder, Mark T., Aida I. Ramos, and Gerardo Marti. 2017. *Latino Protestants in America: Growing and Diverse*. Lanham, MD: Rowman & Littlefield.

National Catholic Reporter. 2021. "In Defiance of Vatican, US Bishops Vote to Advance Communion Document." https://www.ncronline.org/news/defiance-Vatican-Us-bishops-vote-advance-communion-document

Newport, Frank. 2022a. "The Religion of the Supreme Court Justices." https://news.gallup.com/opinion/polling-matters/391649/religion-supreme-court-justices.aspx

Newport, Frank. 2022b. "Slowdown in the Rise of Religious Nones." https://news.gallup.com/opinion/polling-matters/406544/slowdown-rise-religious-nones.aspx

Orcés, Diana. 2022. "Where Do Catholics' Views Stand Today?" https://www.prri.org/spotlight/where-do-catholics-views-stand-today/

Perry, Samuel L., and Cuyrus Schleifer. 2019. "Are the Faithful Becoming Less Fruitful? The Decline of Conservative Protestant Fertility and the Growing Importance of Religious Practice and Belief in Childbearing in the US." *Social Science Research* 78:137–55.

Pew Research Center. 2015. "America's Changing Religious Landscape." https://www.pewresearch.org/religion/2015/05/12/chapter-2-religious-switching-and-intermarriage/#retention-of-childhood-members-hindus-muslims-and-jews-most-successful-at-retaining-adherents

Picciotti-Bayer, Andrea. September 22, 2022. "Counterfeit Catholicism, Left and Right." *Wall Street Journal*. https://www.wsj.com/articles/counterfeit-catholicism-left-and-right-secularism-sectarianism-integralists-america-church-vatican-ii-markets-subsidiarity-11663875550

Ramos, Aida I., Robert D. Woodberry, and Christopher G. Ellison. 2017. "The Contexts of Conversion among U.S. Latinos." *Sociology of Religion* 78(2):119–45.

Sander, William. 1995. *The Catholic Family: Marriage, Children, and Human Capital*. Boulder, CO: Westview Press.

Sandstrom, Aleksandra. 2021. "Faith on the Hill." https://www.pewresearch.org/religion/2021/01/04/faith-on-the-hill-2021/

Sherkat, Darren E. 2014. *Changing Faith: The Dynamics and Consequences of Americans' Shifting Religious Identities*. New York: New York University Press.

Skirbekk, Vegard, Eric Kaufmann, and Anne Goujon. 2010. "Secularism, Fundamentalism, or Catholicism? The Religious Composition of the United States to 2043." *Journal for the Scientific Study of Religion* 49(2):293–310.

Smith, Christian, Kyle Longest, Jonathan Hill, and Kari Christoffersen. 2014. *Young Catholic America: Emerging Adults in, out of, and Gone from the Church*. New York: Oxford University Press.

Smith, Gregory. 2021. "About Three-in-Ten U.S. Adults Are Now Religiously Unaffiliated." https://www.pewresearch.org/religion/2021/12/14/about-three-in-ten-u-s-adults-are-now-religiously-unaffiliated/

Smith, Gregory A. 2020. "8 Facts About Catholics and Politics in the U.S." https://www.pewresearch.org/fact-tank/2020/09/15/8-facts-about-catholics-and-politics-in-the-U-S/

Stark, Rodney. 2008. *What Americans Really Believe*. Waco, TX: Baylor University Press.

Stone, Lyman, and W. Bradford Wilcox. 2021. "The Religious Marriage Paradox: Younger Marriage, Less Divorce." Institute for Family Studies. https://ifstudies.org/blog/the-religious-marriage-paradox-younger-marriage-less-divorce

Taylor, Paul, Mark Hugo Lopez, Jessica Martínez, and Gabriel Velasco. 2012. "Politics, Values and Religion." https://www.pewresearch.org/hispanic/2012/04/04/v-politics-values-and-religion/

Westoff, Charles F., and Elise F. Jones. 1979. "The End of 'Catholic' Fertility." *Demography* 16:209–17.

Wilde, Melissa J. 2020. *Birth Control Battles: How Race and Class Divided American Religion*. Berkeley: University of California Press.

Wuthnow, Robert. 1990. *The Restructuring of American Religion: Society and Faith since World War II*. Princeton, NJ: Princeton University Press.

Zech, Charles E., Mary L. Gautier, Mark M. Gray, Jonathon L. Wiggins, and Thomas P. Gaunt. 2017. *Catholic Parishes of the 21st Century*. New York: Oxford University Press.

Zeitz, Josh. 2015. "When America Hated Catholics." *Politico*. https://www.politico.com/magazine/story/2015/09/when-america-hated-catholics-213177/

CHAPTER 2

Agius Vallejo, Jody. 2012. *Barrios to Burbs: The Making of the Mexican-American Middle Class*. Palo Alto: Stanford University Press.

Alba, Richard, and Victor Nee. 2003. *Remaking the American Mainstream: Assimilation and Contemporary Immigration*. Cambridge, MA: Harvard University Press.

Alba, Richard, Albert J. Raboteau, and Josh DeWind, eds. 2009. *Immigration and Religion in America: Comparative and Historical Perspectives*. New York: New York University Press.

Amin, Nadia, and Darren E. Sherkat. 2013. "Religion, Gender, and Educational Attainment among U.S. Immigrants: Evidence from the New Immigrant Survey." In *Religion and Inequalities*, edited by L. A. Keister and D. E. Sherkat. New York: Cambridge University Press.

Berger, Mark C. 1989. "Demographic Cycles, Cohort Size, and Earnings." *Demography* 26:311–21.

Bergmann, Barbara R. 2011. "Sex Segregation in the Blue-Collar Occupations: Women's Choices or Unremedied Discrimination?" *Gender and Society* 25:88–93.

Bialik, Kristen, and Richard Fry. 2019. "Millennial Life: How Young Adults Today Compare with Prior Generations." https://www.pewresearch.org/social-trends/2019/02/14/millennial-life-how-young-adulthood-today-compares-with-prior-generations-2/

Biddle, Catharine, and Ian Mette. 2017. "Education and Information." In *Rural Poverty in the United States*, edited by A. R. Tickamyer, J. Sherman, and J. Warlock, 322–48. New York: Columbia University Press.

Blau, Francine D., and Lawrence M. Kahn. 2017. "The Gender Wage Gap: Extent, Trends, and Explanations." *Journal of Economic Literature* 55(3):789–865.

Brooks, Clem, and Catherine Bolzendahl. 2004. "The Transformation of US Gender Role Attitudes: Cohort Replacement, Social-Structural Change, and Ideological Learning." *Social Science Research* 33(1):106–33. doi:10.1016/s0049-089x(03)00041-3

Carlson, Edward, and Justin Goss. 2016. *The State of the Urban/Rural Digital Divide* Washington, DC: USDA National Telecommunications and Information Administration.

Carr, Patrick J., and Maria J. Kefalas. 2009. *Hollowing out the Middle: The Rural Brain Drain and What It Means for America*. Boston: Beacon.

Chaves, Mark. 2017. *American Religion: Contemporary Trends, Second Edition*. Princeton, NJ: Princeton University Press.

Chetty, Raj, Nathaniel Hendren, Patrick Kline, and Emmanuel Saez. 2014. "Where Is the Land of Opportunity? The Geography of Intergenerational Mobility in the United States." *Quarterly Journal of Economics* 129:1553–623.

Civettini, Nicole H. W., and Jennifer Glass. 2008. "The Impact of Religious Conservatism on Men's Work and Family Involvement." *Gender & Society* 22(2):172–93.

Cobb, Robert A., Walter G. McIntire, and Phillip A. Pratt. 1989. "Vocational and Educational Aspirations of High School Students: A Problem for Rural America." *Research in Rural Education* 6(2):6.

Connelly, Rachel. 1986. "A Framework for Analyzing the Impact of Cohort Size on Education and Labor Earnings." *Journal of Human Resources* 21:543–62.

D'Antonio, William V., James D. Davidson, Dean R. Hoge, and Katherine Meyer. 2001. *American Catholics: Gender, Generation, and Commitment*. Walnut Creek, CA: Altamira Press.

Davis, Darren W., and Donald B. Pope-Davis. 2017. *Perseverance in the Parish?: Religious Attitudes from a Black Catholic Perspective*. New York: Cambridge University Press.

Diamant, Jeff, Besheer Mohamed, and Joshua Alvarado. 2022. "Black Catholics in America." Pew Research Center. https://www.pewresearch.org/religion/2022/03/15/black-catholics-in-america/

Dimock, Michael. 2019. "Defining Generations: Where Millennials End and Generation Z Begins." https://www.pewresearch.org/fact-tank/2019/01/17/where-millennials-end-and-generation-z-begins

Duncan, Cynthia M. 2015. *Worlds Apart: Poverty and Politics in Rural America*. New Haven, CT: Yale University Press.

Eagle, David, Lisa A. Keister, and Jen'nan Ghazal Read. 2017. "Household Charitable Giving at the Intersection of Gender, Marital Status, and Religion." *Nonprofit and Voluntary Sector Quarterly*. doi:10.1177/0899764017734650.

Easterlin, Richard A., Christine MacDonald, and Diane J. Macunovich. 1990. "How Have American Baby Boomers Fared? Earnings and Economic Well-Being of Young Adults, 1964–1987." *Population Economics* 3:277–90.

Easterlin, Richard A., Christine M. Schaeffer, and Diane J. Macunovich. 1993. "Will the Baby Boomers Be Less Well Off Than Their Parents? Income, Wealth, and Family Circumstances over the Life Cycle in the United States." *Population and Development Review* 19:497–522.

Economic Research Service. 2019a. *Rural America at a Glance*. Washington, DC: Department of Agriculture.

Economic Research Service. 2019b. *Rural Employment and Unemployment*. Washington, DC: Department of Agriculture.

Elder, Glen H. 1974. *Children of the Great Depression: Social Change in Life Experience*. Chicago: University of Chicago Press.

Ellison, Christopher G., and John P. Bartkowski. 2002. "Conservative Protestantism and the Division of Household Labor among Married Couples." *Journal of Family Issues* 23:950–85.

England, Paula, Jonathan Bearak, Michelle J. Budig, and Melissa J. Hodges. 2016. "Do Highly Paid, Highly Skilled Women Experience the Largest Motherhood Penalty?" *American Sociological Review* 81(6):1161–89.

England, Paula, Andrew Levine, and Emma Mishel. 2020. "Progress toward Gender Equality in the United States Has Slowed or Stalled." *Proceedings of the National Academy of Sciences* 117(13):6990–97. doi: https://doi.org/10.1073/pnas.2003878117

Feliciano, Cynthia. 2005. "Does Selective Migration Matter? Explaining Ethnic Disparities in Educational Attainment among Immigrants' Children." *International Migration Review* 39:841–71.

Feliciano, Cynthia. 2006. *Unequal Origins: Immigrant Selection and the Education of the Second Generation*. New York: LFC Scholarly Publishing.

Forest, Kay B., Phyllis Moen, and Donna Dempster-McClain. 1995. "Cohort Differences in the Transition to Motherhood: The Variable Effects of Education and Employment before Marriage." *Sociological Quarterly* 36:315–36.

Fry, Richard. 2013. *A Rising Share of Young Adults Live in Their Parents' Home*. Washington, DC: Pew Research Centers Social and Demographic Trends.

Fry, Richard, and Kim Parker. 2018. "Early Benchmarks Show 'Post-Millennials' on Track to Be Most Diverse, Best-Educated Generation Yet." https://www.pewresearch.org/social-trends/2018/11/15/early-benchmarks-show-post-millennials-on-track-to-be-most-diverse-best-educated-generation-yet/

Gibbs, Robert M., and John B. Cromartie. 1994. "Rural Youth Outmigration: How Big Is the Problem and for Whom?" *Rural Development Perspectives* 10:9–16.

Glass, Jennifer, and Jerry Jacobs. 2005. "Childhood Religious Conservatism and Adult Attainment among Black and White Women." *Social Forces* 84(1):555–79.

Golden, Claudia, and Lawrence F. Katz. 2008. *The Race between Education and Technology*. Cambridge, MA: Belknap.

Gray, Mark M., Mary Gautier, and Thomas Gaunt. 2014. "Cultural Diversity in the Catholic Church in the United States." https://www.usccb.org/issues-and-action/cultural-diversity/upload/cultural-diversity-cara-report-phase-1.pdf

Greeley, Andrew M. 1977. *The American Catholic: A Social Portrait*. New York: Basic Books.

Greeley, Andrew M. 1989. *Religious Change in America*. Cambridge, MA: Harvard University Press.

Greeley, Andrew M. 2004. *The Catholic Revolution: New Wine, Old Wineskins, and the Second Vatican Council*. Berkeley: University of California Press.

Hamilton, Lawrence C., Leslie R. Hamilton, Cynthia M. Duncan, and Chris R. Colocousis. 2008. *Place Matters: Challenges and Opportunities in Four Rural Americas*. Durham, NH: Carsey Institute Report on Rural America.

Hoeffel, Elizabeth M., Sonya Rastogi, Myoung Ouk Kim, and Hasan Shahid. 2012. *The Asian Population 2010*. Washington, DC: Census Bureau.

Hondagneu-Sotelo, Pierette. 2008. *God's Heart Has No Borders: How Religious Activists Work for Immigrant Rights*. Berkeley: University of California Press.

Horwitz, Ilana M. 2022. *God, Grades, and Graduation: Religion's Surprising Impact on Academic Success*. New York: Oxford University Press.

Hout, Michael. 2016. "Saint Peter's Leaky Boat: Falling Intergenerational Persistence among U.S.-Born Catholics since 1974." *Sociology of Religion* 77(1):1–17.

Igielnik, Ruth, and Abby Budiman. 2020. "In Battleground States, Hispanics Grew More Than Other Racial or Ethnic Groups as a Share of Eligible Voters." https://www.pewresearch.org/2020/09/23/the-changing-racial-and-ethnic-composition-of-the-u-s-electorate/

Jennings, Jennifer E., and Candida G. Brush. 2013. "Research on Women Entrepreneurs: Challenges to (and from) the Broader Entrepreneurship Literature?" *Academy of Management Annals* 7:663–715.

Johnson, Kenneth M. 2012. *Rural Demographic Trends in the New Century*. Durham, NH: Carsey Institute.

Jones, Nicholas, Rachel Marks, Roberto Ramirez, and Merarys Rios-Vargas. 2021, "2020 Census Illuminates Racial and Ethnic Composition of the Country." https://www.census.gov/library/stories/2021/08/improved-race-ethnicity-measures-reveal-united-states-population-much-more-multiracial.html;

https://www.census.gov/library/stories/2021/08/improved-race-ethnicity-measures-reveal-united-states-population-much-more-multiracial.html

Kaplan, Elaine Bell. 2020. "The Millennial/Gen Z Leftists Are Emerging: Are Sociologists Ready for Them?" *Sociological Perspectives* 63(3):408–27.

Keister, Lisa A. 2000. *Wealth in America: Trends in Wealth Inequality*. New York: Cambridge University Press.

Keister, Lisa A., Jody Agius Vallejo, and E. Paige Borelli. 2014. "Mexican American Mobility: An Exploration of Wealth Accumulation Trajectories." *Social Forces* 89:763–74.

Keister, Lisa A., James W. Moody, and Tom Wolff. 2021. "Rural Kids and Wealth." *RSF: The Russell Sage Foundation Journal of the Social Sciences* 8(4):155–82. https://doi.org/10.7758/rsf.2022.8.4.07

Kennickell, Arthur B. 2000. "An Examination of Changes in the Distribution of Wealth from 1989–1998: Evidence from the Survey of Consumer Finances." *Federal Reserve Board Bulletin*.

Lachance-Grzela, Mylène, and Geneviève Bouchard. 2010. "Why Do Women Do the Lion's Share of Housework? A Decade of Research." *Sex Roles* 63(11–12):767–80. doi:10.1007/s11199-010-9797-z

Lichter, Daniel, and Deborah Graefe. 2011. "Rural Economic Restructuring: Implications for Children, Youth, and Families." In *Economic Restructuring and Family Wellbeing in Rural American*, edited by K. E. Smith and A. R. Tickamyer, 25–39. University Park: Pennsylvania State University Press.

Lichter, Daniel T., Vincent Roscigno, and Dennis J. Condron. 2003. "Rural Children and Youth at Risk." In *Challenges for Rural America in the Twenty-First Century*, edited by 97–108. University Park: Pennsylvania State University Press.

Lichter, Daniel, and K. Schafft. 2016. "People and Places Left Behind: Rural Poverty in the New Century." In *The Oxford Handbook of the Social Science of Poverty*, edited by D. Brady and L. M. Burton, 317–40. New York: Oxford University Press.

Lin, Ken-Hou, and Donald Tomaskovic-Devey. 2013. "Financialization and U.S. Income Inequality, 1970–2008." *American Journal of Sociology* 118:1284–329.

MacTavis, Katherine, and Sonya Salamon. 2003. "What Do Rural Families Look Like Today?" In *Challenges for Rural America in the Twenty-First Century*, edited by 73–85. University Park: Pennsylvania State University Press.

Macunovich, Diane J., Richard A. Easterlin, Christine M. Schaeffer, and Eileen M. Crimmins. 1995. "Echoes of the Baby Boom and Bust: Recent and Prospective Changes in Living Alone among Elderly Widows in the United States." *Demography* 32:17–28.

Masci, David, and Gregory A. Smith. 2018. "Seven Facts About American Catholics." https://www.pewresearch.org/fact-tank/2018/10/10/7-facts-about-american-catholics/

McLaughlin, Diane K., Carla Shoff, and Mary-Ann Demi. 2014. "Influence of Perceptions of Current and Future Community on Residential Aspirations of Rural Youth." *Rural Sociology* 79(4):453–77.

Mulder, Mark T., Aida I. Ramos, and Gerardo Marti. 2017. *Latino Protestants in America: Growing and Diverse*. Lanham, MD: Rowman & Littlefield.

Natarajan, Anusha, and Carolyne Im. 2022. "Key Facts About Hispanic Eligible Voters in 2022." https://www.pewresearch.org/fact-tank/2022/10/12/key-facts-about-hispanic-eligible-voters-in-2022/

National Women's Business Council. 2012. "Fact Sheet: Gender Differences in U.S. Business." https://s3.amazonaws.com/nwbc-prod.sba.fun/wp-content/uploads/2012/01/05044441/fact-sheet-gender-differences-in-us-business.pdf

Passel, Jeffrey S., Mark Hugo Lopez, and D'Vera Cohn. 2022. "U.S. Hispanic Population Continued Its Geographic Spread in the 2010s." https://www.pewresearch.org/fact-tank/2022/02/03/u-s-hispanic-population-continued-its-geographic-spread-in-the-2010s/

Pew Research Center. 2012a. "Asian Americans: A Mosaic of Faiths." https://www.pewresearch.org/religion/2012/07/19/asian-americans-a-mosaic-of-faiths-overview/

Pew Research Center. 2012b. *The Rise of Asian Americans*. Washington, DC: Pew Research Center, Pew Social and Demographic Trends, Pew Forum on Religion and Public Life.

Portes, Alejandro, and Ruben G. Rumbaut. 2006. *Immigrant America: A Portrait,* 3rd ed. Berkeley: University of California Press.

Probst, Janice C., Jessica D. Bellinger, Katrina M. Walsemann, James Hardin, and Saundra H. Glover. 2011. "Higher Risk of Death in Rural Blacks and Whites Than Urbanites Is Related to Lower Incomes, Education, and Health Coverage." *Health Affairs* 30:1872–79.

Ramos, Aida I., Robert D. Woodberry, and Christopher G. Ellison. 2017. "The Contexts of Conversion among U.S. Latinos." *Sociology of Religion* 78(2):119–45.

Reskin, Barbara, and Michelle Maroto. 2011. "What Trends? Whose Choices?" *Gender and Society* 25:81–7.

Riley, Matilda White. 1973. "Aging and Cohort Successions." *Public Opinion Quarterly* 37:35–49.

Rodriguez, James. 2023. "Sorry Millennials, You're Never Getting a Good Home." *Business Insider*. https://www.businessinsider.com/millennials-house-home-real-estate-mortgage-rates-rent-debt-boomers-2022-9

Rumbaut, Rubén G. 2008. "The Coming of the Second Generation: Immigration and Ethnic Mobility in Southern California." *Annals of the American Academy of Political and Social Science* 620:196–236.

Ryder, Norman B. 1965. "The Cohort as a Concept in the Study of Social Change." *American Sociological Review* 30:843–61.

Sabelhaus, John, and Joyce Manchester. 1995. "Baby Boomers and Their Parents: How Does Their Economic Well-Being Compare in Middle Age?" *Journal of Human Resources* 30:791–806.

Sanchez, Boris. October 15, 2022. "The Latino Voter Shift Comes into Focus in South Texas." https://www.cnn.com/2022/10/14/politics/latino-voters-texas-15th/index.html

Saurav, Pathak, Sonia Goltz, and Mari Buche. 2013. "Influences of Gendered Institutions on Women's Entry into Entrepreneurship." *International Journal of Entrepreneurial Behavior and Research* 19:478–502.

Sherkat, Darren E. 2014. *Changing Faith: The Dynamics and Consequences of Americans' Shifting Religious Identities*. New York: New York University Press.

Sherman, Jennifer, and Rayna Sage. 2011. "Sending Off All Your Good Treasures: Rural Schools, Brain-Drain, and Community Survival in the Wake of Economic Collapse." *Journal of Research in Rural Education* 26:1–14.

Smith, Chelsea, Robert Crosnoe, and Shih-Yi Chao. 2016. "Family Background and Contemporary Changes in Young Adults' School-Work Transitions and Family Formation in the United States." *Research in Social Stratification and Mobility* 46:3–10.

Smith, Christian, Kyle Longest, Jonathan Hill, and Kari Christoffersen. 2014. *Young Catholic America: Emerging Adults in, out of, and Gone from the Church*. New York: Oxford University Press.

Smith, Gregory A. 2020. "8 Facts About Catholics and Politics in the U.S." https://www.pewresearch.org/fact-tank/2020/09/15/8-facts-about-catholics-and-politics-in-the-u-s/

Stark, Rodney. 2008. *What Americans Really Believe*. Waco, TX: Baylor University Press.

Stockard, Jean, Jo Anna Gray, Robert O'Brien, and Joe Stone. 2009. "Race Differences in Cohort Effects on Non-Marital Fertility in the United States." *Social Forces* 87(3):1449–79.

Thébaud, Sarah, and Laura Halcomb. 2019. "One Step Forward? Advances and Setbacks on the Path toward Gender Equality in Families and Work." *Sociology Compass* 13(6):e12700. doi:https://doi.org/10.1111/soc4.12700

Thiede, Brian C., Hyojung Kim, and Tim Slack. 2017. "Marriage, Work, and Racial Inequalities in Poverty: Evidence from the U.S." *Journal of Marriage and Family* 79:1241–57.

Thiede, Brian C., Daniel T. Lichter, and Tim Slack. 2018. "Work, but Poor: The Good Life in Rural America?" *Journal of Rural Studies* 59:183–93.

Tsvetkova, Alexandra, Mark Partridge, and Michael Betz. 2017. "Entrepreneurial and Employment Responses to Economic Conditions across the Rural-Urban Continuum." *Annals of the American Academy of Political and Social Science* 672:83–102.

Voas, David, and Mark Chaves. 2016. "Is the United States a Counterexample to the Secularization Thesis?" *American Journal of Sociology* 121:517–56.

von Reichert, Christiane, John B. Cromartie, and Ryan O. Arthun. 2011. "Returning Home and Making a Living: Employment Strategies of Returning Migrants to Rural U.S. Communities." *Journal of Rural and Community Development* 6:35–52.

Waite, Linda J. 1995. "Does Marriage Matter?" *Demography* 32:483–507.

Walters, Nathan P., and Edward N. Trevelyan. 2011. *The Newly Arrived Foreign-Born Population of the United States: 2010*. American Community Survey Briefs. Washington, DC: U.S. Census Bureau.

Warner, Judith, Nora Ellmann, and Diana Boesch. 2018. "The Women's Leadership Gap." *Center for American Progress*. https://www.americanprogress.org/issues/women/reports/2018/11/20/461273/womens-leadership-gap-2/

Western, Bruce, and Jake Rosenfeld. 2011. "Unions, Norms, and the Rise in U.S. Wage Inequality." *American Socioligical Review* 76:513–37.

Wiggins, Jonathon L., Mary L. Gautier, and Thomas P. Gaunt. 2021. "A Realignment of the Catholic Church in the United States: A Tale of Four U.S. Cities." *Theology Today* 38(3):267–75.

Wilde, Melissa J. 2007. *Vatican II: A Sociological Analysis of Religious Change*. Princeton, NJ: Princeton University Press.

Wolff, Edward N. 2002. *Top Heavy: A Study of the Increasing Inequality of Wealth in America*. New York: New Press.

Xie, Yu, and Kimberly Goyette. 2012. *Asian Americans: A Demographic Portrait*. Ann Arbor: University of Michigan, Population Studies Center, Institute for Social Research.

Yamokoski, Alexis, and Lisa A. Keister. 2006. "The Wealth of Single Women: Marital Status and Parenthood in the Asset Accumulation of Young Baby Boomers in the United States." *Feminist Economics* 12:167–94.

Yang, Yang, and Linda C. Lee. 2009. "Sex and Race Disparities in Health: Cohort Variations in Life Course Patterns." *Social Forces* 87:2093–2124.

Yavorsky, Jill E., Lisa A. Keister, and Yue Qian. 2020. "Gender in the One Percent." *Contexts* 19(1):12–17. doi:https://doi.org/10.1177/1536504220902196

Yavorsky, Jill E., Lisa A. Keister, Yue Qian, and Mike Nau. 2019. "Women in the One Percent: Gender Dynamics in Top Income Positions." *American Sociological Review* 84(1):54–81.

Zagorsky, Jay L. 1999. "Young Baby Boomers' Wealth." *Review of Income and Wealth* 45:135–56.

Zech, Charles E., Mary L. Gautier, Mark M. Gray, Jonathon L. Wiggins, and Thomas P. Gaunt. 2017. *Catholic Parishes of the 21st Century*. New York: Oxford University Press.

Zhou, Min. 2009. *Contemporary Chinese America: Immigration, Ethnicity, and Community Transformation*. Philadelphia: Temple University Press.

CHAPTER 3

Adserà, Alícia. 2015. "Fertility, Feminism, and Faith: The Influence of Secularism and Economic Conditions." In *Whither the Child? Causes and Consequences of Low Fertility*, edited by E. P. Kaufmann and W. B. Wilcox, 1–28. Oxfordshire, UK: Routledge.

Catholic Church. 2000. *Catechism of the Catholic Church*. 2nd Edition https://www.usccb.org/sites/default/files/flipbooks/catechism/.

Catholics for Choice. 2023. "The Legacy of Humane Vitae." https://www.catholicsforchoice.org/resource-library/humanae-vitae/the-legacy-of-humanae-vitae/

Center for Applied Research in the Apostolate (CARA). 2023. "Nineteen Sixty-Four Blog." https://nineteensixty-four.blogspot.com/search?q=marriage

Cooksey, Elizabeth C. 1997. "Consequences of Young Mothers' Marital Histories for Children's Cognitive Development." *Journal of Marriage and the Family* 59:245–61.

Curtis, Kristen Taylor, and Christopher G. Ellison. 2002. "Religious Homogamy and Marital Conflict: Findings from the National Survey of Families and Households." *Journal of Family Issues* 23(4):551–76.

Dillon, Michele. 1999. *Catholic Identity: Balancing Reason, Faith, and Power*. New York: Cambridge University Press.

Dillon, Michele. 2018. *Postsecular Catholicism: Relevance and Renewal*. New York: Oxford University Press.

Ellison, Christopher G., Nicholas H. Wolfinger, and Aida I. Ramos-Wada. 2013. "Attitudes toward Marriage, Divorce, Cohabitation, and Casual Sex among Working-Age Latinos: Does Religion Matter?" *Journal of Family Issues* 34:295–322.

Freedman, Ronald, Pascal K. Whelpton, and John W. Smit. 1959. *Family Planning, Sterility, and Population Growth*. New York: McGraw-Hill.

Freedman, Ronald, Pascal K. Whelpton, and John W. Smit. 1961. "Socio-Economic Factors in Religious Differentials in Fertility." *American Sociological Review* 26:608–14.

Gao, George. 2015. "Americans' Ideal Family Size Is Smaller Than It Used to Be." https://www.pewresearch.org/fact-tank/2015/05/08/ideal-size-of-the-american-family/

Hahn, Kimberly. 2001. *Life-Giving Love: Embracing God's Design for Marriage*. Cincinnati, OH: Servant Books.

Hout, Michael, Andrew Greeley, and Melissa J. Wilde. 2001. "The Demographic Imperative in Religious Change in the United States." *American Journal of Sociology* 107(2):468–500.

Jones, Rachel K. 2020. "People of All Religions Use Birth Control and Have Abortions." https://www.guttmacher.org/article/2020/10/people-all-religions-use-birth-control-and-have-abortions

Kalmijn, Matthijs. 1991. "Shifting Boundaries: Trends in Religious and Educational Homogamy." *American Sociological Review* 56:786–800.

Kennedy, Sheela, and Steven Ruggles. 2014. "Breaking up Is Hard to Count: The Rise of Divorce in the United States, 1980–2010." *Demography* 51(2):587–98.

Konieczny, Mary Ellen. 2013. *The Spirit's Tether: Family, Work, and Religion among American Catholics*. New York: Oxford University Press.

Kuperberg, Arielle. 2019. "Premarital Cohabitation and Direct Marriage in the United States: 1956–2015." *Marriage and Family Review* 55(5):447–75.

Landale, Nancy S., and R. S. Oropesa. 2007. "Hispanic Families: Stability and Change." *Annual Review of Sociology* 33:381–405.

Lehrer, Evelyn L. 2004. "The Role of Religion in Union Formation: An Economic Perspective." *Population Research and Policy Review* 23(2):161–85.

Lehrer, Evelyn L., and Carmel U. Chiswick. 1993. "Religion as a Determinant of Marital Stability." *Demography* 30:385–404.

Mahoney, Annette, Kenneth I. Pargament, Nalini Tarakeshwar, and Aaron B. Swank. 2008. "Religion in the Home in the 1980s and 1990s: A Meta-Analytic Review and Conceptual Analysis of Links between Religion, Marriage, and Parenting." *Psychology of Religion and Spirituality* 1:63–101.

Manning, Wendy D. 2004. "Children and the Stability of Cohabiting Couples." *Journal of Marriage and Family* 66:674–89.

Manning, Wendy D., Susan L. Brown, and Krista. K Payne. 2014. "Two Decades of Stability and Change in Age at First Union Formation." *Journal of Marriage and Family* 76(2):247–60.

Marcum, John P. 1986. "Explaining Protestant Fertility: Belief, Commitment, and Homogamy." *Sociological Quarterly* 27:547–58.

Morgan, S. Philip. 1991. "Late Nineteenth-and Early Twentieth-Century Childlessness." *American Journal of Sociology* 97:779–807.

Mosher, William D., Linda Hendershot, and David P. Johnson. 1992. "Religion and Fertility in the United States: New Patterns." *Demography* 29:199–214.

Myers, Scott M. 2006. "Religious Homogamy and Marital Quality: Historical and Generational Patterns, 1980–1997." *Journal of Marriage and Family* 68:292–304.

Perry, Samuel L. 2015. "A Match Made in Heaven? Religion-Based Marriage Decisions, Marital Quality, and the Moderating Effects of Spouse's Religious Commitment." *Social Indicators Research* 123:203–15.

Perry, Samuel L. 2022. "American Religion in the Era of Increasing Polarization." *Annual Review of Sociology* 48:87–107.

Perry, Samuel L., and Cyrus Schleifer. 2019. "Are the Faithful Becoming Less Fruitful? The Decline of Conservative Protestant Fertility and the Growing Importance of Religious Practice and Belief in Childbearing in the US." *Social Science Research* 78:137–55.

Pope John Paul II. November 30, 1986. "Homily Perth, Australia." https://www.vatican.va/content/john-paul-ii/en/homilies/1986/documents/hf_jp-ii_hom_19861130_perth-australia.html

Pope John Paul II. 2006. *Man and Woman He Created Them: A Theology of the Body*. Translated by M. Waldstein. Alexandria, VA: Pauline Books and Media.

Pope Paul VI. 1968. *Humanae Vitae*. Washington, DC: USCCB.

Qian, Yue. 2018. "Educational Assortative Mating and Income Dynamics in Couples: A Longitudinal Dyadic Perspective." *Journal of Marriage and Family* 80(3):607–21.

Sassler, Sharon, and Daniel T. Lichter. 2020. "Cohabitation and Marriage: Complexity and Diversity in Union-Formation Patterns." *Journal of Marriage and Family* 82(1):35–61.

Sherkat, Darren E. 2000. "That They Be Keepers of the Home: The Effect of Conservative Religion on Early and Late Transitions into Housewifery." *Review of Religious Research* 41:344–458.

Sherkat, Darren E. 2004. "Religious Intermarriage in the United States: Trends, Patterns, and Predictors." *Social Science Research* 33(4):606–25.

Sherkat, Darren E. 2014. *Changing Faith: The Dynamics and Consequences of Americans' Shifting Religious Identities*. New York: New York University Press.

Sherkat, Darren E., and Christopher G. Ellison. 1999. "Recent Developments and Current Controversies in the Sociology of Religion." *Annual Review of Sociology* 25:363–94.

Simon, Robin W. 2002. "Revisiting the Relationship among Gender, Marital Status, and Mental Health." *American Journal of Sociology* 107:1065–96.

Skirbekk, Vegard, Eric Kaufmann, and Anne Goujon. 2010. "Secularism, Fundamentalism, or Catholicism? The Religious Composition of the United States to 2043." *Journal for the Scientific Study of Religion* 49(2):293–310.

Smith, Lyman. 2020. "The Rise of Childless America." https://ifstudies.org/blog/the-rise-of-childless-america

Stokes, Charles E., and Christopher G. Ellison. 2010. "Religion and Attitudes toward Divorce Laws among U.S. Adults." *Journal of Family Issues* 31:1279–304.

Stone, Lyman, and W. Bradford Wilcox. 2021. "The Religious Marriage Paradox: Younger Marriage, Less Divorce." Institute for Family Studies. https://ifstudies.org/blog/the-religious-marriage-paradox-younger-marriage-less-divorce

Vaaler, Margaret L., Christopher G. Ellison, and Daniel A. Powers. 2009. "Religious Influences on the Risk of Marital Dissolution." *Journal of Marriage and Family* 71(4):917–34.

Waite, Linda J. 1995. "Does Marriage Matter?" *Demography* 32:483–507.

Waite, Linda J., and Evelyn L. Lehrer. 2004. "The Benefits from Marriage and Religion in the United States: A Comparative Analysis." *Population and Development Review* 29(2):255–75. https://doi.org/10.1111/j.1728-4457.2003.00255.x

Wilde, Melissa J. 2001. "From Excommunication to Nullification: Testing and Extending Supply-Side Theories of Religious Marketing with the Case of Catholic Marital Annulments." *Journal for the Scientific Study of Religion* 40:235–49.

Wilde, Melissa J. 2020. *Birth Control Battles: How Race and Class Divided American Religion*. Berkeley: University of California Press.

Winters, Michael Sean. 2018. "In Defense of 'Humanae Vitae.'" *National Catholic Reporter*. https://www.ncronline.org/opinion/distinctly-catholic/defense-humanae-vitae

Wright, Matthew R., Susan L. Brown, and Wendy D. Manning. 2021. "A Cohort Comparison of Midlife Marital Quality: A Quarter Century of Change." *Journal of Family Issues* 44(2):538–59.

Zagorsky, Jay L. 2005. "Marriage and Divorce's Impact on Wealth." *Journal of Sociology* 41:406–24.

CHAPTER 4

Agius Vallejo, Jody. 2012. *Barrios to Burbs: The Making of the Mexican-American Middle Class*. Palo Alto: Stanford University Press.

Agius Vallejo, Jody, and Jennifer Lee. 2009. "Brown Picket Fences." *Ethnicities* 9:5–31.

Alba, Richard. 2009. *Blurring the Color Line: The New Chance for a More Integrated America*. Cambridge, MA: Harvard University Press.

Aldrich, Howard E., Linda A. Renzulli, and Nancy Langton. 1998. "Passing on Privilege: Resources Provided by Self-Employed Parents to Their Self-Employed Children." *Research in Social Stratification and Mobility* 16:291–317.

Amin, Nadia, and Darren E. Sherkat. 2013. "Religion, Gender, and Educational Attainment among U.S. Immigrants: Evidence from the New Immigrant Survey." In *Religion and Inequalities*, edited by L. A. Keister and D. E. Sherkat, 52–74. New York: Cambridge University Press.

Baber, Ashley. 2023. "Labour Market Engineers: Reconceptualising Labour Market Intermediaries with the Rise of the Gig Economy in the United States." *Work, Employment, and Society*. https://doi.org/10.1177/09500170221150087

Beckert, Jens. 2022. "Durable Wealth: Institutions, Mechanisms, and Practices of Wealth Perpetuation." *Annual Review of Sociology* 48:233–55.

Bendix, Reinhard, and Seymour Martin Lipset. 1966. *Class, Status, and Power*. New York: Free Press.

Bergmann, Barbara R. 2011. "Sex Segregation in the Blue-Collar Occupations: Women's Choices or Unremedied Discrimination?" *Gender and Society* 25:88–93.

Biddle, Catharine and Ian Mette. 2017. "Education and Information." In *Rural Poverty in the United States*, edited by A. R. Tickamyer, J. Sherman, and J. Warlock, 322–48. New York: Columbia University Press.

Bodrožić, Zlatko, and Paul S. Adler. 2018. "The Evolution of Management Models: A Neo-Schumpeterian Theory." *Administrative Science Quarterly* 63(1):85–129.

Brainard, Lael. 2016. "Coming of Age in the Great Recession." In *Economic Mobility: Research and Ideas on Strengthening Families, Communities and the Economy*, edited by A. Brown, D. Buchholz, D. Davis, and A. Gonzalez, 67–76. Washington, DC: Federal Reserve Bank of St. Louis and the Board of Governors of the Federal Reserve System.

Brooks, David. 2015. *The Road to Character*. New York: Random House.

Bryk, Anthony S., Valerie E. Lee, and Peter B. Hollan. 1993. *Catholic Schools and the Common Good*. Cambridge, MA: Harvard University Press.

Burge, Ryan P. 2021. *The Nones: Where They Came from, Who They Are, and Where They Are Going*. Minneapolis, MN: Fortress Press.

Burton, Tara Isabella. 2022. *Strange Rites: New Religions for a Godless World*. New York: PublicAffairs.

Carbonaro, William, and Elizabeth Covay. 2010. "School Sector and Student Achievement in the Era of Standards Based Reforms." *Sociology of Education* 83:160–82.

Center for Applied Research in the Apostolate (CARA). 2023. "Frequently Requested Church Statistics." https://cara.georgetown.edu/faqs

Choi, Jung Hyun, Jun Zhu, Laurie Goodman, Bhargavi Ganesh, and Sarah Strochak. 2018. "Millennial Homeownership: Why Is It So Low, and How Can We Increase It?" https://www.urban.org/sites/default/files/publication/98729/2019_01_11_millennial_homeownership_finalizedv2_0.pdf

Crosa, Beth, Lisa A. Keister, and Howard Aldrich. 2001. "Access to Valuable Resources: Financial, Social, and Human Capital as Determinants of Entrepreneurship." Ohio State University Department of Sociology Working Paper.

Dallavis, Julie. W., Megan Kuhfeld, Beth Tarasawa, and Stephen Ponisciak. 2021. "Achievement Growth in K-8 Catholic Schools Using NWEA Data." *Journal of Catholic Education* 24. doi:http://dx.doi.org/10.15365/joce.2402012021

D'Antonio, William V., Michele Dillon, and Mary L. Gautier. 2013. *American Catholics in Transition*. Lanham, MD: Rowman & Littlefield.

Davis, Kenneth C. 2010. "America's True History of Religious Tolerance." *Smithsonian Magazine*. https://www.smithsonianmag.com/history/americas-true-history-of-religious-tolerance-61312684/?=&no-ist=&page=1

Denton, Melinda L. 2004. "Gender and Marital Decision Making: Negotiating Religious Ideology and Practice." *Social Forces* 82:1151–80.

Dolan, Greg. 2018. "Why Can't the Middle Class Afford Catholic School Anymore?" *Education Next*. https://www.educationnext.org/why-cant-middle-class-afford-catholic-school-anymore/

Dougherty, Kevin D., Jenna Griebel, Mitchell J. Neubert, and Jerry Z. Park. 2013. "A Religious Profile of American Entrepreneurs." *Journal for the Scientific Study of Religion* 52:401–09.

Durkheim, Emile. 1912/1954. *The Elementary Forms of Religious Life*. New York: Free Press.

Ellison, Christopher G., and John P. Bartkowski. 2002. "Conservative Protestantism and the Division of Household Labor among Married Couples." *Journal of Family Issues* 23:950–85.

Ellison, Christopher G., Nicholas H. Wolfinger, and Aida I. Ramos-Wada. 2013. "Attitudes toward Marriage, Divorce, Cohabitation, and Casual Sex among Working-Age Latinos: Does Religion Matter?" *Journal of Family Issues* 34:295–322.

England, Paula, Jonathan Bearak, Michelle J. Budig, and Melissa J. Hodges. 2016. "Do Highly Paid, Highly Skilled Women Experience the Largest Motherhood Penalty?" *American Sociological Review* 81(6):1161–89.

England, Paula, Andrew Levine, and Emma Mishel. 2020. "Progress toward Gender Equality in the United States Has Slowed or Stalled." *Proceedings of the National Academy of Sciences* 117(13):6990–97. https://doi.org/10.1073/pnas.2003878117

Evans, William N., and Robert M. Schwab. 1995. "Finishing High School and Starting College: Do Catholic Schools Make a Difference?" *Quarterly Journal of Economics* 110:941–74.

Featherman, David L. 1971. "The Socioeconomic Achievement of White Religio-Ethnic Subgroups: Social and Psychological Explanations." *American Sociological Review* 36:207–22.

Fitzgerald, Scott T., and Jennifer L. Glass. 2013. "Conservative Protestants, Normative Pathways, and Adult Attainment." In *Religion and Inequalities*, edited by L. A. Keister and D. E. Sherkat, 97–118. New York: Cambridge University Press.

Forbes. 2023. "These High-Profile Billionaires and 300 Others Missed the Cut—For Now." https://www.forbes.com/sites/johnhyatt/2022/09/27/oprah-kanye-charlie-munger-the-american-billionaires-too-poor-to-make-the-2022-forbes-400/?sh=4507c5fa7c24

Fry, Richard. 2013. *A Rising Share of Young Adults Live in Their Parents' Home.* Washington, DC: Pew Research Centers Social and Demographic Trends.

Fry, Richard, and Kim Parker. 2018. "Early Benchmarks Show 'Post-Millennials' on Track to Be Most Diverse, Best-Educated Generation Yet." https://www.pewresearch.org/social-trends/2018/11/15/early-benchmarks-show-post-millennials-on-track-to-be-most-diverse-best-educated-generation-yet/

Gibson-Davis, Christina, Lisa A. Keister, and Lisa Gennettian. 2020. "Net Worth Poverty in Child Households by Race and Ethnicity, 1989–2019." *Journal of Marriage and Family* doi:10.1111/jomf.12742

Glenn, Norval D., and Ruth Hyland. 1967. "Religious Preference and Worldly Success: Some Evidence from National Surveys." *American Sociological Review* 32:73–85.

Gohmann, Stephan F. 2012. "Institutions, Latent Entrepreneurship, and Self-Employment: An International Comparison." *Entrepreneurship Theory and Practice* 36(2):295–321.

Goodman, Laurie S., and Christopher Mayer. 2018. "Homeownership and the American Dream." *Journal of Economic Perspectives* 32(1):31–58.

Greeley, Andrew M. 1969. "Continuities in Research on the 'Religious Factor.'" *American Journal of Sociology* 75:355–59.

Greeley, Andrew M. 1977. *The American Catholic: A Social Portrait.* New York: Basic Books.

Greeley, Andrew, and Michael Hout. 2006. *The Truth About Conservative Christians: What They Think and What They Believe.* Chicago, IL: University of Chicago Press.

Grinstein-Weiss, Clinton Key Michal, and Shannon Carrillo. 2015. "Homeownership, the Great Recession, and Wealth: Evidence from the Survey of Consumer Finances." *Housing Policy Debates* 25(3):419–45.

Hallinan, Maureen T., and Warren N. Kubitschek. 2010. "School Sector, School Poverty, and the Catholic School Advantage." *Catholic Education* 14:143–72.

Hao, Lingxin. 2007. *Color Lines, Country Lines: Race, Immigration, and Wealth Stratification in America.* New York: Russell Sage Foundation.

Harding, John P., and Stuart S. Rosenthal. 2017. "Homeownership, Capital Gains and Self-Employment." *Journal of Urban Economics* 99:120–35.

Horwitz, Ilana M. 2022. *God, Grades, and Graduation: Religion's Surprising Impact on Academic Success.* New York: Oxford University Press.

Horwitz, Ilana, Kaylee Matheny, Krystal Laryea, and Landon Schnabel. 2022. "From Bat Mitzvah to the Bar: Religious Habitus, Self-Concept, and Women's Educational Outcomes." *American Socioligical Review* 87(2):236–372.

Keister, Lisa A. 2003a. "Sharing the Wealth: Siblings and Adult Wealth Ownership." *Demography* 40:521–42.

Keister, Lisa A. 2003b. "Religion and Wealth: The Role of Religious Affiliation and Participation in Early Adult Asset Accumulation." *Social Forces* 82:173–205.

Keister, Lisa A. 2005. *Getting Rich: America's New Rich and How They Got That Way.* New York: Cambridge University Press.

Keister, Lisa A. 2007. "Upward Wealth Mobility: Exploring the Roman Catholic Advantage." *Social Forces* 85(3):1195–225.

Keister, Lisa A. 2008. "Conservative Protestants and Wealth: How Religion Perpetuates Asset Poverty." *American Journal of Sociology* 113:1237–71.

Keister, Lisa A. 2011. *Faith and Money: How Religious Belief Contributes to Wealth and Poverty.* New York: Cambridge University Press.

Keister, Lisa A. 2014. "The One Percent." *The Annual Review of Sociology* 40:347–67.

Keister, Lisa A., and E. Paige Borelli. 2013. "Religion and Wealth Mobility: The Case of American Latinos." In *Religion and Inequalities*, edited by L. A. Keister and D. E. Sherkat, 119–45. New York: Cambridge University Press.

Keister, Lisa A., and Darren E. Sherkat. 2013. *Religion and Inequalities*. New York: Cambridge University Press.

Keister, Lisa A., and Darby E. Southgate. 2022. *Inequality: A Contemporary Approach to Race, Class, and Gender, Second Edition*. New York: Cambridge University Press.

Keister, Lisa A., Sarah Thebaud, and Jill Yavorsky. 2022. "Gender in the Elite." *Annual Review of Sociology* 48:149–69.

Killewald, Alexandra, and Margaret Gough. 2010. "Money Isn't Everything: Wives' Earnings and Housework Time." *Social Science Research* 39 (6): 987–1003.

Kim, Phillip H., Howard E. Aldrich, and Lisa A. Keister. 2004. "Household Income and Net Worth." In *Handbook of Entrepreneurial Dynamics: The Process of Business Creation in Contemporary America*, edited by W. B. Gartner, 49–61. Thousand Oaks, CA: Sage

Konieczny, Mary Ellen. 2013. *The Spirit's Tether: Family, Work, and Religion among American Catholics*. New York: Oxford University Press.

Lachance-Grzela, Mylène, and Geneviève Bouchard. 2010. "Why Do Women Do the Lion's Share of Housework? A Decade of Research." *Sex Roles* 63(11–12):767–80. doi:10.1007/s11199-010-9797-z

Lehrer, Evelyn L. 1995. "The Effect of Religion on the Labor Supply of Married Women." *Social Science Research* 24:281–301.

Lenski, Gerhard. 1961. *The Religious Factor: A Sociological Study of Religion's Impact on Politics, Economics, and Family Life*. Garden City, NY: Doubleday.

Levin, Jeff, Matt Bradshaw, Byron R. Johnson, and Rodney Stark. 2022. "Are Religious 'Nones' Really Not Religious?: Revisiting Glenn, Three Decades Later." *Interdisciplinary Journal of Research on Religion* 18(7):1–29.

Massengill, Rebekah Peeples. 2013. "Nonaffiliation and Socioeconomic Status: Differences in Education and Income between Atheists and Agnostics and "Nothing in Particulars"." In *Religion and Inequalities*, edited by L. A. Keister and D. E. Sherkat, 31–51. New York: Cambridge University Press.

Muller, Chandra, and Christopher G. Ellison. 2012. "Religious Involvement, Social Capital, and Adolescents' Academic Progress: Evidence from the National Education Longitudinal Study of 1988." *Sociological Focus* 34(2):155–83.

Myers, Dowell, Isaac Megbolugbe, and SeongWoo Lee. 1998. "Cohort Estimation of Homeownership Attainment among Native-Born and Immigrant Populations." *Journal of Housing Research* 9:237–69.

Neal, Derek. 1997. "The Effect of Catholic Secondary Schooling on Educational Achievement." *Journal of Labor Economics* 15:98–123.

Ostrander, Susan A. 1984. *Women of the Upper Class*. Philadelphia, PA: Temple University Press.

Padavic, Irene, Robin J. Ely, and Erin M. Reid. 2020. "Explaining the Persistence of Gender Inequality: The Work–Family Narrative as a Social Defense against the 24/7 Work Culture." *Administrative Science Quarterly* 65(1):61–111.

Petersen, Anne Helen. 2019. "14 Millennials Got Honest About How They Afforded Homeownership." https://www.buzzfeed.com/annehelenpetersen/millennials-homeowners-mortgage-buying-house-apartment

Pew Hispanic Center. 2011. *Statistical Portrait of Hispanics in the United States, 2011*. Washington, DC: Pew Hispanic Center.

Pope John Paul II. 1988. *Post-Synodal Apostolic Exhortation Christifideles Laici (Christ's Faithful Laity)*. Washington, DC: USCCB.

Qian, Zhenchao. 2013. *During the Great Recession, More Young Adults Lived with Parents*. Washington, DC: Census Bureau.

Regnerus, Mark D. 2003. "Religion and Positive Adolescent Outcomes: A Review of Research and Theory." *Review of Religious Research* 44(4):394–413.

Renzulli, L. A., H. Aldrich and J. Moody. 2000. "Family Matters: Gender, Networks, and Entrepreneurial Outcomes." *Social Forces* 79(2):523–46. doi:10.2307/2675508

Rietveld, Cornelius A., and Brigitte Hoogendoorn. 2022. "The Mediating Role of Values in the Relationship between Religion and Entrepreneurship." *Small Business Economics* 58:1309–35.

Rivera, Lauren A., and András Tilcsik. 2016. "Class Advantage, Commitment Penalty: The Gendered Effect of Social Class Signals in an Elite Labor Market." *American Socioligical Review* 81:1097–131.

Rodriguez, James. 2023. "Sorry Millennials, You're Never Getting a Good Home." *Business Insider*. https://www.businessinsider.com/millennials-house-home-real-estate-mortgage-rates-rent-debt-boomers-2022-9

Roof, Wade Clark. 1979. "Socioeconomic Differences among White Socioreligious Groups in the United States." *Social Forces* 58:280–89.

Roof, Wade Clark, and William McKinney. 1987. *American Mainline Religion: Its Changing Shape and Future*. New Brunswick, NJ: Rutgers University Press.

Rugh, Jacob S. 2020. "Vanishing Wealth, Vanishing Votes? Latino Homeownership and the 2016 Election in Florida." *Journal of Ethnic and Migration Studies* 46(18):3829–54.

Rumbaut, Rubén G., and Alejandro Portes. 2014. *Immigrant America: A Portrait*. Berkeley, CA: University of California Press.

Sander, William. 1996. "Catholic Grade Schools and Academic Achievement." *Journal of Human Resources* 31:540–48.

Saurav, Pathak, Sonia Goltz, and Mari Buche. 2013. "Influences of Gendered Institutions on Women's Entry into Entrepreneurship." *International Journal of Entrepreneurial Behavior and Research* 19:478–502.

Schnabel, Landon, Cyrus Schleifer, Eman Abdelhadi, and Samuel Perry. 2022. "The Religious Work Ethic and the Spirit of Patriarchy: Religiosity and the Gender Gap in Working for Its Own Sake, 1977–2018." *Sociological Science* 9:75–101.

Seabright, Paul. 2016. "Religion and Entrepreneurship: A Match Made in Heaven?" *Archives de Sciences Socioles des Religions* 61(175):201–20.

Smith, Christian. 1998. *American Evangelicalism: Embattled and Thriving*. Chicago, IL: University of Chicago Press.

Smith, Christian. 2000. *Christian America? What Evangelicals Really Want*. Berkeley: University of California Press.

Smith, Christian, and Robert Faris. 2005. "Socioeconomic Inequality in the American Religious System: An Update and Assessment." *Journal for the Scientific Study of Religion* 44(1):95–104.

Smith, Christian, Kyle Longest, Jonathan Hill, and Kari Christoffersen. 2014. *Young Catholic America: Emerging Adults in, out of, and Gone from the Church*. New York: Oxford University Press.

Spilerman, Seymour, and Francois-Charles Wolff. 2012. "Parental Wealth and Resource Transfers: How They Matter in France for Home Ownership and Living Standards." *Social Science Research* 41:207–23.

Stark, Rodney. 2008. *What Americans Really Believe*. Waco, TX: Baylor University Press.
Stryker, Robin. 1981. "Religio-Ethnic Effects on Attainments in the Early Career." *American Sociological Review* 46:212–31.
Thébaud, Sarah, and Laura Halcomb. 2019. "One Step Forward? Advances and Setbacks on the Path toward Gender Equality in Families and Work." *Sociology Compass* 13(6):e12700. doi:https://doi.org/10.1111/soc4.12700
Tindera, Michela. 2021. "Here's How Much Joe Biden Is Worth?" https://www.forbes.com/sites/michelatindera/2021/06/10/heres-how-much-joe-biden-is-worth/?sh=7fa1b7b7461b
Tsvetkova, Alexandra, Mark Partridge, and Michael Betz. 2017. "Entrepreneurial and Employment Responses to Economic Conditions across the Rural-Urban Continuum." *Annals of the American Academy of Political and Social Science* 672:83–102.
United States Census Bureau. 2021. "Poverty in the United States." https://www.census.gov/library/publications/2022/demo/p60-277.html
Vaisey, Stephen. 2009. "Motivation and Justification: A Dual-Process Model of Culture in Action." *American Journal of Sociology* 114(6):1675–715.
Valdez, Zulema. 2011. *The New Entrepreneurs: How Race, Class, and Gender Shape American Enterprise*. Palo Alto, CA: Stanford University Press.
Wainer, Allison, and Jeffrey Zabel. 2020. "Homeownership and Wealth Accumulation for Low-Income Households." *Journal of Housing Economics* 47:1016–24.
Weber, Max. 1930. *The Protestant Ethic and the Spirit of Capitalism*. New York: Harper Collins.
Wolff, Edward N., Lindsay A. Owens, and Esra Burak. 2011. "How Much Wealth Was Destroyed in the Great Recession?" In *The Great Recession*, edited by D. B. Grusky, B. Western and C. Wimer, 127–58. New York: Russell Sage.
Wright, Erik Olin. 1997. *Class Counts: Comparative Studies in Class Analysis*. New York: Cambridge University Press.
Wuthnow, Robert. 1990. *The Restructuring of American Religion: Society and Faith since World War II*. Princeton, NJ: Princeton University Press.
Yavorsky, Jill E., Lisa A. Keister, Yue Qian, and Sarah Thebaud. 2023. "Separate Spheres in the New Gilded Age: Mapping the Gender Division of Labor by Income and Wealth. Soad061." *Social Forces*. https://doi-org.proxy.lib.duke.edu/10.1093/sf/soad061
Zeitz, Josh. 2015. "When America Hated Catholics." *Politico*. https://www.politico.com/magazine/story/2015/09/when-america-hated-catholics-213177/
Zhou, Min. 2007. "Revisiting Ethnic Entrepreneurship: Convergencies, Controversies, and Conceptual Advancements." In *Rethinking Migration: New Theoretical and Empirical Perspectives*, edited by A. Portes and J. DeWind, 37–61. New York: Berghahn Books.
Zhou, Min, Jennifer Lee, Jody Agius Vallejo, Rosaura Tafoya-Estrada, and Yang Sao Xiong. 2008. "Success Attained, Deterred, and Denied: Divergent Pathways to Social Mobility in Los Angeles' New Second Generation." *Annals of the American Academy of Political and Social Science* 620:37–61.

CHAPTER 5

Barron, Robert. 2020. *Renewing Our Hope: Essays for the New Evangelization*. Washington, DC: Catholic University of America Press.
Bullivant, Stephen. 2022. *Nonverts: The Making of Ex-Christian America*. New York: Oxford University Press.

Burge, Ryan P. 2021. *The Nones: Where They Came from, Who They Are, and Where They Are Going*. Minneapolis, MN: Fortress Press.
Cavins, Jeff. 2022. *My Life on the Rock: A Rebel Returns to the Catholic Faith, 2nd Edition*. West Chester, PA: Ascension Press.
Cavins, Jeff. June 2, 2023. "The Jeff Cavins Show." In *Why I Left the Catholic Church* https://podcasts.apple.com/us/podcast/the-jeff-cavins-show-your-catholic-bible-study-podcast/id1201282412?i=1000615463573. West Chester, PA: Ascension Press.
D'Antonio, William V., Michele Dillon, and Mary L. Gautier. 2013. *American Catholics in Transition*. Lanham, MD: Rowman & Littlefield.
Diamant, Jeff. 2019. "The Countries with the 10 Largest Christian Populations and the 10 Largest Muslim Populations." https://www.pewresearch.org/short-reads/2019/04/01/the-countries-with-the-10-largest-christian-populations-and-the-10-largest-muslim-populations/
Djupe, Paul A., Jacob R. Neiheisel, and Kimberly H. Conger. 2018. "Are the Politics of the Christian Right Linked to State Rates of the Nonreligious? The Importance of Salient Controversy." *Political Research Quarterly* 71(4):910–22. doi:https://doi.org/10.1177/1065912918771526.
Frey, William H. 2020. "Now, More Than Half of Americans Are Millennials or Younger." Brookings Institution. https://www.brookings.edu/blog/the-avenue/2020/07/30/now-more-than-half-of-americans-are-millennials-or-younger/
Gecewicz, Claire. 2019. "Key Takeaways About How Americans View the Sexual Abuse Scandal in the Catholic Church." https://www.pewresearch.org/short-reads/2019/06/11/key-takeaways-about-how-americans-view-the-sexual-abuse-scandal-in-the-catholic-church/
Glass, Jennifer L., April Sutton, and Scott T. Fitzgerald. 2015. "Leaving the Faith: How Religious Switching Changes Pathways to Adulthood among Conservative Protestant Youth." *Social Currents* 2:126–43.
Greeley, Andrew M. 1989. *Religious Change in America*. Cambridge, MA: Harvard University Press.
Heft, James L., and Jan E. Stets, eds. 2021. *Empty Churches: Non-Affiliation in America*. New York: Oxford University Press.
Holland, Tom. 2019. *Dominion: How the Christian Revolution Remade the World*. New York: Basic Books.
Hout, Michael, and Claude S. Fischer. 2002. "No Religious Preference: Politics and Generations." *American Sociological Review* 67(2):165–90.
Kramer, Stephanie, Conrad Hackett, and Marcin Stonawski. 2022. "Modeling the Future of Religion in America." https://www.pewresearch.org/religion/2022/09/13/modeling-the-future-of-religion-in-america/
Lipka, Michael. 2016. "Why America's 'Nones' Left Religion Behind." https://www.pewresearch.org/short-reads/2016/08/24/why-americas-nones-left-religion-behind/
MacGregor, Carol Ann, and Ashlyn Haycook. 2021. "Lapsed Catholics and Other Religious Non-Affiliates." In *Empty Churches: Non-Affiliation in America*, edited by J. L. Heft and J. E. Stets, 79–105. New York: Oxford University Press.
McCarty, Robert J., and John M. Vitek. 2018. *Going, Going, Gone: The Dynamics of Disaffiliation in Young Catholics*. Winona, MN: St. Mary's Press.
Newport, Frank. 2022. "Slowdown in the Rise of Religious Nones." https://news.gallup.com/opinion/polling-matters/406544/slowdown-rise-religious-nones.aspx
Norris, Pippa, and Ronald Inglehart. 2011. *Sacred and Secular: Religion and Politics Worldwide*. New York: Cambridge University Press.

Pew Research Center. 2015. "America's Changing Religious Landscape." https://www.pewresearch.org/religion/2015/05/12/chapter-2-religious-switching-and-intermarriage/#retention-of-childhood-members-hindus-muslims-and-jews-most-successful-at-retaining-adherents

Sherkat, Darren E. 1991. "Leaving the Faith: Testing Theories of Religious Switching Using Survival Models." *Social Science Research* 20:171–87.

Sherkat, Darren E. 2001. "Tracking the Restructuring of American Religion: Religious Affiliation and Patterns of Religious Mobility, 1973–1998." *Social Forces* 79:1459–93.

Sherkat, Darren E. 2014. *Changing Faith: The Dynamics and Consequences of Americans' Shifting Religious Identities*. New York: New York University Press.

Skirbekk, Vegard, Eric Kaufmann, and Anne Goujon. 2010. "Secularism, Fundamentalism, or Catholicism? The Religious Composition of the United States to 2043." *Journal for the Scientific Study of Religion* 49(2):293–310.

Smith, Christian, Kyle Longest, Jonathan Hill, and Kari Christoffersen. 2014. *Young Catholic America: Emerging Adults in, out of, and Gone from the Church*. New York: Oxford University Press.

Smith, Christian, Bridget Ritz, and Michael Rotolo. 2020. *Religious Parenting: Transmitting Faith and Values in Contemporary America*. Princeton, NJ: Princeton University Press.

Voas, David, and Mark Chaves. 2016. "Is the United States a Counterexample to the Secularization Thesis?" *American Journal of Sociology* 121:517–56.

Wilson, John, and Darren E. Sherkat. 1994. "Returning to the Fold." *Journal for the Scientific Study of Religion* 33:148–61.

Wuthnow, Robert. 1990. *The Restructuring of American Religion: Society and Faith since World War II*. Princeton, NJ: Princeton University Press.

Wuthnow, Robert. 1999. *Growing up Religious: Christians and Jews and Their Journeys of Faith*. Boston: Beacon Press.

CHAPTER 6

Alwin, Duane. 2007. *Margins of Error: A Study of Reliability in Survey Measurement*, 1st ed. Hoboken, NJ: Wiley-Interscience.

Baldassarri, Delia and Amir Goldberg. 2014. "Neither Ideologues nor Agnostics: Alternative Voters' Belief System in an Age of Partisan Politics." *American Journal of Sociology* 120(1):45–95.

Baldassarri, Delia, and Barum Park. 2020. "Was There Ever a Culture War? Partisan Polarization and Secular Trends in U.S. Public Opinion." *Journal of Politics* 82(3):809–27.

Bartkowski, John P., and Susan E. Grettenberger. 2018. *The Arc of Faith-Based Initiatives: Religion's Changing Role in Welfare Service Provision*. Cham, Switzerland: Springer.

Bellah, Robert N. 2011. *Religion in Human Evolution: From the Paleolithic to the Axial Age*. New York: Belknap.

Boutyline, Andrei, and Stephen Vaisey. 2017. "Belief Network Analysis: A Relational Approach to Understanding the Structure of Attitudes." *American Journal of Sociology* 122(5):1339–615.

Brenan, Megan. 2023. "Belief in Five Spiritual Entities Edges Down to New Lows." https://news.gallup.com/poll/508886/belief-five-spiritual-entities-edges-down-new-lows.aspx

Bruce, Tricia C. 2020. *How Americans Understand Abortion: A Comprehensive Interview Study of Abortion Attitudes in the U.S.* South Bend, IN: University of Notre Dame Press.

Burge, Ryan P. 2021. *The Nones: Where They Came from, Who They Are, and Where They Are Going.* Minneapolis, MN: Fortress Press.

CCC. 2000. *Catechism of the Catholic Church*, 2nd ed. https://www.usccb.org/sites/default/files/flipbooks/catechism/

D'Antonio, William V., James D. Davidson, Dean R. Hoge, and Mary L. Gautier. 2007. *American Catholics Today: New Realities of Their Faith and Their Church.* Lanham, MD: Rowman and Littlefield.

D'Antonio, William V., Michele Dillon, and Mary L. Gautier. 2013. *American Catholics in Transition.* Lanham, MD: Rowman & Littlefield.

Davis, Nancy J., and Robert V. Robinson. 1996. "Are the Rumors of War Exaggerated? Religious Orthodoxy and Moral Progressivism in America." *American Journal of Sociology* 102(3):756–87.

Day, Maureen K., ed. 2018. *Young Adult American Catholics: Explaining Vocation in Their Own Words.* Mahwah, NJ: Paulist Press.

Day, Maureen, James Cavendish, Paul Perl, Mary Gautier, and Michele Dillon. Forthcoming. *Catholicism at a Crossroads: The Present and Future of America's Largest Church.*

Dillon, Michele. 1999. *Catholic Identity: Balancing Reason, Faith, and Power.* New York: Cambridge University Press.

Durkheim, Emile. 1912/1954. *The Elementary Forms of Religious Life.* New York: Free Press.

Ellison, Christopher G., Gabriel A. Acevedo, and Aida I. Ramos-Wada. 2011. "Religion and Attitudes toward Same-Sex Marriage among U.S. Latinos." *Social Science Quarterly* 92(1):35–56.

Ellison, Christopher G., Nicholas H. Wolfinger, and Aida I. Ramos-Wada. 2013. "Attitudes toward Marriage, Divorce, Cohabitation, and Casual Sex among Working-Age Latinos: Does Religion Matter?" *Journal of Family Issues* 34:295–322.

Galek, Kathleen C., Kevin J. Flannelly, Christopher G. Ellison, Nava R. Silton and Katherine R.B. Jankowski. 2015. "Religion, Meaning and Purpose in Life, and Mental Health." *Psychology of Religion and Spirituality* 7:1–12.

Gorski, Philip S., and Samuel L. Perry. 2022. *The Flag and the Cross: White Christian Nationalism and the Threat to American Democracy.* New York: Oxford University Press.

Greeley, Andrew M. 1977. "How Conservative Are American Catholics?" *Political Science Quarterly* 92(2):199–218.

Green, John C., James L. Guth, Corwin E. Smidt, and Lyman A. Kellstedt. 1996. *Religion and the Culture Wars.* Lanham, MD: Rowman & Littlefield.

Hahn, Kimberly. 2001. *Life-Giving Love: Embracing God's Design for Marriage.* Cincinnati, OH: Servant Books.

Hoffmann, John P., Christopher G. Ellison, and John P. Bartkowski. 2017. "Conservative Protestantism and Attitudes toward Corporal Punishment, 1986–2014." *Social Science Research* 63:81–94.

Horowitz, Jason, and Ruth Graham. August 30, 2023. "Pope Says a Strong U.S. Faction Offers a Backward, Narrow View of the Church." *New York Times.* https://www.nytimes.com/2023/08/30/world/europe/pope-francis-american-conservatives.html

Hout, Michael. 2016. "Saint Peter's Leaky Boat: Falling Intergenerational Persistence among U.S.-Born Catholics since 1974." *Sociology of Religion* 77(1):1–17.

Hout, Michael, and Claude S. Fischer. 2002. "No Religious Preference: Politics and Generations." *American Sociological Review* 67(2):165–90.

Hout, Michael, and Andrew M. Greeley. 1987. "The Center Doesn't Hold: Trends in Church Attendance, 1940–1984." *American Sociological Review* 52:325–45.

Jozkowski, Kristen N., Brandon L. Crawford, and Mary E. Hunt. 2018. "Complexity in Attitudes toward Abortion Access: Results from Two Studies." *Sexuality Research and Social Policy* 15:464–82.

Jozkowski, Kristen N., Brandon L. Crawford, and Malachi Willis. 2021. "Abortion Complexity Scores from 1972 to 2018: A Cross-Sectional Time-Series Analysis Using Data from the General Social Survey." *Sexuality Research and Social Policy* 18:13–26.

Kaplan, Anna. 2022. "Pelosi Joins Biden, Kerry, Giuliani and Other Catholics Threatened with No Communion Because of Abortion Support." *The Economist*. https://www.forbes.com/sites/annakaplan/2022/05/24/pelosi-joins-biden-kerry-giuliani-and-other-catholics-threatened-with-no-communion-because-of-abortion-support/?sh=60eb35501d58

Keister, Lisa A. 2023. "Beliefs About Poverty and Inequality: Du Bois and Ethnic Differences among Catholics." *Journal for the Scientific Study of Religion* 62(S1):163–82.

Koenig, Harold, Dana King, and Verna B. Carson. 2012. *Handbook of Religion and Health*, 2nd ed. New York: Oxford University Press.

Konieczny, Mary Ellen. 2013. *The Spirit's Tether: Family, Work, and Religion among American Catholics*. New York: Oxford University Press.

Krok, Dariusz. 2015. "The Role of Meaning in Life within the Relations of Religious Coping and Psychological Well-Being." *Journal of Religion and Health* 54(6):229–308.

Levin, Jeff, Matt Bradshaw, Byron R. Johnson, and Rodney Stark. 2022. "Are Religious "Nones" Really Not Religious?: Revisiting Glenn, Three Decades Later." *Interdisciplinary Journal of Research on Religion* 18(7):1–29.

Lipka, Michael. 2016. "Why America's 'Nones' Left Religion Behind." https://www.pewresearch.org/short-reads/2016/08/24/why-americas-nones-left-religion-behind/

McCall, Leslie. 2013. *The Undeserving Rich: American Beliefs About Inequality, Opportunity, and Redistribution*. New York: Cambridge University Press.

McCammon, Sarah. 2021. "An Issue Dividing Catholics: Should Abortion Rights Supporters Be Denied Communion?" *National Public Radio*. https://www.npr.org/2021/11/15/1055749036/an-issue-dividing-catholics-should-abortion-rights-supporters-be-denied-communion

National Catholic Reporter. 2021. "In Defiance of Vatican, US Bishops Vote to Advance Communion Document." https://www.ncronline.org/news/defiance-vatican-us-bishops-vote-advance-communion-document

Norris, Pippa, and Ronald Inglehart. 2011. *Sacred and Secular: Religion and Politics Worldwide*. New York: Cambridge University Press.

Orcés, Diana. 2022. "Where Do Catholics' Views Stand Today?" https://www.prri.org/spotlight/where-do-catholics-views-stand-today/

Perry, Samuel L. 2022. "American Religion in the Era of Increasing Polarization." *Annual Review of Sociology* 48:87–107.

Perry, Samuel L., Joshua T. Davis, and Joshua B. Grubbs. 2023. "Controlling the Past to Control the Future: Christian Nationalism and Mandatory Patriotic Education in Public Schools." *Journal for the Scientific Study of Religion* 62(3):694–708.

Perry, Samuel, Elizabeth McElroy, Landon Schnabel, and Joshua Grubbs. 2022. "Fill the Earth and Subdue It: Christian Nationalism, Ethno-Religious Threat, and Nationalist Pronatalism." *Sociological Forum* 37(4):995–1017.

Perry, Samuel, Landon Schnabel, and Joshua Grubbs. 2022. "Christian Nationalism, Perceived Anti-Christian Discrimination, and Prioritizing 'Religious Freedom' in the 2020 Presidential Election." *Nations and Nationalism* 28(2):714–25.

Pew Research Center. 2008. "U.S. Religious Landscape Survey: Religious Beliefs and Practices." https://www.pewresearch.org/religion/2008/06/01/chapter-1-religious-beliefs-and-practices/

Pew Research Center. 2015. "America's Changing Religious Landscape." https://www.pewresearch.org/religion/2015/05/12/chapter-2-religious-switching-and-intermarriage/#retention-of-childhood-members-hindus-muslims-and-jews-most-successful-at-retaining-adherents."

Pope Paul VI. 1975. *Evangelii Nuntiandi (on Evangelization in the Modern World).* Washington, DC: USCCB.

Rowland, Susan K. 2017. "Seven Things Catholics Should Know About Divorce." St. Anthony Messenger, Franciscan Media. https://www.franciscanmedia.org/st-anthony-messenger/june-2017/seven-things-catholics-should-know-about-divorce/.

Schwadel, Philip. 2013. "Changes in Americans Strength of Religious Affiliation, 1974–2010." *Sociology of Religion* 74(1):107–28.

Schwadel, Philip, and Christopher G. Ellison. 2017. "Period and Cohort Changes in Americans' Support for Marijuana Legalization: Convergence and Divergence across Social Groups." *Sociological Quarterly* 58:405–28.

Sherkat, Darren E. 2017. "Politics, Religion, and Confidence in Science." *Politics and Religion* 10:137–60.

Sherkat, Darren E. 2021. "Cognitive Sophistication, Religion, and the Trump Vote." *Social Science Quarterly* 102:179–97.

Silton, Nava R., Kevin J. Flannelly, Kathleen C. Galek, and Christopher G. Ellison. 2014. "Beliefs About God and Mental Health among American Adults." *Journal of Religion and Health* 53:1285–96.

Smith, Gregory A. 2020. "8 Facts About Catholics and Politics in the U.S." https://www.pewresearch.org/fact-tank/2020/09/15/8-facts-about-catholics-and-politics-in-the-u-s/

Stark, Rodney. 2008. *What Americans Really Believe.* Waco, TX: Baylor University Press.

Stokes, Charles E., and Christopher G. Ellison. 2010. "Religion and Attitudes toward Divorce Laws among U.S. Adults." *Journal of Family Issues* 31:1279–304.

Tope, Daniel, Brittany Rawlinson, Justin Pickett, Amy M. Burdette, and Christopher G. Ellison. 2017. "Religion, Race, and Othering Obama." *Social Currents* 4:51–70.

Voas, David, and Mark Chaves. 2016. "Is the United States a Counterexample to the Secularization Thesis?" *American Journal of Sociology* 121:517–56.

Wilson, George, Vincent Roscigno, Carsten Sauer, and Nick Petersen. 2022. "Mobility, Inequality, and Beliefs about Distribution and Redistribution." *Social Forces* 100(3):1053–79.

CHAPTER 7

Bekkers, René, and Pamala Wiepking. 2011. "Who Gives? A Literature Review of Predictors of Charitable Giving Part One: Religion, Education, Age and Socialisation." *Voluntary Sector Review* 2(3):337–65.

Brenan, Megan. 2020. "Americans Remain More Liberal Socially Than Economically." https://news.gallup.com/poll/311303/americans-remain-liberal-socially-economically.aspx

Brooks, Arthur C. 2003. "Religious Faith and Charitable Giving." *Policy Review* 121:39–50.

D'Antonio, William V., Michele Dillon, and Mary L. Gautier. 2013. *American Catholics in Transition*. Lanham, MD: Rowman & Littlefield.

Dionne Jr., E. J. 2000. "There Is No 'Catholic Vote.' and Yet, It Matters." https://www.brookings.edu/articles/there-is-no-catholic-vote-and-yet-it-matters/

Eagle, David, Lisa A. Keister, and Jen'nan Ghazal Read. 2017. "Household Charitable Giving at the Intersection of Gender, Marital Status, and Religion." *Nonprofit and Voluntary Sector Quarterly* 47(1):185–205. https://doi.org/10.1177/0899764017734650

Ellison, Christopher G., Nicholas H. Wolfinger, and Aida I. Ramos-Wada. 2013. "Attitudes toward Marriage, Divorce, Cohabitation, and Casual Sex among Working-Age Latinos: Does Religion Matter?" *Journal of Family Issues* 34:295–322.

Farmer, Adam, Blair Kidwell, and David M. Hardesty. 2020. "Helping a Few a Lot or Many a Little: Political Ideology and Charitable Giving." *Journal of Consumer Psychology* 34:614–30. doi:https://doi.org/10.1002/jcpy.1164.

Gaunt, Thomas. 2022. *Faith and Spiritual Life of Young Adult Catholics in a Rising Hispanic Church*. Collegeville, MN: Liturgical Press.

Greater Good Science Center. 2017. "The Science of Generosity." https://ggsc.berkeley.edu/images/uploads/ggsc-jtf_white_paper-generosity-final.pdf

Greeley, Andrew M. 1977. "How Conservative Are American Catholics?" *Political Science Quarterly* 92(2):199–218.

Havens, John J., Mary A. O'Herlihy, and Paul G. Schervish. 2006. "Charitable Giving: How Much, by Whom, to What, and How?" In *The Non-Profit Sector: A Research Handbook*, edited by W. W. Powell and R. Steinberg, 542–63. New Haven, CT: Yale University Press.

Himes, Kenneth R. 2019. "Catholic Social Teaching, Economic Inequality, and American Society." *Journal of Religious Ethics* 47(2):283–310.

Indiana University Lilly Family School of Philanthropy. 2021. "Everyday Donors of Color: Diverse Philanthropy During Times of Change." https://scholarworks.iupui.edu/server/api/core/bitstreams/829fe636-91b6-4ea1-a683-e501148e2620/content

Krogstad, Jens Manuel, and Luis Noe-Bustamante. 2021. "Key Facts About U.S. Latinos for National Hispanic Heritage Month." https://www.pewresearch.org/fact-tank/2021/09/09/key-facts-about-u-s-latinos-for-national-hispanic-heritage-month/

Manza, Jeff, and Clem Brooks. 1997. "The Religious Factor in U.S. Presidential Elections, 1960–1992." *American Journal of Sociology* 103(1):38–81.

Newport, Frank. 2020. "Religious Group Voting and the 2020 Election." https://news.gallup.com/opinion/polling-matters/324410/religious-group-voting-2020-election.aspx

Newport, Frank. 2021. "What's Driving Americans' Views of Their Taxes?" https://news.gallup.com/opinion/polling-matters/349955/driving-americans-views-taxes.aspx

O'Brien, John, and Eman Abdelhadi. 2020. "Re-Examining Restructuring: Racialization, Religious Conservatism, and Political Leanings in Contemporary American Life." *Social Forces* 99(2):474–503.

Parker, Kim, Juliana Menasce Horowitz, Ruth Igielnik, J. Baxter Oliphant, and Anna Brown. 2017. "The Demographics of Gun Ownership." https://www.pewresearch.org/social-trends/2017/06/22/the-demographics-of-gun-ownership/

Pope Francis. 2018. *Apostolic Exhortation Gaudete et Exsultate (Rejoice and Be Glad)*. Washington, DC: USCCB.

Pope Francis. 2020. *Apostalic Exhortation Evangelii Gaudium (The Joy of the Gospel)*. Washington, DC: USCCB.

Ramos, Aida I., Robert D. Woodberry, and Christopher G. Ellison. 2017. "The Contexts of Conversion among U.S. Latinos." *Sociology of Religion* 78(2):119–45.

Regnerus, Mark D., Christian Smith, and David Sikkink. 1998. "Who Gives to the Poor? The Influence of Religious Tradition and Political Location on the Personal Generosity of Americans toward the Poor." *Journal for the Scientific Study of Religion* 37(3):481–93.

Sanchez, Boris. October 15, 2022. "The Latino Voter Shift Comes into Focus in South Texas." https://www.cnn.com/2022/10/14/politics/latino-voters-texas-15th/index.html

Smith, Gregory A. 2020. "8 Facts About Catholics and Politics in the U.S." https://www.pewresearch.org/fact-tank/2020/09/15/8-facts-about-catholics-and-politics-in-the-u-s/

Stine, Vincent. 2020. "Is There a Catholic Vote and Does It Matter?" *Political Science Now*. https://politicalsciencenow.com/is-there-a-catholic-vote-and-does-it-matter/

Vatican II. 1965. "Gaudium et Spes (Joy and Hope)." https://www.vatican.va/archive/hist_councils/ii_vatican_council/documents/vat-ii_const_19651207_gaudium-et-spes_en.html

Wiepking, Pamela, and Rene Bekkers. 2012. "Who Gives? A Literature Review of Predictors of Charitable Giving Part Two: Gender, Family Composition, and Income." *Voluntary Sector Review* 3:217–45.

Wuthnow, Robert. 1990. *The Restructuring of American Religion: Society and Faith since World War II*. Princeton, NJ: Princeton University Press.

Yongzheng, Yang, and Liu Peixu. 2021. "Are Conservatives More Charitable Than Liberals in the U.S.? A Meta-Analysis of Political Ideology and Charitable Giving." *Social Science Research* 99. doi:10.1016/j.ssresearch.2021.102598

CHAPTER 8

Arrow, Kenneth J. 1974. *The Limits of Organization*. New York: Norton.

Bekkers, René, and Woods Bowman. 2008. "The Relationship between Confidence in Charitable Organizations and Volunteering Revisited." *Nonprofit and Voluntary Sector Quarterly* 38(5):884–97.

Bhutta, Neil, Jesse Bricker, Andrew C. Chang, Lisa J. Dettling, Sarena Goodman, Joanne W. Hsu, Kevin B. Moore, Sarah Reber, Alice Henriques Volz, Richard A. Windle, Kathy Bi, Jacqueline Blair, Julia Hewitt, and Dalton Ruh. 2020. "Changes in U.S. Family Finances from 2016 to 2019: Evidence from the Survey of Consumer Finances." *Federal Reserve Bulletin*. Washington, DC: Board of Governors of the Federal Reserve System.

Bowman, Woods. 2004. "Confidence in Charitable Institutions and Volunteering." *Nonprofit and Voluntary Sector Quarterly* 33(2):247–70.

Brady, Henry E., and Thomas B. Kent. 2022. "Fifty Years of Declining Confidence and Increasing Polarization in Trust in American Institutions." *Daedelus* https://doi.org/10.1162/DAED_a_01943

Bryant, W. Keith, Haekyung Jeon-Slaughter, Hyojin Kang, and Aaron Tax. 2003. "Participation in Philanthropic Activities: Donating Money and Time." *Journal of Consumer Policy* 26:43–73.

Burge, Ryan P. 2021. *The Nones: Where They Came from, Who They Are, and Where They Are Going*. Minneapolis, MN: Fortress Press.

Carlo, Gustavo, James B. Allen, and Dion C. Buhman. 1999. "Facilitating and Disinhibiting Prosocial Behaviors: The Nonlinear Interaction of Trait Perspective Taking and Trait Personal Distress on Volunteering." *Basic and Applied Social Psychology* 21:189–97.

CCC. 2000. *Catechism of the Catholic Church*, 2nd Edition. https://www.usccb.org/sites/default/files/flipbooks/catechism/.

Cheng, Siwei. 2016. "The Accumulation of (Dis)Advantage: The Intersection of Gender and Race in the Long-Term Wage Effect of Marriage." *American Socioligical Review* 81:29–56.

Coleman, James S. 1988. "Social Capital in the Creation of Human Capital." *American Journal of Sociology* 94:S95–S120.

Day, Maureen K. 2020. *Catholic Activism Today: Individual Transformation and the Struggle for Social Justice*. New York: New York University Press.

Ellison, Christopher G., and John P. Bartkowski. 2002. "Conservative Protestantism and the Division of Household Labor among Married Couples." *Journal of Family Issues* 23:950–85.

Ellison, Christopher G., Nicholas H. Wolfinger, and Aida I. Ramos-Wada. 2013. "Attitudes toward Marriage, Divorce, Cohabitation, and Casual Sex among Working-Age Latinos: Does Religion Matter?" *Journal of Family Issues* 34:295–322.

England, Paula, Jonathan Bearak, Michelle J. Budig, and Melissa J. Hodges. 2016. "Do Highly Paid, Highly Skilled Women Experience the Largest Motherhood Penalty?" *American Socioligical Review* 81(6):1161–89.

Fegan, Colette, and Sarah Cook. 2014. "The Therapeutic Power of Volunteering." *Advances in Psychiatric Treatment* 20(3):217–24.

Gibson-Davis, Christina, Lisa A. Keister, and Lisa Gennettian. 2020. "Net Worth Poverty in Child Households by Race and Ethnicity, 1989–2019." *Journal of Marriage and Family* doi:10.1111/jomf.12742.

Gorski, Philip S., and Samuel L. Perry. 2022. *The Flag and the Cross: White Christian Nationalism and the Threat to American Democracy*. New York: Oxford University Press.

Himes, Kenneth R. 2019. "Catholic Social Teaching, Economic Inequality, and American Society." *Journal of Religious Ethics* 47(2):283–310.

Indiana University Lilly Family School of Philanthropy. 2021. "Everyday Donors of Color: Diverse Philanthropy During Times of Change." https://scholarworks.iupui.edu/server/api/core/bitstreams/829fe636-91b6-4ea1-a683-e501148e2620/content

Keister, Lisa A. 2014. "The One Percent." *The Annual Review of Sociology* 40:347–67.

Keister, Lisa A. 2017. "Why Don't Americans Care About Inequality?" in *Inequality in America: Interdisciplinary Perspectives*, edited by B. Hahn and K. Schmidt (22–30). Berlin: Verlag Press.

Keister, Lisa A., and Darren E. Sherkat. 2013. *Religion and Inequalities*. New York: Cambridge University Press.

Keister, Lisa A., and Darby E. Southgate. 2022. *Inequality: A Contemporary Approach to Race, Class, and Gender, Second Edition*. New York: Cambridge University Press.

Killewald, Alexandra, and Margaret Gough. 2010. "Killewald, Alexandra, and Margaret Gough. 2010. 'Money Isn't Everything: Wives' Earnings and Housework Time.'" *Social Science Research* 39 (6): 987–1003. *Social Forces* 39(6):987–1003.

Killewald, Alexandra, Fabian T. Pfeffer, and Jared N. Schachner. 2017. "Wealth Inequality and Accumulation." *Annual Review of Sociology* 43:379–404.

Lehrer, Evelyn L. 1995. "The Effect of Religion on the Labor Supply of Married Women." *Social Science Research* 24:281–301.

Lehrer, Evelyn L. 2004. "The Role of Religion in Union Formation: An Economic Perspective." *Population Research and Policy Review* 23(2):161–85.

Levin, Jeff, Matt Bradshaw, Byron R. Johnson, and Rodney Stark. 2022. "Are Religious 'Nones' Really Not Religious?: Revisiting Glenn, Three Decades Later." *Interdisciplinary Journal of Research on Religion* 18(7):1–29.

McCall, Leslie. 2013. *The Undeserving Rich: American Beliefs About Inequality, Opportunity, and Redistribution*. New York: Cambridge University Press.

McCall, Leslie, and Lane Kenworthy. 2009. "Americans' Social Policy Preferences in the Era of Rising Inequality." *Perspectives on Politics* 7(3):459–84.Ottani-Wilhelm, Mark, David B. Estell, and Neil H. Perdue. 2014. "Role-Modeling and Conversations About Giving in the Socialization of Adolescent Charitable Giving and Volunteering." *Journal of Adolescence* 37(1):53–66.

Padavic, Irene, Robin J. Ely, and Erin M. Reid. 2020. "Explaining the Persistence of Gender Inequality: The Work–Family Narrative as a Social Defense against the 24/7 Work Culture." *Administrative Science Quarterly* 65(1):61–111.

Parsons, Talcott. 1937. *The Structure of Social Action*. New York: Free Press.

Paxton, Pamela. 2002. "Social Capital and Democracy: An Interdependent Relationship." *American Sociological Review* 67(2):254–7.

Paxton, Pamela. 2007. "Association Memberships and Generalized Trust: A Multilevel Model across 31 Countries." *Social Forces* 86(1):47–76.

Pope John Paul II. 1984. *Apostolic Letter Salvifici Doloris (on the Christian Meaning of Human Suffering)*. Washington, DC: USCCB.

Pope John Paul II. January 27, 1999. "Papal Mass, St. Louis, Missouri." https://www.vatican.va/content/john-paul-ii/en/travels/1999/documents/hf_jp-ii_hom_27011999_stlouis.html

Pope Leo XIII. 1891. *Apostalic Encyclical Rerum Novarum (Rights and Duties of Capital and Labor)*. Washington, DC: USCCB.

Ritzman, Barbara, and Donald Tomaskovic-Devey. 1992. "Life-Chances and Support for Equity as a Counter-Normative Distributional Rule." *Social Forces* 71:745–63.

Sherkat, Darren E. 2000. "That They Be Keepers of the Home: The Effect of Conservative Religion on Early and Late Transitions into Housewifery." *Review of Religious Research* 41:344–458.

Sherkat, Darren E. 2017. "Politics, Religion, and Confidence in Science." *Politics and Religion* 10:137–60.

Taylor, Paul, Cary Funk, and April Clark. 2007. "Americans and Social Trust: Who, Where and Why." https://www.pewresearch.org/wp-conten-t/uploads/sites/3/2010/10/socialtrust.pdf

Thébaud, Sarah, and Laura Halcomb. 2019. "One Step Forward? Advances and Setbacks on the Path toward Gender Equality in Families and Work." *Sociology Compass* 13(6):e12700. doi:https://doi.org/10.1111/soc4.12700

Thomas, Margaret M.C., Daniel P. Miller, and Taryn W. Morrissey. 2019. "Food Insecurity and Child Health." *Pediatrics* 144(4):e20190397. doi:10.1542/peds.2019-0397

Tolbert, Charles M., Thomas A. Lyson, and Michael D. Irwin. 1998. "Local Capitalism, Civic Engagement, and Socioeconomic Well-Being." *Social Forces* 77(2):401–28.

United States Conference of Catholic Bishops (USCCB). 2011. *To Live Each Day with Dignity: A Statement on Physician-Assisted Suicide*. Washington, DC: USCCB.

Vatican II. 1965a. "Gaudium Et Spes (Joy and Hope)." https://www.vatican.va/archive/hist_councils/ii_vatican_council/documents/vat-ii_const_19651207_gaudium-et-spes_en.html

Vatican II. 1965b. "Lumen Gentium (Light of the Nations)." https://www.vatican.va/archive/hist_councils/ii_vatican_council/documents/vat-ii_const_19641121_lumen-gentium_en.html

Welch, Michael R., David Sikkink, Eric Sartain, and Carolyn Bond. 2004. "Trust in God and Trust in Man: The Ambivalent Role of Religion in Shaping Dimensions of Social Trust." *Journal for the Scientific Study of Religion* 43(3):317–43.

Wilson, George, Vincent Roscigno, Carsten Sauer, and Nick Petersen. 2022. "Mobility, Inequality, and Beliefs about Distribution and Redistribution." *Social Forces* 100(3):1053–79.

Winship, Scott. 2013. "How Much Do Americans Care About Income Inequality?" *Brookings Briefs* April 30.

Yamagishi, Toshio, and Midori Yamagishi. 1994. "Trust and Commitment in the United States and Japan." *Motivation and Emotion* 18(2):129–36.

Yang, Y. Claire, Kristen Schorpp, Courtney Boen, Karen Gerken, and Kathleen Mullan Harris. 2020. "Socioeconomic Status and Biological Risks for Health and Illness across the Life Course." *Journal of Gerontology: Series B, Social Sciences* 75(3):613–24.

Yavorsky, Jill E., Lisa A. Keister, Yue Qian, and Sarah Thebaud. 2023. "Separate Spheres in the New Gilded Age: Mapping the Gender Division of Labor by Income and Wealth Soad061." *Social Forces*. https://doi-org.proxy.lib.duke.edu/10.1093/sf/soad061

CHAPTER 9

Barron, Robert. 2020. *Renewing Our Hope: Essays for the New Evangelization*. Washington, DC: Catholic University of America Press.

D'Antonio, William V., Michele Dillon, and Mary L. Gautier. 2013. *American Catholics in Transition*. Lanham, MD: Rowman & Littlefield.

Day, Maureen, James Cavendish, Paul Perl, Mary Gautier, and Michele Dillon. Forthcoming. *Catholicism at a Crossroads: The Present and Future of America's Largest Church*.

Horowitz, Jason, and Ruth Graham. August 30, 2023. "Pope Says a Strong U.S. Faction Offers a Backward, Narrow View of the Church." *New York Times*. https://www.pewresearch.org/short-reads/2019/08/05/transubstantiation-eucharist-u-s-catholics

Smith, Gregory. 2019. "Just One-Third of U.S. Catholics Agree with Their Church That Eucharist Is Body, Blood of Christ." https://www.pewresearch.org/short-reads/2019/08/05/transubstantiation-eucharist-u-s-catholics/

APPENDIX

D'Antonio, William V., James D. Davidson, Dean R. Hoge, and Mary L. Gautier. 2007. *American Catholics Today: New Realities of Their Faith and Their Church*. Lanham, MD: Rowman & Littlefield.

D'Antonio, William V., Michele Dillon, and Mary L. Gautier. 2013. *American Catholics in Transition*. Lanham, MD: Rowman & Littlefield.

Davern, Michael, Rene Bautista, Jeremy Freese, Stephen L. Morgan and Tom W. Smith. 2021. "General Social Survey Documentation and Public Use File Codebook." https://gss.norc.org/documents/codebook/gss%202021%20codebook%20r1.pdf

Gibson-Davis, Christina, Lisa A. Keister, and Lisa Gennettian. 2020. "Net Worth Poverty in Child Households by Race and Ethnicity, 1989–2019." *Journal of Marriage and Family* doi:10.1111/jomf.12742

Greeley, Andrew, and Michael Hout. 2006. *The Truth About Conservative Christians: What They Think and What They Believe*. Chicago, IL: University of Chicago Press.

Jozkowski, Kristen N., Brandon L. Crawford, and Mary E. Hunt. 2018. "Complexity in Attitudes toward Abortion Access: Results from Two Studies." *Sexuality Research and Social Policy* 15:464–82.

Jozkowski, Kristen N., Brandon L. Crawford, and Malachi Willis. 2021. "Abortion Complexity Scores from 1972 to 2018: A Cross-Sectional Time-Series Analysis Using Data from the General Social Survey." *Sexuality Research and Social Policy* 18:13–26.

Perry, Samuel L., and Cuyrus Schleifer. 2019. "Are the Faithful Becoming Less Fruitful? The Decline of Conservative Protestant Fertility and the Growing Importance of Religious Practice and Belief in Childbearing in the Us." *Social Science Research* 78:137–55.

Smith, Christian, Kyle Longest, Jonathan Hill, and Kari Christoffersen. 2014. *Young Catholic America: Emerging Adults in, out of, and Gone from the Church*. New York: Oxford University Press.

Steensland, Brian, Jerry Z. Park, Mark D. Regnerus, Lynn D. Robinson, W. Bradford Wilcox, and Robert D. Woodberry. 2000. "The Measure of American Religion: Toward Improving the State of the Art." *Social Forces* 79:291–318.

United States Census Bureau. 2021. "Poverty in the United States." https://www.census.gov/library/publications/2022/demo/p60-277.html

INDEX

For the benefit of digital users, indexed terms that span two pages (e.g., 52–53) may, on occasion, appear on only one of those pages.

abortion, 145f, 145–48, 146b, 147f, 149, 162, 199, 209, 212
abstinence, 58
actual number of children, 62f, 62, 66
age at first birth, 62–63, 63f, 66
American Voices Project (AVP), 9–10, 117, 205–6, 210–11
anger about inequality, 182–83
Asian Catholics, 24f, 28–29, 196
assisted suicide, 183–85, 185f, 193, 199–200, 209

Baby Boomers
  birth cohorts/gender distribution, 23
  fertility rates, 19–20
  gender differences, 21–23, 22f
  religious mobility motivations, 120
  religious mobility/social origins, 109t
  religious tradition statistics, 20f
  socioeconomic status (SES), 17–18
Barrett, Amy C., 152
beliefs in God/Christianity, 121
Biden, Joseph R., 2, 3–4, 26, 88, 96n.2, 122–23, 152, 157–58, 195
birth cohort variation in, 16
birth control, 57–58, 80
birth control/contraception, 57–58, 80
Black Catholics, 24f, 26f, 29–30, 196
born-again experiences, 135, 149–50
born Catholic, 120–21
Brooks, A. C., 165–66
Bush, George W., 157–58

capital punishment, 185–87, 186f, 199–200
Catholic teaching on family, 41–44
charitable giving
  amount given to charity, 168f, 168
  giving to any cause, 167f, 167
  giving to particular charitable causes, 169f, 169–70
childlessness, 64–66, 65f, 110–12, 111t
children, 44, 57–66
clergy sexual abuse scandal, 120
cohabitation, 44, 47–48, 49f, 49–50, 66, 196–97, 209
cohort crowding, 17–18
completed fertility, 64
contraception, 57–58, 80
converts, 5–6, 100f, 101
COVID-19 pandemic, 9, 87, 162, 206
crime/guns/marijuana, 162–65, 163b, 163f
Cuban Americans, 27, 37–38, 120

death penalty, 185–87, 186f, 199–200
decision-making factors, 173
Dillon, M., 42–44, 129
disaffiliation, 100f, 101, 116–17, 202
divorce, 44, 50–54, 52f, 53f, 86, 110–12, 111t, 142–45, 143f, 150–51, 196–97, 199, 209
dual-earner marriages, 176

economic inequality/poverty, 179–83, 181f
education
    Catholic schools historically, 70–72
    homogamy impacts, 56f
    levels of, 72–74, 73f
    marriage impacts, 45
    religion as predictive of, 69
    religious mobility characteristics, 112–15, 113t
    urban–rural differences, 34–37
    wealth relationships to, 86
Eucharist, 119, 150, 198–99, 200–1
evangelization, 133–35, 134f, 149–50
evangelization/religious experiences, 133–35, 134f, 149–50
extramarital sex, 48, 49

family planning, 58
family processes, 41–44
federal poverty line (FPL), 209–10
feelings about Bible, 138f, 138–39
fertility
    Church doctrine, 58
    completed, 64
    wealth relationships to, 86
full-time work, 74–76, 75f, 113t, 114t

Gaudium et Spes (Joy and Hope), 159
gender
    birth cohort distribution, 21–23
    childcare responsibilities, 79
    Church leavers, 110, 122
    earnings, 78
    education, 17–18, 21, 45, 64
    gender roles/gender equality, 78–81, 175–79, 176f, 192–93
    homogamy, 54
    household division of labor, 78–81, 80f, 175–76
    labor force participation, 17–18, 21, 78–79, 175–76
    marriage/divorce, 7f, 7–8, 45, 47, 50–51
    preferential treatment for women, 176f, 176–78, 181, 192
    religious beliefs, 21–23, 22f, 110
    religious mobility, 109t, 110, 122
    secular practices/attitudes, 21
    social origins, 21–23
    women's ordination, 58
gender roles/gender equality, 175–79, 176f, 192–93
generalized trust/confidence. *See* trust/confidence
General Social Survey (GSS), 5–6, 9, 205, 206–10, 211–12
Generation X
    birth cohorts/gender distribution, 23
    cohabitation/marriage, 47–48
    fertility rates, 19
    gender differences/religious tradition, 21–23, 22f
    religious mobility/social origins, 108–10, 109t
    socioeconomic status (SES), 18
Generation Z
    birth cohorts/gender distribution, 23
    fertility rates, 19–20
    gender differences/religious tradition, 21–23, 22f
    Latinos, 18–19
    religious mobility/social origins, 108–10, 109t
    religious tradition statistics, 20f
God/Afterlife/Pope, 135–38, 136f, 198
God/religion in U.S. politics, 140f, 142
Great Depression, 16–17
Great Recession, 89–90
gun ownership, 162–65, 163b, 163f

high incomes/investment incomes, 82–85, 83f, 85f
high wealth, 88–89, 89f, 112–15, 113t, 114t, 122–23
homeownership, 89–91, 91f
homogamy, 54–57, 56f
homophily, 54
household division of labor, 78–81, 80f, 175–76
"Humane Vitae" 58, 67n.2

ideal family size, 60–62, 61f, 66
income gap, 68, 81–85, 82f, 179–83, 181f
inheritance, 91–92, 92f

Jewish Americans, 58–59, 72, 106f, 107

Kerry, John, 157–58

labor unions, 179–83, 181f
leaving patterns, 108–15, 109t, 111t, 113t, 114t
low income, 82f, 82, 112–15, 113t, 114t

making ends meet, 94f, 94–95
marijuana legalization, 162–65, 163f
marriage, 7f, 7–8, 44, 45–48, 47f, 66, 86, 110–12, 111t, 196–97, 209
Mass attendance, 132f, 132, 149, 150, 198–99
Massengill, R. P., 72
meditation, 131–33, 132f, 149, 150
men. *See* gender
Mexican Americans, 27, 32, 37
Millennials
    birth cohorts/gender distribution, 23
    cohabitation/marriage, 47–48
    fertility rates, 19–20
    gender differences/religious tradition, 21–23
    religious mobility/social origins, 108–10, 109t
mobility. *See* religious mobility
Muslims, 106f, 107

National Eucharistic Revival, 200–1
national problems, 161–62
natural family planning, 58
net worth poverty, 87, 88f, 210

Obama, Barack, 157–58

Panel Study of Income Dynamics (PSID), 9, 205, 210, 212–13
Papal infallibility, 138f, 138–39, 198
party affiliation, 153, 154f, 154–56, 156b
philosophy/science importance, 140f, 141, 149
polarization, 154f, 156, 201
political views, 154f, 157, 170–71
Pope Francis, 49, 120, 145, 166, 201
Pope John Paul II, 42, 79–80, 184
Pope Paul VI, 58
pornography, 142–45, 143f, 149, 150–51

poverty
    rates, 82f, 82
    religious mobility, 112–15, 113t, 114t
prayer, 131–33, 132f, 149, 150
prayer in schools, 140f, 141
preferential hiring/promotion of African Americans, 179–83, 181f
preferential treatment of women, 176f, 176–78, 181, 192
Prewar Generation. *See* Silent (Prewar) Generation
pro-life/pro-choice. *See* abortion
Puerto Rican Americans, 27

race/ethnicity, 50, 208–9
reason/evidence in decision-making, 140f, 141–42
religion/politics/science, 139–45, 140f, 149
religious commitment/fertility relationships, 59–60
religious experiences, 133–35, 134f, 149–50
religious mobility
    aggregate-level, 2f, 99
    individual-level, 99–103, 100f
    magnitude of change, 102, 103t
    multiple changes, 103–4, 104t
religious practices, 131–33, 132f, 149
religious service attendance, 132f, 132, 149, 150
responsibility for addressing inequality, 183
Roe v. Wade, 2, 162, 189–90

Second Vatican Council (Vatican II), 19
self-employment, 35, 76–78, 77f, 197
sex/divorce/pornography, 142–45, 150–51
sexual morality, 142–45, 143f, 150–51
Silent (Prewar) Generation
    birth cohorts/gender distribution, 23
    fertility rates, 19
    gender differences/religious tradition, 21–23, 22f
    religious mobility/social origins, 109t
    religious tradition statistics, 20f
    socioeconomic status (SES), 16–17

socioeconomic status (SES)
  Baby Boomers, 17–18
  class position, 93f, 93–94
  dual-earner marriages, 80–81
  education (*see* education)
  full-time work, 74–76, 75f, 113t, 114t
  gender roles/gender equality, 78–80
  Generation X, 18
  high incomes/investment incomes, 82–85, 83f, 85f
  high wealth, 88–89, 89f, 112–15, 113t, 114t, 122–23
  homeownership, 89–91, 91f
  household division of labor, 78–81, 80f
  income, 68, 81–85, 82f
  inheritance, 91–92, 92f
  low income, 82f, 82, 112–15, 113t, 114t
  making ends meet, 94f, 94–95
  marriage impacts on, 45
  net worth poverty, 87, 88f
  self-employment, 76–78, 77f, 197
  Silent (Prewar) Generation, 16–17
  urban–rural differences, 34–37
  wealth, 68, 69, 85–89, 88f, 112–15, 113t
  wealth mobility, 91–92, 92f
  work, 68, 69, 74–78, 75f
spiritual connection, 132f, 133

strength of religious beliefs, 130f, 130–31, 149, 150, 198
suicide/assisted suicide, 183–85, 185f, 193, 199–200, 209
Survey of Consumer Finances (SCF), 88–89

taxes/government spending, 158–61, 160f, 180, 181f, 181
trust/confidence
  corporations, 189–90
  executive branch/federal government, 189–90
  institutions, 187–90, 188f, 193–94
  organized religion, 188f, 188–89, 189b, 194
  science, 189
  Supreme Court, 189–90

unemployment, 35

Vatican II (Second Vatican Council), 19
volunteering, 190–92, 191f, 194
voting behaviors, 157–58

wealth, 68, 69, 85–89, 88f, 112–15, 113t
wealth mobility, 91–92, 92f
Wilde, M., 57
women. *See* gender
work, 68, 69, 74–78, 75f